Piety and Power

FAITH MEETS FAITH

An Orbis Series in Interreligious Dialogue
Paul F. Knitter, General Editor
Editorial Advisors
John Berthrong
Julia Ching
Diana Eck
Karl-Josef Kuschel
Lamin Sanneh
George E. Tinker
Felix Wilfred

In the contemporary world, the many religions and spiritualities stand in need of greater communication and cooperation. More than ever before, they must speak to, learn from, and work with each other in order both to maintain their vital identities and to contribute to fashioning a better world.

FAITH MEETS FAITH seeks to promote interreligious dialogue by providing an open forum for exchanges among followers of different religious paths. While the Series wants to encourage creative and bold responses to questions arising from contemporary appreciations of religious plurality, it also recognizes the multiplicity of basic perspectives concerning the methods and content of interreligious dialogue.

Although rooted in a Christian theological perspective, the Series does not endorse any single school of thought or approach. By making available to both the scholarly community and the general public works that represent a variety of religious and methodological viewpoints, FAITH MEETS FAITH seeks to foster an encounter among followers of the religions of the world on matters of common concern.

FAITH MEETS FAITH SERIES

Piety and Power
Muslims and Christians
in West Africa

Lamin Sanneh

ORBIS BOOKS

Maryknoll, New York 10545

The Catholic Foreign Mission Society of America (Maryknoll) recruits and trains people for overseas missionary service. Through Orbis Books, Maryknoll aims to foster the international dialogue that is essential to mission. The books published, however, reflect the opinions of their authors and are not meant to represent the official position of the society.

Manuscript editing and typesetting by Joan Marie Laflamme.

Library of Congress Cataloging in Publication Data

Sanneh, Lamin O.
    Piety and power : Muslims and Christians in West Africa / Lamin Sanneh.
      p. cm. — (Faith meets faith series)
    Includes bibliographical references and index.
    ISBN 1-57075-090-4 (alk. paper)
      1. Islam—Africa, West. 2. Christianity—Africa, West. 3. Islam—Relations—Christianity. 4. Christianity and other religions—Islam. I. Title. II. Series: Faith meets faith.
    BP64.A4W3696 1996
    297'.1972—dc20   96-43354
                                                                CIP

To Terry Iles and John Crossley,
for having been my
inter-cultural gatekeepers,
with appreciation and respect

Contents

Acknowledgments

The six chapters in this book bring together the two important strands of my personal and professional life, and for that I gratefully acknowledge my indebtedness to individuals spread over too many years in too many places to list here. However, I begin with those who shaped and directed my personal life, for their examples of compassion, trust, integrity, generosity, and capacity for tolerance and inclusiveness. I never realized how serviceable certain aspects of the heritage of traditional ethics I imbibed would be in a secular world full of promise and material abundance, but also seared by conflict and alienation. My parents had only a vague, indirect intimation of that world which their grandchildren, Kelefa and Sia, would know as their natural home, but they prepared me in ways more crucial than even personal acquaintance could have entitled them. They would, I imagine, be impressed by how I have tried to hold my own in the home of the "Nasara," as they called the West, which treats religion as cultural entitlement under law, a situation that tolerates people to be religiously informed so long as they are not religious themselves.

Like many of my contemporaries, I left home for the West immediately after high school, but in other ways I never left home, even if it is only in the ordinary sense of undertaking frequent return visits in order to keep in touch with relatives and friends. From my father I inherited some of his noble *nyancho* spirit of fierce independence, including his sense that truth and honesty left you with no alternative, however elaborately you may weave and dodge and whatever the consequences. He paid a high price for that himself. From my mother I obtained a powerful sense of community, and the conviction that thinking well of others and assuming the best of their motives are the first rules of human interaction. If an uncharitable thought crossed her mind, for example, she would indicate it by appealing to the Creator's forgiveness (*astafurula*, Arabic *astaghfiru-lláh*) in relation to the affected person or persons, often followed by an act of penance. For my father the priority was terseness and purposefulness, for my mother latitude and discretion. Both were religious, yet how different they were! Some of that dual legacy I have carried with me, so that in that sense, too, I have never left home.

My father's Calvinist scruples combined with my mother's catholic sympathies also condition my handling of career options and choices, the sort of independent scrutiny of different options allied to the need for practical commitment that each would recognize in his or her own way. Their example has thus contributed to defining my professional life.

I am grateful for the many opportunities I have had in the course of time to build on this double legacy, however lopsidedly it has turned out. With friends and colleagues in the Islam in Africa Project, now the Project for Christian-Muslim Relations in Africa (Procmura), an ecumenical interfaith agency, I faced the rewarding challenge of relating my academic work to vocational service. Ecumenical Christian and church leaders constantly reminded me of the need for academic training to have an applied dimension in Africa, for the historical and linguistic study of religion, for example, to illuminate present day issues and challenges. An important effect on me of this counsel was to make me feel personally responsible for the regretful growing gap between the new, young generation of university-educated Africans and traditional Africa. Thus, after my education in the United States and Britain, I decided to return to Africa to serve my people, with still some uncertainty about my future professional career. At any rate, for that counsel I remain grateful, and make special mention in that connection of John Crossley, Hans Haafkens, Tom Beetham, Hugh Thomas, and the stimulating intellectual environment of Ibadan, Nigeria, of the 1960s and '70s. I am also grateful to individuals in the Middle East who deepened my grasp of the subject and encouraged me in other ways. I should mention here other persons whom I came to know in my academic career and whose assurances nurtured my vocational as well as professional interests, persons such as John B. Taylor, Thomas Hodgkin, John Lavers, J. Spencer Trimingham, Humphrey J. Fisher, Kenneth Cragg, Jeremy Hinds, John Ralph Willis, Patrick J. Ryan, John B. Carman, Wilfred Smith, George Rupp, and Andrew F. Walls.

With the much appreciated support of the Pew Charitable Trusts, I was able to undertake a reexamination of the subject and to reassemble the pieces that provide the framework of this book. I have rewritten the material that has appeared before and introduced in several places new material and an updated bibliography and notes. A version of the material I delivered as the Henry Martyn Lectures at the University of Cambridge, England, for which courtesy I wish to acknowledge David Ford, Graham Kings, and their colleagues in the Henry Martyn Trust.

My family has been a source of much encouragement and support even though this book as the reason for neglecting my duties is never justification enough. Bill Burrows has given yeoman service to the cause of publishing this book, service well and truly above and beyond the call of duty. Many readers have read the book in draft form and called my attention to numerous details of interpretation, style, and fact, and I am grateful to them. In acknowledging their help and encouragement, as well as that of others, however, I do not in the least wish to suggest they take responsibility either for the opinions expressed here or for any remaining blemishes and defects. In that regard, I do not ask to be relieved of the responsibility that is properly mine, though I ask for the reader's understanding and indulgence.

Orthography and Bibliographical Note

I have followed in the main the *Encyclopaedia of Islam*, New Edition, in transcriptions from the Arabic, except in a few details. I have indicated the *tá'marbútah* as in Qádiriyáh instead of Qádiriyya, except where it is quoted. In a few exceptions I have yielded to prevailing practice, as in *salát* instead of *saláh*. I have disregarded the French *dj* and *ḵ* of the *Encyclopaedia* for the English *j* and *q* respectively, and I have omitted the ligature. I have followed the German Flügel verse numbering of the Qur'án and, in the main, Arberry's translation, with its distinctive ragged margins and line arrangements. It is the only translation in English that attempts to reproduce the oral and audial impact of the original Arabic, at the cost sometimes of idiomatic convenience.

Glossary of Arabic and African Terms

abayah (Manding for gown, robe)
al-harb wa al-siyásah (Arabic, warfare and politics)
al-Mubárak (Arabic, the blessed one)
ansár (Arabic, helpers, those who "helped" the Prophet immigrate to Medina)
'asabiyáh (Arabic, solidarity)
asháb (Arabic, the companions of the Prophet)
askiya (Songhay word for ruler)
astaghfiru-lláh (Arabic, I beg forgiveness of God)
barakah (Arabic, merit, grace, virtue)
bila kayf (Arabic, without asking how)
commissar (originally official of Soviet Communist Party responsible for
    political education and organization)
danka (Manding word for curse, evil spell)
dár al-harb (Arabic, sphere of warfare, enmity)
dár al-Islám (Arabic, sphere of Islam, truth)
dár al-sultánah (Arabic, royal palace)
fátihah (Arabic, opening chapter of the Qur'án)
fatwa (Arabic, authoritative ruling on a religious matter)
faqíh (Arabic for religious scholar, authority)
*fennu (*Arabic, *funún)* (Fula for higher or advanced studies)
fineditugol (Fula for pronunciation, enunciation of the word)
firugol (Fula for vernacular exegesis)
fí sabíl illáh (Arabic, in the path of God)
hadíth (Tradition of the Prophet)
hajj (Arabic, pilgrimage to Mecca)
hijrah (Arabic, emigration of the Prophet from Mecca to Medina)
hizb (azháb) (Arabic, a rubric division of the Qur'án)
'ilm al-rijal (Arabic, knowledge of the men who transmitted the *Hadíth)*
imám (Arabic, prayer leader)
isláh (Arabic, social benefit)
jangugol (Fula for reading)
jihád (Arabic, holy war, struggle)
jihádist (Arabic, holy warrior)
khalifah-general (religious title: supreme caliph)
kalimah (Arabic, confession of the creed)

khalwah (Arabic, clerical retreat)
Madíh (Arabic praise poem on the Prophet)
madinatu-n-nabi (Arabic, city of the Prophet)
Madrasa (Arabic, Islamic school)
malam (Hausa for Muslim teacher, cleric)
marabout (A French word for cleric, priest)
maslahah (Arabic, welfare)
mi'ráj (Arabic, heavenly ascension of the Prophet)
mu'allim (Arabic, teacher)
muftí (Arabic, authority of Islamic religious law)
muhájirún (Arabic, the emigrants with the Prophets)
muríd (Arabic, novice, disciple)
mullah (Anglicized word for cleric)
Munazzamah al-Mu'tamar al-Islámí (Organization of Islamic Countries,
    literally in Arabic, "Islamic Conference Organization")
naskh (Arabic, abrogation)
nyancho (Manding term, royal warrior clan)
Puja (Hindu purification)
qádí (Arabic, Islamic magistrate)
Qádiri (An initiate of the Qádiriyáh Súfí order)
Qádiryya (Súfí religious order)
qiblah (Arabic, direction of prayer toward the Ka'ba)
razzias (Anglicized word for desert raids)
ru'ya al-sálihah (Arabic, sound or perspicacious dreams)
sa'ádah (Arabic, happiness)
salát (Arabic, canonical prayer rite)
salát al-istikhárah (Arabic, supererogatory prayer of decision making)
salát al-istisqá (Arabic, rogation rite, prayer for rain)
Sarki (Hausa term for ruler, chief)
sayf al-haqq (Arabic, sword of God, truth)
shahádah (Arabic, confession of creed)
Sharí'ah (Arabic, canonical legal code)
shaykh (Arabic, spiritual director)
shirk (Arabic, sin of association, idolatry)
shuyúkh (Arabic plural of *shaykh*)
Síra (Arabic, biography of the Prophet)
Súfí (Arabic, Islamic mystic)
sunnah (Arabic, the custom of the Prophet)
súrah (Arabic, chapter of the Qur'án)
tajdíd (Arabic, gradual, peaceful reform)
taríqah (Arabic, Súfí path, order)
teranga (Wolof for hospitality)
Tijáni (follower of the Súfí Tíjániyah order)
Tijániyya (A Súfí religious order)
'ulamá (Arabic, religious scholars)
ummah (Arabic, the orthodox Islamic community, fellowship of believers)

wáridát (Arabic, divine intimations)
windugol (Fula for writing)
yatím (Arabic for orphan)
yatímah (Arabic, pearl, model of excellence)
yirwa (Manding for blessing, virtue)
zakát (Arabic, almsgiving)

Introduction

This book comprises six chapters, including an appendix, dealing with interfaith relations between Muslim and Christian Africans, principally in West Africa. A slightly amended version of the material at present in chapter 5 and chapter 6 also appears in my *The Crown and the Turban*, which deals with the historical and social aspects of the encounter of Islam and African societies. In this book, by contrast, I concentrate on interfaith issues, largely from the point of view of Muslim communities in the context of growing pluralism. The burgeoning Christian communities of Africa, Catholic, Protestant and Independent Christian, constitute an important element of that pluralism. In the process I wish also to correct certain popular misperceptions about Islam while providing a basis for later comparative reflection with reference to the West.

The matter of Africans as religious agents in their own right is an important foundation of the approach of this book. By religious agents I mean not simply Africans as masters of what happened in religious transmission, but more particularly Africans as mediators in a fluid, dynamic intercultural process. In this sense I modify considerably the familiar, conventional approach to Islam (and Christianity) as a belief system imposed without alteration by outside agents, an approach that assumes that religious truth is simply a straight line from imposed doctrine to dramatic conversion, and back again. Rather, my approach concentrates on the intervening stages, those crucial interstices, in which old forms and symbols are retrieved, and then reinforced, either from being recast or reconfirmed, from interaction with new religious materials and influences. I am less concerned either with the beginning or end than with the process itself, with the levers of change rather than with blueprints. There is logic to this method, however radically different it may be from Cartesian logic, and that logic is the historical one of looking upon religious practices as being socially coherent and personally satisfying, just as blueprints may be for theorists and philosophers. In the dynamic setting of community life, people are less interested in consciously forcing the complexity of experience into the rigid frame of theory, although given the multilayered nature of practical experience theory may be unconsciously assimilated into a range of historical aspirations. For my purposes, however, I seize on the religious process as such as an opportunity for interfaith interaction and for clarifying the nature of the crucial relationship between piety and power, between personal faith and public fiat.

My central concern in this book, then, is to describe how Muslims have interacted with Christians and others in African societies and what we may learn from their experience and example. Using a range of historical, indigenous, and Western sources, I try to show the intelligent and flexible ways in which Muslims have

1

responded to the challenge of pluralism, whether through popular religious practice, the demands of state-building, the law-and-order framework imposed by European colonial administrations, the educational reforms of Western Christian missions, or the pressures of secularization and nation building.

A word of definition. I use *Islam* in this book in three interrelated senses: a. as a religion prescribed in Scripture, law, and tradition; b. as a "territorial" historical phenomenon with its own distinctive civilization, culture, and geographical concentration; and c. as a religion that has undergone and is undergoing profound change and transformation from the impact of an ascendant West. On the first two levels of Islam as prescriptive truth and as a territorial historical phenomenon, we are dealing with the religion in terms of its own internal counsels and self-understanding, but on the third level of the impact of the modern West we are dealing with the power of external forces on Islam's self-image. I have tried in this book to engage this theme of Islam's self-image in the context of Western secular dominance, and, in doing so, to confront three basic issues, as follows:

a. the spread and expansion of Islam in Africa has involved a process of reiterating and interpreting the message of the Qur'án through African social and political institutions and ideas, and, in particular, through interaction with Christian Africans, and that has required Muslim religious agents to be flexible and creative. The fact of the relative success with which Muslims penetrated African societies created a certain confidence about new and strange ideas and societies not being a threat or a danger to prescriptive Islam or in conflict with Islam's historical mandate. This positive situation encouraged representative modernist Muslims to believe that continued cooperation and alliance with indigenous institutions and hierarchies would be rewarding. In most places, therefore, Muslims embraced local versions of pluralism and tolerance rather than committing themselves and others to inflexible compliance with the religious code;

b. the role of the Prophet Muhammad in both formal and informal situations in Islam assumed pivotal importance in indigenous African communities now caught up in the acute process of islamization and the transition from a kin-based notion of religion to a creed-based form of it. Under the new requirements of Islam, it was individuals, baptized and instructed in the faith as such, who were qualified for membership in the religious community. So Islam represented the transition from a kin-based territoriality to a faith-based territoriality, and from mythic legends to sacred texts and documented history as the religious frame of reference. Thus the biography and tradition of the Prophet, and, by extension, of holy figures, came to constitute something of a religious and social *axis mundi*, a new center of personal understanding and social interaction;

c. Islam's historical course as a world religion with a program of world conversion that allowed it to establish a commanding presence in several Sub-Saharan African communities eventually brought it into contact with the European powers which were seeking control of Africa. Under colonialism Muslims and Islamic educational and legal institutions enjoyed a certain privileged status in spite of initial misgivings and even resistance. But Islam's "territorial" gains under colonialism were now felt to be threatened by the forceful logic of nationalism and its self-confident program of the establishment of a national secular state.

The Muslims' ambivalence toward the politics of nationalism tended to crystallize into a *Sharí'ah*-fused general debate about the adequacy of a normative national secular state vis-à-vis the claims of religion. Thus the debate about the national secular state has become the crucible in which the changes and transformations of modern Islam are being forged. Africa constitutes an important arena for the meeting of Islamic civilization and Western secular dominance. It is a complex process: Africa has helped to mediate between the world of Islam and that of the West, and in so doing has itself received the imprints of the two influences while adding its own accent. Furthermore, international Islamic organizations, acting as catalysts for Pan-Islamism, have increasingly entered the scene and raised the stakes. In any case, my interest here is to indicate how a modified African Islam and a modified African Christianity have together, and separately, helped to soften the sharp tones of an aggressive Western secularism without denying that Western secularism has profoundly affected everything and everyone it has encountered. Indeed, in the secular national state the West has virtually been unassailable. However, the fundamental issue for Africans who are the recipients of Western influence is whether Western secularism can adapt and accommodate religion and thus preempt theocratic extremism from the right and prescriptive atheism from the left.

Some explanation may be due here for the way I have treated the final and major theme of the book. The principle of analysis is the religious case for democratic political liberalism. I wish to demonstrate not merely that, understood that way, religion is compatible with democratic liberalism, but that religion is necessary to the conception of democratic liberalism at all. I am therefore selective both in my choice of political system and of religious tradition. I have a very specific project in hand, namely, how democratic liberalism as one highly successful political option belongs with the culture of religious voluntarism as an equally successful religious option. Thus, while I focus on democratic liberalism and on religious voluntarism, I by no means wish to assert that there are no alternative political systems and religious traditions, or even that within Christianity and Islam there are not significant divergences. In fact, I mention the two that are among the most prominent counter-examples, namely, theocratic territoriality at one extreme and prescriptive atheism at the other. I imagine an equally plausible case can be made about the connection between theocratic territoriality and political totalitarianism, if not in terms of a common monistic source then at least in terms of method. But I beg the reader, please, to understand how that is not my subject, though even there such a connection would mirror exactly my procedure in treating democratic liberalism and religious voluntarism as kindred themes. The main issue, however, for the reader to decide is whether I have succeeded in proving what I contend; namely, that Muslim religious thought, understood first by its own prescriptive rules and then additionally by its modern-day Westernized tendencies, has enough of a voluntarist impetus in it to fit in with democratic liberalism in which religion is de-theocratized without being disenfranchised. I think so, but at any rate that issue is important to my final view that religion can offer a public rationale for interfaith encounter in the public sphere shaped by Western secular ideas.

1

Interfaith Issues in Muslim *Da'wah* in Africa

The Potential for Solidarity

Mission has become a controversial subject today, with people disposed to see it as an example of intolerance and cultural imperialism. There was, of course, a time when mission enjoyed much wider public confidence and attracted to itself considerable support. But times have changed and the days of missionary enthusiasm have been replaced by a paralyzing guilt complex. Yet while mainline missions have by and large lost their original appeal, the practice of mission continues, particularly by new evangelical groups as well as in other world religions. In these circumstances, then, it may be useful to state the general case for mission and to deal with it where it is still practiced. I would like to do so from a particular point of view, that is to say, from the point of view of religious mission as an intercultural process in which religious materials are reconstituted and have new cultural forms pressed on them. Since what is revealed by this intercultural process may represent a new experience, and often a radical subversion of the rhetoric of religious triumphalism, it suggests that the current mainline criticism of mission may not be as stringent as the internal comprehensive scrutiny that has accompanied mission as an intercultural process.

It is in these terms that I would like to explore mission in its Islamic form and consider from that vantage point pertinent issues in the encounter between Muslim and Christian Africans. Such encounter has a long history, most of which has been harmonious, and that history of interreligious harmony is a precious legacy in our own more jaded generation.

In pre-colonial Africa, it is often the case that Muslims have arrived in African societies with little advanced knowledge among their hosts of who these Muslims are and what they believe. Consequently, with little preparation, the local Pagan populations had no basis to engage in mutual exchange and understanding with their Muslim guests. With time, however, other religious groups, of which Christians formed a significant part, started entering the continent and that resulted in a new form of intercommunal relationship. Before too long, then, Muslims were encountering Christians and finding scope for mutual interpretation and understanding. This interreligious theme is what I would like to explore here.

A significant aspect of Muslim-Christian relations in Africa is that the two communities have been immersed in a rich and long tradition of sharing and thus stand revealed to each other in their differences as much as in their similarities. Yet the impressive literature and discussion on interreligious dialogue that has appeared in the West has not paid much attention to this fact, a neglect that tends to strengthen the view that dialogue separates practice from lived experience, which does nothing except belittle the experience of persons who are themselves the subjects of interreligious encounter. It has left dialogue vulnerable to popular mistrust, something specialists do, the fringe activity of a small minority that is itself on the fringes of its own religious tradition.

Cut off from the concrete lives of persons in community, dialogue is charged with attempting to create a speculative syncretism in order to undermine faith in the interests of interfaith harmony. It has not helped matters that those who favor dialogue have tended to oppose mission. They claim that dialogue is tolerant, enlightened, and open-minded while mission is imperialistic, intolerant, and harmful. Such polarization is bad for mutual confidence, for if you engage in dialogue you must deal with religious differences as well as with similarities and leave open the possibility of changing your mind; in other words, leave open the possibility of convincing others and being in turn convinced. Otherwise it would make no sense to undertake either dialogue or mission. Religions are exclusive in the sense of their unique, particular claims and their historical expression; they are also inclusive in the sense of those religious elements that find echoes in other traditions, and pluralist in terms of their own internal diversity and dynamism, but above all in meeting complex human needs and situations. What religions offer in terms of salvation and ultimate truth cannot in the nature of the case be separated from the practices laid down to attain truth, and dialogue must not drive a wedge between the means and end of religion, between the path and the goal. The view we have of God is not unconnected to the path by which we ascend to that view, so that dialogue must be about the path as well as about witness to the truth the path leads to. Dialogue and witness, therefore, belong together.

In any case, we must expect Muslims engaged in dialogue to be committed to Islam as a living, historical tradition as well as to the God with whom tradition is continuously engaged, with a similar commitment on the part of Christians to avoid a disequilibrium. Interfaith engagement proceeds by what is common to being religious as well as by the exigencies of complex human needs and situations, but most indisputably by what is unique and determinative of faith tradition. On those three grounds of common faith, common experience of life, and historical particularity, we have necessarily been involved with each other, whether by mutual foreclosure or by active solicitation. However we view religion, we cannot be content with one side talking just to itself about the other.

I would like to maintain that religious differences as instances of particularity may prove a source of encouragement provided we see those differences from the right perspective. Thus we can say that Christianity and Islam are united perhaps less by the things they have in common than by what divides them. It is true that both religions teach doctrines of the virgin birth and of the messianic role of Jesus, among other things, and yet the Crusades took place when these facts were common knowledge. On the reverse of the coin, the Muslim prescription of the *Sharí'ah* as the required rule of human obedience and duty toward God and toward each other is in contrast to the Christian teaching about the person of Christ and the sacraments based on his life and work. The risk of misunderstanding appears less in matters of difference than in matters of similarity. Christians are more tempted to allege that Islam is an imitation of Christianity in matters of similarity between the two, while Muslims face an identical temptation precisely where the two religions share areas of overlap. Christians react to a "delinquent Islam," where the similarities fall short of a full concession, and Muslims denounce a heretical Christianity, where a common truth about God splinters into a corrupt trinity. That is why our medieval Christian predecessors viewed Muslim borrowings as sheep-stealing, while their Muslim counterparts saw it as Christian religious laundering. In sum, it did not help the cause of interreligious tolerance that both religions could claim a common prophetic tradition or a shared view of the world as created *ex nihilo*, with human beings held to historical accountability for it. Muslims and Christians still developed exclusive attitudes, determined to prove each other wrong. Believing that they knew where the other side stood, Muslims and Christians "cluttered themselves with aggravating issues" at each other's expense. The closeness of the two religions to each other, instead of making them truly neighborly, produced suspicion and contention. It stoked the fuels of "unifying controversy," the controversy that dispenses with difference by taking it over. Religious rivalry, we know, has an undiscriminating appetite; it will feed as lavishly on shared lineage as on separate bonds. All it requires is proximity. As G. K. Chesterton in 1908 put it in "On the World Getting Smaller": "Modern hostility is a base thing, and arises, not out of a generous difference, but out of a sort of bitter and sneering similarity. It is because we are all copying each other that we are all cursing each other."

If you did not intend to make a sectarian point of it, you could say that in religion genuine difference, which is constitutive of particularity, safeguards genuine identity, and genuine identity promotes pluralism as well as mutual trust. Thus in the common ground between Islam and Christianity where differences disappear there is what Kenneth Cragg has called "a conflict of jealousies," in Islam a jealousy for the Oneness of God as reiterated in the Muslim creed, and in Christianity a jealousy for the Oneness of God as affirmed in the doctrine of the Incarnation.[1] Thus the agreement of the two traditions on the importance of "One" in regard to God does not remove contention or hostility, all going to show that the coalescence and unity of religions will come, if it comes at all, not through the denial of difference but from the joyful celebration of it.

In the "One Worldism" of Wendell Willkie (1892-1944), for example, we have an inspired belief in shared interest in human progress and in the unification of

---

[1] Kenneth Cragg, *The Arab Christian: A History in the Middle East* (Louisville: Westminster/John Knox Press, 1991), 89.

the world by science, technology, and communication. Such a world, Willkie taught, would come about from better acquaintance among the peoples of the world, which would lead naturally to better understanding, and from that understanding would stem love and peace and solidarity and the overcoming of all differences. This simple faith is tied to noble ends, but, alas! it is too simple. With acquaintance may come distrust, and with knowledge may come fear or antagonism. A narrow, inflexible view of the world, which snaps at anything different or foreign, gains no elasticity from being stretched beyond its self-reinforced orbit of self-approval. Only understanding, based on sympathy, can lead to appreciation of differences and to mutual respect. But let us be quite clear about this: understanding is only a tool at the service of truth rather than a contender for truth.

Whatever the case, we can at least be confident that we can only start from where we are, because that is what has conditioned not only what we know about ourselves but about the other, and, furthermore, that is what we have in common. Our capacity for mutual appreciation, or antagonism, remains a matter of our given particularity; that is to say, we reject, concede, or affirm religious points depending on the shape and force of our own particularity. Thus Catholics and Quakers, say, would vary in their attitude to Puja in Hinduism, or Baptists and Orthodox to the *Sharí'ah* in Islam. In the nature of the case, interfaith mutuality presumes religious committedness or at least the validity of particularity. I am not saying that religions must remain fixed in their own self-identity, with no possibility of speaking to outsiders. Rather, I am arguing that we should not delude ourselves into thinking that we can speak to others only if we give up what we believe, for denying one religion, even our own, does not increase religious tolerance. Thus in explaining our faith to others, that is to say, in religious apologetics, we encounter genuine difference, with the challenge to adjust and refocus.

It happens that with Islam and Christianity such apologetics has been going on for centuries, from the time of St. Francis of Assisi and the blessed Raymond Lully to Louis Massignon and Kenneth Cragg, as it must, given the fact that both religions have a missionary tradition, that they have tried to express themselves through cultures not their own, in that way providing an opportunity for genuine mutual understanding. In this sense, Christians and Muslims have in their respective histories seen what risks as well as new possibilities arise when the faith crosses new frontiers. The Qu'rán in its original Arabic takes incalculable risks in the vast missionary range it covers by embracing Kosovo and Kantora, the Tigris and the Tugela, whereas because the Bible is borne upon a stream of infinite idioms and accents, from Alur to Kutchin, and from Ga to Kaka, the Christian message is as good as the tongues that speak it, tongues that unite and permeate the message in a kinship network of soil, song, and symbol. To take just the Christian side for now, it is well to remember that in preliterate societies, mother tongues do not conform to our rational, linear notions of language, with a linguistic concept representing a corresponding thing or object. Rather, these mother tongues are a supple, flexible cultural resource, and with them people express themselves in speech forms steeped in body, social, and natural images. In these cultures language sticks close to the soil, its dynamism an expression of lived reality, the whole of living being taken up in it. Thus in mission Christianity is recast in mother-tongue reiteration. It is thus impossible for either Christianity or Islam to attempt such monumental cultural leaps as in missions without exposing infelicities, not to say inadequacies, in religious intention as well as practice. Missionary work, then, is no respecter of motives; with the best will in the world, missionary agents are at the mercy of first language flux and reflux.

Thus, the evidence that meets us everywhere in the mission field of approximations to truth, some of it inspiring and some dispiriting, is symbolic of religious limitation and is for that reason useful material for learning lessons of realism and humility. Possessing a missionary tradition, therefore, can be a salutary check to facile or arrogant optimism.

We may say, consequently, that far from setting up harmful rivalry or complacent stalemate, one the result of the sectarian spirit and the other of isolation, the missionary ambitions of Islam and Christianity can open new areas of dialogue, particularly at points where both are engaged in self-interpretation through the idiom of other cultures. Whatever the dangers of missionary insensitivity, of which we have grim enough catalogues, the obligation to witness on which both religions insist can be turned to good account. For example, witness would demand making an effort to understand and be understood by others, with persuasion the rule in intercultural relations. To reject that way is to rely on indifference, silence, and chauvinism as the norm in cultural interaction, and that is unworthy of all our insights. Therefore, witness can be a safeguard against our turning ethnocentric in our isolation. By thus reflecting on the image of themselves projected by other peoples, Islam and Christianity may be able to come to grips with aspects of their heritage normally hidden from them from the habit and emphasis of Scripture and creed.

SOME THOUGHTS ON COOPERATION

I shall in the main body of this chapter examine the stimulus of the African environment on missionary Islam and how the resultant interaction constitutes a positive gain for world Islam. My emphasis will be on Africans as missionary pioneers and spokesmen at royal courts and in towns and villages. In the concluding section I shall suggest how the Christian understanding of Islamic religious activity could be a deepening and enriching experience. However, a few general thoughts on bilateral cooperation between the two faiths may be appropriate at this stage.

CONTRAST AND SIMILARITY

(1) *Christian teaching about the cross and the divinity of Christ on the one hand, and, on the other, Islamic teaching about the Qur'ánic revelation and the Divine Law (Sharí'ah) show a fundamental contrast of religious conception.* The Christian encounter with Muslims in contemporary Africa has often resulted in the sharpening of theological contrast and differences between the two religions. In that respect, the Christian pursuit of philanthropic goals has been motivated by

submitting to the imperative of incarnate truth, which demands ethical commitment for the amelioration of the human condition. In that way, Christians have come to believe in a fundamental continuity between the divine mandate and the human enterprise, expressed by the sentiment that humanity was created in the image of God. By contrast, Muslims have insisted on unqualified divine transcendence mediated by a line of prophets culminating with the Prophet Muhammad, whose earthly life and teachings, enshrined in the *Hadíth* literature, provide believers with the definitive example and inspiration. Because Muslims see humanity in the first place as created for submission and obedience, with no inherent rights against God, they view the human enterprise as essentially different from the divine, except insofar as humanity is subordinate to the exalted law. Christians for their part have sought the authentic vindication of truth without an agreed plan for establishing a religious state. This fact ensures a bewildering variety and diversity of situations and contexts, and, Muslims charge, leaves Christians with religion as a will-o'-the-wisp.

In contrast, Muslims have insisted on the unrivaled supremacy of the code, in particular on the forms and practices that have received uniform and universal recognition throughout the Muslim world, whatever the variations of local accent and style. Ibn Khaldún made some observations on the nature of Christian mission which are pertinent to comparative analysis, because he had in mind explicitly the contrasting case with Islamic mission. Ibn Khaldún argued that Christianity is not a true "missionary religion" because, unlike Islam, it does not embrace religion as a state idea, and without the state religious truth lacks the necessary political instrument to establish and maintain it. Religious mission requires political protection, so said Ibn Khaldún.[2] He went further and argued that a militant temperament is necessary for religious mission. "If the power of wrathfulness were no longer to exist in (man), he would lose the ability to help the truth become victorious. There would no longer be holy war or glorification of the word of God" (Khaldún 1968, 1:415). The supremacy of the code in this sense requires personal aggressiveness and the state instrument. It follows from this that the God of justice requires a just society, and it is reasonable, therefore, that such a God will furnish in religion legal provisions for the just society.

However, Muslim canonical tradition is also impressive for its flexibility in enjoining observance. For example, in minority situations where armed invasion or state support is impractical, believers may be encouraged to cultivate the ethic of retreat (*hijrah*), and, thus, the retrieval and restoration (*isláh*) of the *sunnah* as the heritage of the faithful. In any case, if the interreligious contrasts and differences that have been described here can constrain and encourage at the same time, then a genuine interreligious solidarity would become more than a theoretical possibility. With both their roots in time and eternity, they could broaden each other's horizon by the mere fact of proceeding from their respective elevations. That is bound to be as stimulating as the discovery of common ground once promised.

---

[2] Ibn Khaldún, *Al-Muqaddimah: An Introduction to History*, 3 vols., tr. Franz Rosenthal (Princeton: Princeton University Press for the Bollingen Series, 1968), vol. i, pp. 187f., 322.

(2) *A similar phenomenon of contrast also characterizes the attitude and response to the evangelical demands of witness and service.* It is important to call attention to the way in which Muslims and Christians have gone about the business of transmitting their respective heritages. However much they may trust in natural advantages like birth, territorial location, cultural assimilation, and political and legal warrant to sustain faith practice, Christians and Muslims have nevertheless assigned the care of souls to a class of professional specialists raised and trained for the purpose. Such specialists have in principle constituted the missionary order in the two religions, even if in fact they may engage primarily in priestly and diocesan duties. In this situation, the motivation and source of missionary life arise from a common understanding and experience; truth is given to human custody and must be instilled as well as commended, imbibed as well as informed. The call to repentance is common to both religions. In Islam that call is grounded in the unity of God and of Muhammad as his final, if not his only, envoy, with the consequent affirmation of the supremacy of the religious code, to which it is not permissible to add or from which to subtract, at least in theory. In Christianity, similarly, the call to repentance receives its authority from the ideal of sacrificial love, from undertaking action worthy of it, and from identifying with a community organized for the purpose. In both religions, men and women are challenged to transcend their natural status and grasp the ultimate imperative of life with God. Human beings, qua Muslim and Christian, must encounter the world from the vantage point not of natural or cultural advantage but of the prophetic word spoken to them from beyond time. According to the teachings of the two traditions, worldly imperfection does not exonerate from moral responsibility. Faith and action, word and deed, God and creation, are inseparable, though they are not synonymous. It is this ambivalence, of making a moral connection between faith and action without reverting to a literal connection, that defines the open-ended character of faith and witness. This prompts a question which is best taken up in the concluding section of the chapter; namely, whether interested observers could learn from the Muslim version of faith and witness, and if so, whether this can help illuminate the common search for wholeness of which each side has its own distinctive and contrasting understanding.

(3) *In the historical encounter of Islam—or Christianity—with Africa, several assumptions have been made which we need briefly to question and evaluate.* One of the most widespread assumptions about Islam and Christianity in Africa is that, as foreign religions, both denigrated and devalued the African culture they neither understood nor respected. This attitude is most evident with regard to Christianity in Africa, but it is also true of Islam. A few words on this are necessary.

First of all, it seems not a disadvantage that such criticism was made, for where would Islam and Christianity themselves be if they had never been attacked and condemned by opponents! But more seriously the proponents of easy and unfair missionary conquest seem curiously to be themselves underrating the acute religious sense of the African and to be unheedful of the richly documented cases of communities which actively resisted or successfully adapted the incoming religion.

Second, it is an unfair caricature of the indigenous religions to say they melted away under fire of Muslim or Christian criticism because they lacked intrinsic originality or an inner religious or theological core to survive the challenge of scriptural religion. The tenacity with which these indigenous religions have continued to exercise a grip on African populations is proof that the early missionaries were not fighting an imagined or easy battle and that their well-deserved successes were often protracted, less often sure, and everywhere marked by give and take.

The third point, more fundamental than the preceding two, assumes, correctly, that the missionary religious scene in Africa is occupied by two major categories of people: the people who bring in the religion as transmitters and the people who embrace it as receivers. It further assumes, this time incorrectly, that the more important of the two categories is that of the transmitters, more so with Christian missionaries, while the receivers play a passive role, adopting what is introduced. Allegedly lacking in critical religious judgment, the receivers succumb to force and persuasion and even misguidedly facilitate the attack on local religious customs. Hence the popularity with which many educated Africans today, following Western social anthropologists, have answered the call for "indigenizaton" and Africanization in Christianity, though the call is more muted for Islam. Yet once we reverse the order and allow for the fact that Africans as receivers exercised a far more important role than the agents of transmission, it would take the distraction of the offense to ethnic pride out of the discussion and allow us to get to grips with the subject in its vernacular field setting. Indigenization becomes the critical process of the transposition of the message into local idioms, with local populations the source of that original genius that allows the message to take root and prosper. If we were thus predisposed, we would not have to plead for a nationalist uprising against missionaries for the message to be authentic.

In the case of Islam, one consequence of looking at the African as the more central of the two main classes of people is that the stress which medieval Arabic sources placed on the foreign trader as pioneer par excellence of Islam need not be taken uncritically. It is an understandable occupational hazard that a visiting pioneer, earnest for the purpose, would as likely look a gift horse in the mouth, the gift horse in this case being local converts falling short of imported scruples. Whatever the connection between commerce and Islam, it certainly is not the limpet-like closeness we would like to claim. Sir Thomas Arnold did us yeoman service in detaching Islam from the yoke of the sword and attaching its preaching power to the short- and long-range exploits of the trader.[3] We need to travel further along the same road and separate Islam from theories of economic determinism and other causal factors in order to grasp how the religion drew upon its own internal resources to lay a claim on loyalty and affection by prescribing for human need and aspiration.

CONVERSION

One of the earliest pieces of tangible evidence for the conversion of Africans to Islam comes from the account of al-Bakrí, written in 1067 A.D. He says that the

---

[3] See his *The Preaching of Islam* (London, 1896; repr. Lahore 1967).

ruler of ancient Mali turned to a Muslim cleric for help after a catastrophic drought descended on his land. The king had first tried in vain traditional religious options. As a precondition to attending to his request, the cleric required him to undergo Muslim catechism and to embrace Islam, which he did. Then he and his Muslim patron adjourned to a spot outside the town and undertook what is normally the prayer ritual for rain, *salát al-istisqá*, and the following day, in answer to prayer, dramatic rain clouds developed and filled the heavens. The traditional priests, having been exposed by their failure to bring rain, lost their privileges and were banished by the king, their shrines confiscated. Al-Bakrí adds that numerous people, many of them substantial citizens, followed the king's lead and embraced Islam.[4]

A striking feature of al-Bakrí's account is the natural affinity a fledgling Islam seems to share with organized political societies. Islam takes command of prominent centers of public life, and from there proceeds to extend its sway over the rest of society. However, the trail by which Islam arrives has been blazed by traditional religions, specifically by their showing rainmaking to be essential to what true religion is. Once established, Islam might then go on to apply more stringent aspects of its own code to society, but it would by then have signaled an important concession to indigenous religious forms. There is nothing in this story of an easy or simple triumphalist conquest by Islam. In a situation of genuine stalemate, Islam had to wait for its turn, which came after traditional options had been tried without effect. The fact that traditional worship was not dismantled before Islam had proved its efficacy suggests that old religious attitudes persisted beyond the point of outward adherence to Islam.

We should at the same time underscore the commercial setting of the king's capital, the chief metropolis for stranger commercial communities and their clients. Islam was thus following a well-trodden path. However, although there is more than a hint of a heartfelt affair in the report of the king's conversion, there is little evidence that his act resulted in turning his realm into an Islamic state, in giving what Ibn Khaldún called "the power of wrathfulness" in matters of religion state expression. Indeed, the subsequent history of Mali showed no state-mandated *jihád*, no programs of forcible conversion, and no centrally imposed *Sharí'ah* code on the population. The state encouraged the spread of Islam but otherwise did not enforce it.

My second example, relating to a twelfth-century incident, comes from the seventeenth-century chronicle, the *Ta'ríkh al-Súdán*, by 'Abd al-Rahmán al-Sa'dí. The ruler of the ancient Sudanic city of Jenne, Kanbara, decided one day to embrace Islam. He summoned in his presence all the leading scholars of the city, numbering above forty-two thousand. In their midst he relinquished traditional religious worship and adopted Islam, and, almost as a bargain, promptly put three requests before them. First, that anyone coming to Jenne to seek refuge might find in the city ease and abundance and might as a consequence forget his former country. Second, that foreigners might flock to Jenne as their home and their

---

[4] Al-Bakrí, *Kitáb al-Masálik wa'l-Mamálik*, tr. and ed. M. G. de Slane (Algiers: A. Jourdan, 1913; repr. Paris, 1965), text pp. 74ff., tr. pp. 178ff.

numbers outstrip the original inhabitants. Finally, that merchants traveling to the city might lose patience with conditions prevailing there and, eager to leave it, might be compelled to dispose of their merchandise at derisory prices to the benefit of the inhabitants.

The difficulty of this threefold request might be seen not so much in its range of demands as in how the first and last could be reconciled to effect. The congregation concluded the meeting with a recitation of the *fātihah* as a prayer seal. The chronicler was in no doubt that the requests were granted, his own patriotic faith standing to be vindicated. Following this public conversion of the king and as a sign of his good faith his royal palace *(dār al-sultānah)*, perhaps more the *locus* of the imperial cult, was demolished and a community mosque raised on the site. A second edifice, most probably the residence of the new religious functionaries, was constructed adjacent to the mosque.[5]

It is clear in this account that Islam had long been in contention with traditional worship, and so was establishing its sway over well-charted religious territory. Instead of creating a fresh power base, Islam merely occupied the space and status vacated by its rival. What part internal or material factors played in the disintegration of the old religion is a matter for debate, but that Islam arrived on the scene quietly, without the drama of military confrontation, is self-evident. Indeed, the prayer technique employed to confirm Islam in the city is a replica of the role traditional worship has played. Like the account of al-Bakrí, al-Sa'di's story has deep resonances with the commercial ethos of the town, and although it would be extreme to suggest that it was produced to promote the commercial interests of the town, we would be gullible to ignore that motive altogether. Indeed, commercial calculations might not be entirely absent from the motivations of the ruler, and it would be natural that he would wish his capital to become the nerve center of regional trade. We must, nevertheless, take at face value the stress in the account on the role of the clerics in setting the religious pace for the town and in keeping a safe distance from political authority.

KINGS AND CLERICS

A third example, still on Islamic influence on rulers, comes from ancient Mali and is given by Mahmúd al-Ka'ti in his book, the *Ta'ríkh al-Fattásh*. The local Muslim clerics founded a settlement on the Bafing River called Diakhaba which acquired immense stature as a clerical missionary center dedicated to the spread and practice of Islam. So powerful was this clerical tradition that the ruler of Mali was banned from entering it except once a year, on the 27th Ramadan when, as the deferential guest of the *qádí*, the chief judge and also the city's highest official, the king undertook certain religious obligations. He arranged for meal offerings to be prepared. He placed these in a large bowl which he carried on his head. Calling together Qur'án students and little boys, he distributed the food from his head in a standing position. After consuming the food, the pupils called down

---

[5] Mahmúd al-Ka'tí, *Ta'ríkh al-Súdán*, tr. and ed. Octave Houdas (Paris, 1964; originally published 1913-14), text pp.12-14, tr. pp. 23-24.

blessings on the king as a concluding act. The *Ta'ríkh al-Fattásh* says that Diakhaba ('Ja'ba') remained a redoubtable clerical stronghold so that even those who were guilty of acts of hostility against the king could claim inviolable sanctuary within its borders. It continues: "They gave it the epithet, 'the city of God—*yaqál lahu balad Alláh.*'"[6] The phrase "city of God" enshrines a fundamental implicit principle, namely, the repudiation of religion as a state construct.

Although clearly possessing extraordinary authority as a religious missionary center, Diakhaba was by no means untypical. A similar arrangement existed in Gunjúr, another clerical center founded by emigrants from Diakhaba. There also power was exercised by the *qádí,* to whom the ruler, residing in a different place, paid his respects in his annual religious retreat to the center. Both places were founded by a West African clerical clan, the Jakhanké,[7] whose religious life and practice I have described in another work.

This account of the *Ta'ríkh al-Fattásh* introduces many novel features about clerical Islam which need not detain us here. Some obvious parallels with the preceding examples stand out: the town was an important nexus on the trading artery of the riverain trading system and its organized religious hierarchy made it appropriate for the king to visit it, and on terms, too, that suited the resident clerics. Something of the peaceful reputation of the settlement assured it kingly attention, if not protection. War, or Ibn Khaldún's "power of wrathfulness," seems to play an insignificant role in all the accounts, that is to say, at the point of religious change there was little indication of military upheaval or dramatic violent change. Also the role of Africans as recipients and missionary agents of Islam is underlined. Finally, Islam appears as a less self-secure religion, pursuing a defensive course alongside traditional worship until it is able sufficiently to undermine it from within and eventually to replace it. That a ruler takes on the mien of a humble pilgrim and, in an unregal balancing posture, looks to the prayers of young innocents for his earthly and heavenly security smacks too much of local genius to need an external explanation. The original model for this practice must be lodged deep in the bosom of the African religious environment, in particular, in its sacramental sense of mediating grace.

Another example, also from the *Ta'ríkh al-Fattásh,* spotlights the importance of the cleric vis-à-vis the ruler. The present example improves on earlier ones by giving the cleric the upper hand in a confrontation with the ruler. After many attempts to assert his authority over Timbuktu, the Askiya Muhammad Turé, king of Songhay, visits the city in person and summons the *qádí,* Mahmúd b. 'Umar, to an audience. In the ensuing discussion the *askiya* demanded to know why the *qádí* had resisted his orders and turned away his message-bearers. After a flurry of short questions and answers between the two of them, the *qádí* explained his conduct in these words:

---

[6] *Ta'ríkh al-Fattásh,* tr. and ed. M. Delafosse and O. Houdas (1913-14; Paris, 1964), text p. 179, tr. p. 314.

[7] See "The Origins of Clericalism in West African Islam," *Journal of African History* XVII, 1 (1976), pp. 49-72.

Have you forgotten, or are you feigning ignorance, how one day you came to my house and, crawling up to me, you took me by the feet and held on to my garments and said, "I have come so that you may place yourself in safety between me and the fire of damnation. Help me and hold me by the hand lest I stumble into hell fire. I entrust myself in safe-keeping to you." It is for this reason that I have chased away your message-bearers and resisted your commands (text pp. 60-61, tr. pp. 116-17).

A remarkable position with which the king, more remarkably still, unreservedly concurred. He declared in turn:

By God, it is true that I have forgotten this, but you have now reminded me and you are absolutely right. By God, you deserve great reward for you have saved me from harm. May God exalt your rank and make you my security against the fire. What I have done has provoked the wrath of the All-Powerful, but I beg His forgiveness and turn in penitence to Him. In spite of what I have done I still invoke your protection and attach myself to you. Confirm me in this position under you and God will confirm you (and through you) defend me (text p. 61, tr. p. 117).

It is just possible that the chronicler may in this passage be attempting to paint an exaggeratedly pious image of the *askiya,* but if so then he is employing a device which shows his royal patron being challenged with impunity by a subordinate official. Unless the story is true, the king stands more to lose by it than to benefit from it. That such an encounter took place, perhaps in less dramatic circumstances, I think we can safely accept. It is credible in the context of the separation of religion from political authority. It also shows, furthermore, the esteem in which religion is held by Africans, king and commoner alike.

In incidents reported by the chronicles, political rulers had a hard time securing the subordination of religious functionaries, as we have already seen. A well-known case involves the king of Songhay, Askiya Da'wúd (reigned 1549-1582), who appointed, as was his royal prerogative, the *qádí* of Timbuktu. The official, the revered scholar, Muhammad Baghayogho, refused the appointment. The city's leading jurists subsequently interceded with him on the king's behalf, but even that failed to secure the appointment. It is said that the scholar agreed to be *qádí* only after the king threatened to offer the job to an ignoramus! That particular dispute lasted over a year, with the king forced to find a stop gap (*Ta'ríkh al-Súdán,* 176). In another incident, the king is said to have felt slighted when the prestigious Sankore mosque was being built, because he was not informed. He found out only when the project was nearing completion. Undeterred, he sent a generous donation, which was not turned down as such, only it was not used for the mosque but on repairs to an adjoining cemetery. The king could not have missed the pointed symbolism.

All this evidence points to the complex relationship between religion and the state. The organized, hierarchical nature of Islam qualifies it for co-option, but not for takeover, by the state, and in turn makes the state attractive to Islam.

However, in the prevailing social conditions, Islam and the state could not combine without the overhaul of the moral patronage system control led by the clerics. This clerical power strove to keep its distance from state control, and it did so by reaffirming religious neutrality in secular affairs. It demanded a similar hands-off policy from the state.

MILITANCY

Thus far we have considered one method of maintaining Islam, namely, the quietist way, which places emphasis on the structural aspects of establishing Islam, a reform process to which the name *tajdíd* is given. This method fosters a reputation for trade and for accommodation with secular authority. We shall return to it later, but another important method of Islamic expansion is through the adoption of *jihád*, when the policy of accommodation is overthrown and coercive measures are adopted "to help the truth become victorious," to return to Ibn Khaldún. This is the more dramatic but certainly less frequent strategy of maintaining Islam's missionary strength. Yet even in *jiháds* there was great concern that weak Muslims should be enabled to escape falling deeper into grave error rather than that non-Muslims should forcibly be converted, and sometimes, though not always, this concern was paramount over the desire for conquest and booty.

In this sense one of the greatest missionary movements in African Islam was that led by the Fulani reformer Shaykh 'Uthmán b. Fudi (1754-1817), more commonly known as Shehu Usuman dan Fodio, or simply as the Shehu (from the Arabic *shaykh* meaning "teacher" or "scholar"), and his lieutenants. Beginning about 1786 until his death in 1817, the Shehu toured widely in the Hausa states of North Nigeria preaching Islam and extending the frontiers of his authority. He established the caliphate during this time, with the capital at Sokoto, although he himself withdrew from active politics and allowed his son and brother, Muhammad Bello and 'Abd Alláh dan Fodio, to take the reins of power. Like other Muslim clerics, the Shehu confronted local political rulers with demands and requests, which were mostly granted. For example, he required, and obtained, the submission to Islam of the vacillating sultan of Gobir, Bawa. The latter also bowed to the Shehu's request to free the ruler of a neighboring state with which Gobir was at loggerheads. In fact, the Shehu counseled Bawa during some of the sultan's more difficult military campaigns, and a local chronicle says that Bawa lost his life (1790) in an operation in which he foolhardily exceeded the counsels and limits the Shehu had set.[8]

The Shehu as an individual is outstanding, but he is neither unique nor representative of the broad pattern of islamization and missionary expansion. Many individuals stood in the same militant tradition, devout men who unsheathed the sword of righteousness against unbelief, corruption, and charlatanry. As one writer observes, while it is true that Islam took on the color of water in many societies, it is also true that in others "it is dyed with blood." The *jihád* was adopted as a stern

---

[8] Mervyn Hiskett, *The Sword of Truth: The Life and Times of Shehu Usuman dan Fodio* (New York: Oxford University Press, 1973), pp. 42-46.

and irrevocable duty against polytheists and those venal *malams* (scholars) who encouraged détente with unjust rulers. The *jihádists* were particularly scathing toward such Muslim scholars who had compromised the faith, misled unwary Muslims, and titillated the fancy of oppressive rulers, all this on the basis of bogus credentials![9] All dead wood to be cut down.

The Shehu is also unrepresentative of the broad pattern of islamization. Recent research, in which the present writer has had a share, has revealed the existence in West Africa of a strong quietist clerical clan with a long history of missionary endeavor, and with a pacific and politically neutral reputation to boot. The tantalizing references to Islam in ancient Ghana and Mali, with particular reference to the Serakhullé (also known as the Soninké) inhabitants of Ghana, can now be more meaningfully gathered together, though that is best done elsewhere. The Serakhullé clerics are the most powerful and enduring group in Black African Islam. Better known as the Jakhanké, who founded Diakhaba and Gunjúr already referred to, the clerics established a missionary career based on scrupulous abjuration of war and of politics *(al-harb wa al-siyásah),* including chieftaincy office for themselves. In modern times they created a prosperous center at Touba in Guinea (1803). The town was invaded and occupied without opposition by the French in 1911. The Málikí *muftí* of Senegal and the *muftí* of Burkina Faso were both of Jakhanké clerical stock. The clerics are reputed to have spread Islam to Hausaland in the fifteenth century and today they or their disciples can be found in various parts of Africa. Characteristic of their mode of expansion is the creation of what they call a *majlis,* essentially a clerical/educational parish from which Islam is taken to surrounding areas. Names for such *majlis* centers sometimes suggest their missionary purpose: *Nibrás* (lantern light), *Touba* (blessedness, tree of Paradise), *Taybatu* (sweet-smelling, an epithet for Medina), *Nema (ni'mah,* grace, blessing), *Dár Salám* (abode of peace, sphere of Islam), and so on.

In the same peaceful if controversial vein could be fitted the Ahmadiyah Muslim missionary movement in many parts of West Africa. The Ahmadís have been very warily received, if not repudiated, by Sunni Muslim communities in West Africa,[10] and their inclusion here is only for the purpose of emphasizing that even in a distant tributary of Islam the missionary ardor was far from being quenched. Their involvement in modern schools and medical care is an example of Muslim awareness of opportunities for service, just as Christians discovered in their pioneer years.

---

[9] Mervyn Hiskett, "The Islamic Tradition of Reform in the Western Sudan from the 16th to the 18th Century," *Bulletin of the School of Oriental and African Studies* XXV, 3 (1962), pp. 575-96.

[10] Al-Hájj Muhammad Fádilu Fadera, of Senegambia, has strongly condemned the Ahmadiyah in a closely written forty-five-page booklet, *Kitáb Tahdhíru Ummati 'I-Muhammadiyát min Ittibái 'l-firqati Ahmadiyát (A Warning to the Muslim Community on the Dangers of Following the Ahmadiyah Sect),* printed in Dakar, n.d. During fieldwork in 1972 the present writer saw evidence of the document being disseminated along travel routes.

INTERRELIGIOUS UNDERSTANDING

It remains now to consider, in this final section, how Christians might understand and respond to such complex Islamic missionary activity. This is best done by outlining first the stages through which Muslim-Christian relations have passed.

In the early stages of contact between the two communities, there was scant interest in dialogue or mutual understanding. This was true from the late fifteenth century to the end of the eighteenth century, when the pace for the abolition of the slave trade picked up. We might call this stage one of indifference, although both sides had dormant images of each other that were caricatures. This was subsequently followed by the era of great rivalry, which lasted through much of the nineteenth century. Christians and Muslims regarded each other with something bordering on hysteria as each side billeted recruits to wage its campaign. The Christian missionary movement, insofar as it was controlled by foreign bodies, found itself sharing aims with the colonial administration in certain places. One aim in which both cooperated was the attempt to check the spread of Islam as an anti-Christian and an anticolonial force. The missionaries were also acting from fear, fear of losing African converts to Islam and of seeing Christianity defeated by Islam as an unworthy rival. It was a similar motive which led some later missionaries to acquiesce grudgingly in the apparent ease with which Islam was gaining followers. Gradually, however, Christian missionaries came to acquire a reserved tolerance for Islam on the grounds that it established a tender bridge to a higher revelation which the African was incapable of reaching in one brief stride. A paradox developed here: the call to Christian service must be obeyed toward Africans for whom the claims of a rival religion were admitted to be more suitable! The other side of the paradox cut against the church, which labored under a self-inflicted pessimism in the face of alleged Islamic expansion in Africa. And yet the picture it painted, or allowed to be painted, of Islamic strength in Africa and of its own not inconsiderable contribution to the missionary enterprise concealed the true nature of the process of religious change in the two religions. It also paved the way for a vocal, but by no means representative, reaction to Christianity as a religion imposed institutionally from outside and maintained by Western colonial patronage, thus reinforcing the now questionable supposition that Western transmitters of the faith were superior to Africans as receivers.

The era of rivalry had its colonial version too. The French, perhaps more than the British, Portuguese, or Germans, were deeply involved with Islam in North and West Africa. At one stage so resolved were the French to scotch what they alarmingly called "the Islamic peril" that they staged what a French scholar/administrator termed "the St. Bartholomew's massacre of the marabouts."[11] In fact, this was mainly a round-up operation of the leading Muslim scholars of Guinea precedent to their incarceration in Mauritania. This was the incident described above, when the French invaded Touba in 1911 and arrested the leading Jakhanké

---

[11] Paul Marty, *L'Islam en Guinée* (Paris: E. Leroux, 1921), p. 117. See also Mourey and Terrier, *L'Expansion Francaise et la Formation Territoriale* (Paris, 1910), p. 234.

clerics along with others on suspicion of fomenting a maraboutic insurrection. It was clear that the French were acting upon an articulate policy toward Islam. For example, a French officer serving in the Algerian colonial service was once dispatched to West Africa with specific orders to report on the most effective means to be employed to halt the march of Islam in lands slowly coming under French protection. Particularly, the French wanted to know the feasibility of a *cordon sanitaire* being set up in Islam's path. All these efforts were ironically facilitated by the propensity of African Muslims to withdraw into obscure enclaves to practice the faith.

One of the best examples of the coalescence of such Christian missionary fear of Islam and colonial mistrust was Freetown where, in the mid-nineteenth century, a policy was evolved to try to check the flow of Muslims from the hinterland into the Freetown peninsula, and once there to segregate the two groups in demarcated residential areas. This was called the Parish Scheme. But a short time later the situation was dramatically altered, chiefly as a result of the single-handed efforts of Dr. Edward Blyden, the great black nationalist.[12]

The era of rivalry between the two religions was followed by what we may loosely term the years of confinement, lasting through the active phase of colonial expansion into the first decades of the twentieth century. Islam's retreat before encroaching colonialism had become a precondition of its self-image by the time strong local Christian communities were established on the coast, and the two sides remained in comparative isolation, an entente even if it was not cordial. Christianity nestled along the coast, supported, and more often checked, by a strong commercial population, while Islam cultivated the virtue of rustic cloisters. Walter Miller, for example, the pioneer missionary of the Church Missionary Society in North Nigeria, observed censoriously that the Muslim leaders believed that "their isolation from the world was almost hermetic, and only the merest breath of information stole through the few, not quite closed doors."[13] But even Muslims in full retreat were asking if the period of isolation looming ahead need be an inevitable or permanent stalemate. One European pioneer was asked by a group of keen Muslims, "Why dost thou not respect our prophet as an envoy from the Most High, since we acknowledge Christ as such?"[14]

This era of confinement, while it lasted, had a disastrous effect on the work of Christian bridge-builders like Dr. Blyden, whose attempts to establish modern schools among Muslims, with the necessary government support, were resisted by Muslim isolationists like Legally Savage. While it is true that Christians have unwarrantedly feared or, in isolation, misrepresented the strengths and weaknesses of Islam, it is also true, almost as a necessary corollary, that Muslims have had

---

[12] Dr. Blyden's formative work was on this subject: *Christianity, Islam and the Negro Race* (London, 1887; repr. Edinburgh: Edinburgh University Press, 1967).

[13] Walter Miller, *Reflections of a Pioneer* (London: CMS, 1936), p. 23. Miller was writing in about 1900.

[14] Gaspard Mollien, *Travels in Africa to the Sources of the Senegal and Gambia in 1818* (London, 1820), p. 51.

like perceptions of Christianity. Such attitudes thrive from the renewable resource
of mutual mistrust.

The apparent failure, however, of people like Dr. Blyden or Legally Savage
points to a real need for both communities to emerge from confinement and isolation, which came about from the consequences of nationalism and independence.
The retreat which imperial rule precipitated among Muslims was extended by the
emergence of nationalist politics and independence. The relative inability of traditional Muslim élites to compete successfully for jobs in modern states has robbed
them further of many of those ideals which prompted their withdrawal. The phenomenon of Muslim constituents, under the direction of the traditional *'ulamá*
(scholars), voting into power men with whom they share little or no confessional
solidarity is a demonstration of the withdrawal attitude. This only postpones some
of the issues which confinement has created.

A partial withdrawal, which relies on the amenability of local politicians to
Muslim demands and interests, could prepare the way for loosening the chains of
confinement. Muslim interests might be seen to lie more and more in the arena of
modern options, as numerous groups and organizations in Freetown and elsewhere are discovering, and with such a gradual shift of the center of Muslim
activity there might come an increase in Christian contact already underway in
many places. In fact, what has happened is that, beginning in the mid-1970s,
Muslim political activism erupted into the open, demanding national attention.
The *Sharí'ah* has been a catalyst for this. Muslims have organized behind it with
calls for its adoption as public law. With little experience of running a religious
state, Christians have found themselves outflanked and outmaneuvered, and any
response they have given has necessarily been a variation or modification of
Muslim initiatives. There could be no mistaking which side has been setting the
pace.

AFRICAN CHRISTIAN INDEPENDENCY

The closest Christian Africans have come to Islamic religious militancy has
been in the history of African Christian Independency, for that was one of the
most sustained attempts at applied religion. The rise and growth of Independency
thus echoed the standard themes of Muslim *jihád*. Historians concerned only with
the political basis of African Christianity have stressed the populist, anti-élitist
nature of Independency. That may be true, but Independency is a complex movement whose features we may summarize as follows, taking in the Muslim *jihád*
comparison at the same time.

The Apocalyptic Theme

We may begin with the apocalyptic theme and say: i) Independency has made
striking use of apocalyptic materials from the Bible and combined these with a
messianic creed. ii) Independency and *jihád* strove after a millenarian version of
religion, with an apocalyptic anticipation of divine intervention and triumph in
human affairs. iii) Both movements used dreams and visions to supplement stan-

dard revelation. iv) Both encouraged withdrawal from the world and both used the office of prophesy to proclaim the impending arrival of God's reign. v) To emphasize their break with and disdain of the world, both movements employed divinatory techniques of obtaining guidance and giving instructions and orders to secure allegiance. vi) In heralding the coming of the expected millennium, both preached a triumphalist message in which their version of sin and injustice determined where and against whom the sword of truth was to be unsheathed.

Structural Factors

Second, there were structural factors concerning organizing and mobilizing a popular movement, namely, i) Both movements stressed the role of the minority community as the carrier of religious truth and insisted on the need to overtake and recast mainstream values and institutions. This minority status of the virtuous community was invested with a historical mission to change the world and thus to transcend itself. Thus in its transitory condition the community of *jihád* and Independency adhered to strict codes of behavior and observance and fed upon rituals that the larger community had inexcusably corrupted or forsaken. ii) In strikingly identical language, *jihád* and Independency denounced the status quo and the leadership that fostered it. iii) Both made membership in their movement a prerequisite of sound faith. iv) Both movements riveted on their followers the heavy chains of discipline and personal sacrifice. v) Organizationally, Independency and *jihád* relied on charismatic concepts of authority vested in the founder's family, with succession reverting to the founder's children.

MODERNIST REACTION

In a similar way, *jihád* and Independency were a reaction in their respective historical contexts. In the case of the *jihád*, that context was the persistence of indigenous structures and idioms among local Muslims, while in Independency it was the intrusion of modernist forces into traditional life, symbolized by missionary overlordship. Eventually, as in the movement of al-Hajj 'Umar al-Fútí (d. 1864), the *jihád* reacted with military force against growing European power in hinterland Africa, while Christian Independency was born out of the clash with colonial and missionary authorities, beginning in Freetown in the 1820s and continuing for over a century there and elsewhere.

THE COMPARATIVE DIMENSION

However, not to ignore differences, the *jihád* combined physical combat with spiritual warfare and directed itself to setting up a theocratic state, whereas Independency contented itself with waging only a spiritual struggle of mass experience and personal transformation, but without the slightest hint of a program to create and run a religious state. That was the telling difference.

Thus the emergence of Independency has directed the attention of Christian Africans to the inward jurisdiction, to the control and subduing of unholy human impulses, and away from the outward program of world conquest. Independency was a committed search for healing and holiness, for the rule and gifts of God in the temple of a transformed humanity. All of that would express itself in vernacular accents and in local styles. Thus Independency revealed a vigorous field of interaction between the church and its preponderant African context. Hence the renewed interest in the church in customary religious practices in Africa. A new field of dialogue has been discovered almost within the walls of the church.

A similar situation has existed in Islam, which means the two sides can meet on the religious level. One brief example may suffice. Local accounts say that when Islam was first introduced to Yorubaland (perhaps in the eleventh or twelfth century) by a Hausa Muslim, the people of Ife at first resisted the new faith, but afterward retrieved the sack of the missionary containing a copy of Qur'án, covered it with a pot and began to worship it as Odudua. Thus began the cult of Odudua among the Yorubas.[15] Of course this is only a story and may not actually describe a historical incident. But it does show how Islam can be conceived among traditional worshipers, namely, as a religion on which indigenous conceptions might act as stimulus and articulator.

INTERRELIGIOUS INITIATIVES

The field of dialogue which Independency has widened is one which the churches in Africa have recently begun to explore and expand. In 1960 it was agreed to institutionalize this concern for dialogue with Islam, and thus was created the Islam-in-Africa Project, later to become the Project for Christian-Muslim Relations in Africa (Procmura, for short). It grew out of the concern of the churches to train their people with integrity so that they can carry out their responsibility toward their Muslim neighbors, with the demand especially to nurture interreligious trust and understanding. If religion matters to Africans, as it evidently does, then persons who are ill-informed or ill-motivated may miss completely its important connections and influences in personal life and social practice, with grave loss for intercommunal solidarity and real risk of mutual distortion and unilateral judgment. This would be as true for Christians as for Muslims. In the event, Procmura has felt it to be in the interest of both sides that religious communities take the lead in fostering knowledge and respect for each other's tradition, and that Christian and Muslim Africans not shy away from open religious conversation in the mistaken belief that avoiding religion will advance tolerance on more secure foundations, all this without being driven by the forces of political expedience. The evidence Procmura has produced has shown impressive interfaith sensitivity among Africans, and nothing dramatizes that fact better than the widespread attitude of Muslim and Christian Africans supporting each other's faith: with donations, labor, personal visits, and participation in each other's feasts. Thus, for example, have churches and mosques and other religious structures been preserved and maintained in friendly proximity. The fact is that Christian and Muslim Africa is for the most part enfolded within the larger setting of the old

---

[15] R. E. Dennett, *Nigerian Studies* (London, 1910; repr. London: Frank Cass, 1968), p. 75. Dennett reproduces a local account.

Africa, with its deep-rooted hospitality, tolerance, and generosity, and it would be surprising if nothing of that admirable heritage did not survive in the new religions. Both sides are involved in a creative transformation process, and it cannot be stressed enough how much Christian and Muslim Africans owe to traditional Africa, whatever the rhetoric of religious propaganda.[16] Less than that common debt would be reason enough for the two communities to compare and exchange views as a matter of mutual trust. As it is, signs are hopeful, for much of the literature Procmura has produced has been in almost equal demand by Muslims and Christians: factual accounts of the two religions, the challenge of identification with the nonliterate traditional religions of Africa, and imaginative, sympathetic descriptions of the spiritual life. Public meetings, lectures, and talks, drawing both Muslims and Christians, have also been in demand.

Procmura, then, as a modest contribution of the churches in Africa to bilateral harmony between the two faiths has clearly filled a need. In this sense it has also helped prepare the way for the next stage in interfaith relations, that is, encounter. The confident, though conciliatory, approach that Procmura has shaped and encouraged in dialogue is itself a contributory factor to genuine encounter. It would be unflattering to Islam to suggest that it can be encountered only when the full claims of Christianity are mitigated by a desire for a temporary or illusory solidarity, and vice versa. To demand the removal of boundaries as a precondition to meeting is to deny beforehand the possibility of meeting at all. True friendship can penetrate those boundaries and render false or harmful ones dispensable, replacing them with genuine tolerance and celebration of difference. The unity that comes about under those circumstances would not be at each other's expense, or anyone else's.

RESPONSE

If a question is asked about the interreligious response to Muslim religious activity, three things may be said in the light of experience. The first is the unquestioned importance of Muslim Africa for interreligious understanding and engagement and how the African setting seems to have accentuated the theological and moral aspects of faith practice. That is to say, religion carried little overt political threat, except as restraint. The devout and humble clerics held emperors, kings, and princes to account through the clerics' frail grasp and partial glimpse of the Creator. There is, of course, the danger of religion being set up as a consolidated power structure and being deified or demonized as such. But that danger, common in fact to all human endeavor, is not avoided by denying religion through the countless evasive and alternative techniques offered us by secular culture. In a good deal of Africa, religion in all its immense diversity and with all its momentous capacity for good as well as for ill, continues to thrive and prosper, requiring

---

[16] Pope Paul VI spoke to this spirit of mutual trust when he called for openness and honesty in dialogue. See Francis O. Nwaiwu, *Inter-Religious Dialogue in African Context: Christianity, Islam and African Religion* (Munich: African University Studies, 1990).

only that we overcome our self-imposed scruples to expound it fairly and sensitively. Consequently, all persons of goodwill may be encouraged and instructed by the frank and direct way Muslim Africans appear to have understood and discharged their missionary obligation.[17]

The second is that in spite of the close identity of Islam and the African religious scene, there was a fundamental unity of thought and practice with world Islam. The Arabic language of the Qur'án and the commentaries, the prayer postures, the Islamic lunar calendar, and the figure and example of the Prophet have all helped strengthen the universal missionary appeal of Islam. The Christian could derive ecumenical profit from this confessional solidarity of Muslims.

A third observation relates to religious jingoism which both Christians and Muslims have separately espoused, with or without political instruments. Although triumphalist movements have dramatized legitimate objections to this world as the ultimate and absolute, there are nevertheless pitfalls. But first a word about motives. It is right that people should be led by ethical commitment to oppose an unjust, oppressive, and callous social and political order. The stark dichotomy between a world deeply scarred by cruelty, exploitation, poverty, and injustice on the one hand and, on the other, a vision of another unsullied and radiant through righteous and ethical action, is enough to stir people of conscience in the deepest recesses of their sense of duty and loyalty. That is the stuff of which the psalms are made and by which the prophets are defined.

Nevertheless, there have been difficulties, as we have seen. Religious programs to remedy such an inadequate world have failed in their turn. An elevated vision of the kingdom of God has been no guarantee of its realization, and the records of both Muslims and Christians have been littered with the broken hopes and betrayed trust of religious idealism. Religion may inspire and challenge, but always with its antidotes of humility, self-criticism, and self-denial. Faith carries with it as a permanent peril the sedulous defect of cultural arrogance. The question asked above may now be taken up again: to what extent may religious people hold firmly to the promise of the kingdom to come and still participate meaningfully, if critically, in an imperfect world? If believers have made a fetish of success in the past, and reaped retributive failure in consequence, are they not in equal danger today of normatizing inertia and evasive indifference?

Three things to say on this. First, the historical record of the Western missionary movement has come under stringent investigation, with a special focus on Western cultural superiority as the basis of much of missionary motivation. It has

---

[17] Commenting on the visit of Pope John Paul II to Muslim West Africa in May 1991, Cokkie van't Leven reported that the Holy Father could not help but notice the pervasive influence of *teranga*, the Wolof for hospitality and respect, in society. Back in Rome and still reflecting on his West African experience, the pope instructed Cardinal Francis Arinze to communicate his personal gratitude and appreciation to the Muslim and Christian community leaders, whose welcome he had grown to cherish (Cokkie van't Leven, "Africa's Tradition of Peaceful Co-existence: Threatened Dream or Lasting Reality?," in Ge Speelman, Jan van Lin, and Dick Mulder, eds., *Muslims and Christians in Europe: Breaking New Ground: Essays in Honour of Jan Slomp* (Kampen: Uitgeverij, 1993).

occasioned much contrition and retreat among the mainline Western churches, who have acknowledged that the trumpeted call to evangelical commitment did not prevent a mixed baggage of ethical principle, humanitarian impulse, political cynicism, and cultural hubris to be assembled in the West and unpacked in the mission field. The West has still not recovered sufficiently from that legacy, and Muslim missionary endeavor has shown no signs of being an exception to this historical experience of ambivalence and ambiguity.

Second, understanding the impressive history of Islamic *da'wah* in Africa has been stimulating and challenging for those in the West who have reflected on the matter, stimulating because it has demonstrated to any interested observer how seriously Muslims have taken the vocation of witness. The devotion and sense of self-sacrifice which Muslims have shown in obedience to the call to spread and establish the faith have been a poignant reminder of what lies at the heart of religious commitment. Almost from their earliest contact with Muslim groups, Western observers have written admiringly of the public practice of Islam. The muezzin's brisk and clear call to prayer, the simple daily gestures of surrender and self-abasement before the Creator in the prayer ritual, and the donning of the garb of poverty, self-denial and personal sacrifice in the fast of Ramadan are some of the things specially noted. Even a well-seasoned Muslim traveler like Ibn Battúta was astonished in 1352 A.D. when he saw the esteem in which local Muslims in West Africa held Qur'ánic learning, and their punctilious observance of Friday worship made an equally favorable impression on him.[18] The challenge consists in learning through commitment an identical lesson of humility. The Muslim reformers discovered that their confidence in the supremacy of the revealed law had to be tempered with the experience of people's ambivalence or weakness even when they professed the creed, thus suggesting that the path to absolute submission is a difficult and often elusive one.

The third and final point, arising out of the preceding one, is that Islam's victories in the *jihád* wars made it vulnerable to men with worldly ambition, and schismatic consequences followed. The community of the faithful, spread over vast lands of wealth and power, succumbed to internal dissension and factionalism. Rebellions broke up the unity forged in the fire of faith and reform, a poignant reminder to utopian champions everywhere, too, that this world cannot be a substitute for the true reign of God. Once religious militancy turned to institution-building in the caliphate, the reformers found that the face they would give to truth was tarnished by numerous blemishes of greed, insincerity, and compromise. Their habit of keeping record of the failures of their opponents now served to remind them of worse scandals among themselves. It turns out that "the glorification of the word" by the sword is a dubious moral undertaking, because the impeccable standards of revealed truth to which theocrats would hold the world burden them with spectacular liabilities.

Ethical commitment, then, has to reckon with the fact that the broken records of past attempts, the broken vessels of human communication by which ethical

---

[18] Ibn Battúta, *Travels in Asia and Africa*, tr. and ed. H. A. R. Gibb (London, 1929; repr. London: Routledge & Kegan Paul, 1957), p. 330.

concerns seek practical expression, this brokenness must condition all primary human motivation rather than being seen as a denial of commitment. For a significant portion of Muslim Africa, people seem content to live in a provisional ethical order, to tarry in the broad, temporal space between revealed imperative and its deferred final consummation. Their hope is fixed in that consummation which makes worthwhile the struggle of attempts at obedience. It was courage, born of deep personal trust, that enabled small, pioneering Muslim communities to pitch tent in obscure frontier corners of Africa. Yet it was also the gracious hospitableness, the *teranga*, of host communities that offered precious haven, a secure threshold, to stranger Muslims. Africa's old sanctions thus bear the seeds of such threshold encounter as proof and vindication, with Muslims and others profiting therefrom. However, *teranga* may not survive the stringent choice Muslims are disposed to force.

In those circumstances the Muslim reform would appeal to arguments that purists use to divide the world between truth and falsehood, between ideals and compromise, with an implicit appeal to the political instrument as guarantor of virtue and righteousness. It is in their nature, however, for ideals to look and sound superior, while practice looks untidy and ambiguous. Consequently, the modernist Muslim appeal to practice is vulnerable to logical assault from radical idealists and their essentialist creed. Yet that idealist scheme is to the same degree at risk from practice, for implementing the ideal code will reveal intrinsic weaknesses in the human schematization of it. It will blur the line between winners and losers, between the oracles of rectitude and the foot soldiers of policy. In practice, then, differences would emerge that would implicate past motives and carry retroactive stigma. Not even the sources would be safe from spoilt ideals. Thus, even if we believe that revealed injunction establishes the folly of seeking alternative sources of truth and guidance, we should recognize that religion as a state idea has nevertheless to reckon with the inadequacies of human instrumentality and the invidiousness of human insinuation. The reasonable course would be to accept that not all was bad in the old order, that its heritage of hospitableness, which encouraged minority communities to grow and flourish, had something of abiding value, and that you do not quarantine truth merely by tempering it with the political sword. That is why the attempt to have strict, practical models hewn out of ideals has typically created debate and controversy in the religious community. Nowhere has such controversy flourished better than in the overlap between religion and state authority, an overlap which the classical separation of church and state has evaded or else sought to abolish. But whether it ignores it or takes it over, the state instrument in any case falls far short of the religious apprehension of truth. I shall return to this matter in later parts of this work.

CHAPTER BIBLIOGRAPHY

'Ali, Michael Nazir. *Frontiers in Muslim-Christian Encounter.* Oxford: Regnum Books, 1987; repr. 1991.
_____. *Islam: A Christian Perspective.* Philadelphia: Westminster Press, 1984.

Bakrí, al-. *Kitáb al-Masálik wa'l-Mamálik (Book of Routes and Realms)*. Edited by M. G. de Slane. Algiers: A. Jourdan, 1913.

Battúta, Ibn. *Travels in Asia and Africa*. Translated and edited by H. A. R. Gibb. London, 1929; repr. London: Routledge & Kegan Paul, 1957.

Blyden, Edward W. *Christianity, Islam and the Negro Race*. London 1887; repr. Edinburgh: Edinburgh University Press, 1967.

Carriere, Rene, and Paul Holle. *De la Senegambie Française*. Paris, 1955.

Dennett, R. E. *Nigerian Studies*. London, 1910; repr. London: Frank Cass, 1968.

Fadera, al-Hájj Muhammad Fádilu. *Kitáb Tahdhíru Ummati 'I-Muhammadiyát min Ittibái 'l-firqati Ahmadiyát (A Warning to the Muslim Community on the Dangers of Following the Ahmadiyah Sect)*. Printed in Dakar, n.d.

Hiskett, Mervyn. *The Development of Islam in West Africa*. London: Longman, 1984, chaps. 13, 16, and 17.

_____. "The Islamic Tradition of Reform in the Western Sudan from the 16th to the 18th Century." *Bulletin of the School of OrientalAfrican Studies* XXV, 3 (1962).

_____. *The Sword of Truth: The Life and Times of Shehu Usuman dan Fodio*. New York: Oxford University Press, 1973.

Ka'ti, Mahmúd al-. *Ta'ríkh al-Fattásh*. Translated and edited by O. Houdas and M. Delafosse. Paris: Librairie d'Amérique et d'Orient Adrien-Maisonneuve, 1964.

Lugard, Lady (*nee* Flora Shaw). *A Tropical Dependency*. London, 1906; repr. London, 1964.

Marty, Paul. *L'Islam en Guinee*. Paris: E. Leroux, 1921.

Miller, Walter. *Reflections of a Pioneer*. London: CMS, 1936.

Mollien, Gaspard. *Travels in Africa to the Sources of the Senegal and Gambia in 1818*. London, 1820.

Mourey and Terrier. *L'Expansion Française et la Formation Territoriale*. Paris, 1910.

Sa'dí, 'Abd al-Rahmán al-. *Ta'ríkh al-Súdán*. Translated and edited by O. Houdas. Paris: Librairie d'Amérique et d'Orient, Adrien-Maisonneuve, 1964.

Sanneh, Lamin. "The Origins of Clericalism in West African Islam," *Journal of African History* XVII, 1 (1976).

Stock, Eugene. *A History of the Church Missionary Society*. Vols. ii and iii. London, 1916.

Zwemer, Samuel. *Arabia: The Cradle of Islam*. New York, 1900.

_____, ed. *The Mohammedan World of Today*. New York, 1906.

2

Muhammad's Significance for Christians

Biography, History, and Faith

My earliest memories as a child growing up in Muslim West Africa have the image of the Prophet Muhammad stamped on them, not simply as the casual frill of an impressionable religious mind, but as the solid etched image of a historical personality, someone who actually broke surface and commanded men and women while angels held their breath. Muhammad erupted into my life almost at the same time as I myself burst into the life of my community. My baptismal name, Karamo, meaning "scholar," given to me on the eighth day of my birth, was suspended until the women on my mother's side performed a separate ceremony in which they conferred on me the name Ma-Lamin, a local variant of Muhammad al-Amín, as befitted a firstborn son. That name, in its shortened form, Lamin, stuck.

New mothers with their infants are held in house quarantine until the eighth day after birth. On that day the imam officiates at a religious ceremony which is held in the morning. The time for it may be signaled by the sound of the kettle drum otherwise used for summoning worshipers to Friday worship. The infant's head is shaved and water poured over it. The imam and the assembled gathering seat themselves facing east and recite the *fátihah*, the Lord's Prayer of Islam, followed by the *kalimah* or *shahádah*, the Muslim creed, which the imam alone intones and then spits into the ears of the child, first into the right ear and then into the left. The creed witnesses to the sovereignty of God and to the Prophet's blessed uniqueness. The *kalimah* as creed is not a tariff of belief so much as a proclamation of what one takes to be the case. With a blessing, the imam then lays his right hand on the child's head and pronounces its name as instructed by the parents. When he has done that, he picks up the child with both hands and raises it to shoulder height by way of public presentation, at the same time declaring its newly acquired name. He invites the assembly to join in a prayer of safety and thanksgiving for the child and its parents. Normally, kola-nuts and unleavened bread would be distributed as an offering. That would conclude the formal parts of the rite of baptism. An informal, rather boisterous reception would follow, with pancakes and nonalcoholic ginger beer, marking a contrast to the earlier and more sedate religious ceremony.

The second stage of the name-giving ceremony belonged to the domain of women and combined religion with secular celebration: there was drumming, singing, dancing, and participation in a communal feast. The year of my birth, which occurred during the Second World War, a war in which my mother's brother was drafted and killed, though never acknowledged as such by the government, coincided with the introduction of the farthing coin as a new currency unit in British colonial Africa, and people changed their pennies as well as shillings into four or forty-eight times as many farthing coins to create a sense of affluence and good times. The women decorated themselves with pieces of the new coin attached to an assortment of colorful threads and strung from their heads, and the men attended the ceremony in their finery. The birth of this Muhammad as another Ma-Lamin was occasion for communal jollification as much as for honoring anew God's exalted Envoy whose own birth brought glad tidings to the world. In that way, the Prophet's *barakah*, his grace and virtue, was celebrated on the numerous occasions when firstborn sons received his name in public collective ceremonies. Thus Muhammad became the established rule of social conduct, the rule that made first claim on the pride of the tribe. The Prophet's grand historical mission of bringing God's message to humanity was thus affirmed on the numerous occasions when families and communities dedicated to him male children to obtain his *barakah* and to express their gratitude.

As I grew up, relatives, friends and even casual acquaintances referred to me by a variety of salutations—Saïbo, "the companion," Mustafa, "the chosen," "al-Amín," "the faithful one," among others—all by virtue of bearing the Prophet's name. It was often discipline enough to be told that your conduct in a given situation was unworthy of the man whose name you bore. By the same token, if people wanted to compliment you they would salute you by an attribute of the Prophet. In course of time you yourself began to think of such compliments as the pattern of conduct that was right and proper to follow. A further refinement might occur with the sense that if you had even a morsel of the Prophet's *barakah*, your conduct would reflect his example and precept without your straining, and that the fragrance of his *barakah* would infuse your whole being to such an extent that your actions and deeds would exude his sweetness.

I recognize that such religious sentiments are regarded with embarrassment bordering on scandal among some Christians, and certainly among our theological experts for whom such sentiments smack too much of religious mystification to be acceptable. My own encounter with that version of Western skepticism was the way I was first greeted in the church when I sought Christian baptism. After I was shown an alternative door in the neighboring Catholic church, which ignored me, I was accepted in the Protestant church on condition that I read books on the historical-critical method as applied to the texts of the New Testament. The heart of that procedure is that God is not a demonstrable cause and so cannot be a subject for history. In the logic of causation, then, religion must be predicated of human subjects, which allows religion to be constituted in terms of cause and effect.

A statement I recently came across expresses this sentiment that faith is the ideal representation of things that need have no historical existence, that the mind has powers of invention greater than what is historically or naturally feasible. The statement asserts, "As a trained theologian and pastor, I am not concerned with whether there was an Abraham, a Noah, a 40-year trek in the wilderness or an invasion of Palestine. The stories were created to convey the theological truth that God empowers, guides and saves. Faith is the key."[1] Even today, it is striking how such a claim rests on no surer foundation than a flare of cotton waste, with the divine centerpiece torn out of it, a sort of utility piece that allows us to embroider on it whatever image we choose. The sort of God we stitch on it, being merely our own doublet, cannot do any of those things that we cannot do for ourselves. And what use is a see-through God, or, for that matter, a key that merely repeats the pattern of our own wishful thinking? It is vain pretense.

In any case, in my situation I followed the advice of my church and studied the critical method, in part because my upbringing had instilled in me a deep respect for elders and for those in authority, and in part because religion had been such a primary force in my life that even the secondary forms of it that I encountered in the historical-critical method failed to intimidate or deter me. My Christian teachers were in disbelief, because here I was exposed to the icons of an enlightened brilliant critical tradition (I was referred to Hume and Kant), one which had in other respects so stimulated me, and I was still clinging to a religious worldview. So they responded with an embargo of their own. When I asked for permission to study theology in University, I was refused. The reason given was baffling, namely, that a liberal arts program would be more beneficial because it would offer the background and depth for which theology would be a fitting conclusion. This is obviously sound practice, though it is not the British practice. However, I was too intimidated to argue. I was in too much awe of liberal Christianity to question openly its announced position, and having been taught to obey first and complain later, surrender came naturally, if not permanently.

In fact, I made a virtue of necessity. I behaved in a way to express my appreciation for the opportunity of study, any study, and a sense that many others never had such a chance. Here I was being drawn so generously into the rich tradition of critical study, sharpening my wits against the detractors and despisers of truth. Besides, admission into the church fulfilled a deep compelling desire, one I could not suppress in spite of the obstacles, while critical historical discipline helped set the path I would follow as a lifelong career. I would thank God for opportunities unplanned and blessings unmerited.

The surrender which came so naturally with regard to the advice of my superiors was part and parcel of the equally natural religious disposition which even the historical-critical tradition, developed with regard to the New Testament, did not weaken but instead deepened, helping me to appreciate all the more the importance of history to faith, and vice versa. The conflict that so many writers saw

---

[1] "The Bible: Fact or Fiction," *Time* (January 15, 1996), p. 11.

between fact and opinion, between objective data and subjective feelings, between scientific evidence and religious invention, or between history and myth, did not exist for me. Even as a child I saw how a community's symbols, the object and subject of its history, could shape and motivate, and in turn be shaped and motivated by its actions and reflection, by its conduct and intention, its deeds and aspirations. As a student about to embark for college, I also sensed a deeper problem with the kind of historical skepticism the West had otherwise so brilliantly pioneered, a critical skepticism with momentous consequences for the emancipation of the individual and for modernity. That deeper problem was the tendency of an enlightenment West to be indifferent to, intolerant even of non-Western cultures. My church, which felt compelled to stand firm on historical form criticism as a condition for being Christian, felt no similar obligation with regard to the abundant non-Western cultural materials that surrounded it on all sides, in music, song, dance, art, idioms, dreams, ritual ceremony, and general way of life. And thus you have the paradox of a missionary church proposing to pursue its calling with the effective hand of outreach tied behind its back. It was not a convincing situation, and even the church knew it.

Thus, standing today within what the critical method has fashioned of Christianity and at the opposite end of my childhood upbringing, I return to the subject of Muhammad in order to stress again the crucial worldly character of his religious mission and how he established religious claims as the defining rule of social conduct and historical practice. For Muhammad, God was truth, and faith in such a God was demonstrated by the way one lived, or was supposed to live, that is to say, the creature is related to the Creator only on the basis of submission and obedience, rather than on the basis of the creature replacing the Creator or being equal to the Creator. In the human attempts at faithfulness lies the possibility of surmounting the downward pull of the impulses of our animal nature. The commandments of God, thus, are the door by which the creature rises and arrives into the state of divine approval. Indeed, the Prophet himself, by virtue of his office, demonstrated God's truth by his submission and obedience. His story is the God-filled story of the triumph of good over evil, of faith over unbelief, of sincerity over hypocrisy. The qualities of the Prophet that we admired as children, qualities such as compassion, truthfulness, reliability, courage, insight, devotedness, and generosity, had attached to them the ring and dust of actual events. If Muhammad was remote, it was remoteness of historical uniqueness, not of metaphysical difference from us. He was exalted in his humanity, not in spite of it. As Ernest Renan said of Islam's roots in space and time, the religion was born in the full glare of history. He continued: "Its roots are at surface level, the life of its founder is as well known to us as those of the Reformers of the sixteenth century."

Muhammad's person also became the subject of rich religious feeling, the vessel in which was received and refined an immense outpouring of spiritual tribute. In a stirring testimony, a little-known Swahili poet takes up the theme of Muhammad as tribute for all humanity:

The very existence of this universe, its cause was our Hashemite.

Muhammad is the lord of two worlds, the earth and the heavens and the animated beings, spirits and men of every sort, from the Arabs for the foreigners. It is our prophet who rules, ordering good things and denying bad ones, he is the one who defeats people and kills them by saying: "No" or: "So be it." He is the beloved of his Lord, we may hope for his intercession, he is the right guide of his Community, in the midst of terror and turmoil. He has called people toward the true religion, and whoever follows him and believes in him, has an important reason for his trust: God will save him at the resurrection. He surpasses all the other prophets in appearance, character, and nature, they do not even approach him in appearance, nor in his knowledge, nor in his capacity to work miracles. All the other prophets have their rank assigned to them in relation to the prophet; they possess one handful of water from the ocean of his knowledge, or one sip, and that is all, where there is the great and beneficial rainfall. They are all just standing near their lord, each one like a single dot in the great volume of all knowledge, in the celestial tablet. They are just like one vowel mark in the great book of wisdom.

He is the confessor, the form and meaning which have been completed; finally the Omniscient placed him apart to be the beloved of the Generous. In his goodness he has no rival, either among the prophets or the angels, God cleansed him so became pure, His jewel, His dear beloved. Leave off speaking, I forbid you, the word of praise of the Christians for the prophet Jesus. You may render complete homage to the prophet, praise in any form you like his good qualities. Any form you like for his essence, do not fear, attribute his nobility to his descent, attribute it also to his rank, any form you like for rendering him homage. Because his virtues are very many, their number has no conceivable limit; any form of praise a person can mention, they will never be completed no matter how long that person speaks. If his rank and the miracles he performed would be duly praised, a person, if so able, would have died and even rotted, being called by his name still while still persisting.

He did not come to bring us fear; his whole religion contains God's riches, and we merely have to listen to him and to obey, we do not have to feel doubt nor suspicion. The intelligence of the people is being pressed down, they do not know the reality of the prophet, far away and near by he is the same, the human eye does not accept to look at him. . . . He is like the sun because of his virtues, and they are like the stars, this we know, in order for their light to shine, it is necessary that the sun has not yet come out, that there is darkness. Noble in his mien is the prophet, his character is well disposed. He has gathered goodness, he is exceedingly kind, always appearing cheerful and smiling. His mildness is like a lovely flower, and his nobleness like the full moon, his generosity is like an ocean, his solicitude is like time. The prophet, if you would see him in his full splendour, would be quite unique, like a king, surrounded by many warriors. Like a pearl in its oyster shell, when he begins to speak it emerges, and its place, my brothers, is when he speaks and smiles. There is no perfume that matches the sand on which he lay down, a tree in Paradise it is, for him who may enjoy the smell, it is his bliss.[2]

In his still influential biography of the Prophet, Tor Andrae observed that poetic hyperbole is natural to religious memory and reminiscence, and constitutes a common bond among religions. For that reason, he argued, religious history must take the kernel of simple facts along with the elaborate elements of pious imagination to understand not only what might then just be a relic but also how the faithful might obtain succor from it. His apologia finds more than an echo in the particular example of the Prophet of Islam.

"Our earliest Gospel (Mark)," he writes, "begins with the baptism of Jesus at the Jordan, and his consecration to the office of the Messiah. The authentic history of Mohammed begins in like fashion with his appearance as a prophet in Mecca. What is related of his earlier experiences is mainly legendary. If I do not here completely ignore these pious legends, which otherwise belong more properly to the history of the beliefs of his followers than to the biography of the Prophet, my reason is that it is important, merely from the historical point of view, to become acquainted with the great personalities of the world religions dressed in those garments in which the pious faith of their followers have clothed them. The manger of Bethlehem and the song of the angels belong to the portrait of Jesus, and the fourfold contact with suffering and renunciation of the pleasures of the palace to the portrait of Buddha. Something of the magic of their personalities, which we might not understand in any other way, speaks to us through the poetry of faith."[3]

Muhammad's birth, for example, has the element of the marvelous all around it. A typical account speaks of how the thrones of royalty were overturned, the idols of heathendom fell on their faces, the wild animals of East and West as well as creatures of the sea prophesied good tidings when the happy news of his birth was announced. His mother was told in a dream to call his name Muhammad because his final reward will be *praised* (Ar. *ahmad*).

He was born pure, circumcised; his umbilical cord was cut by the hand of Divine Power. He was born fragrant and endued with pomade, his eyes coloured with kohl of divine care . . . the glowing stars became more brilliant and with their light the depth and height of the sacred and of forbidden things became illuminated. With him light came forth which shone for him over the castles of imperial Syria. And whoever had the valley of Mecca for

---

[2] Cited in Jan Knappert, *Swahili Islamic Poetry* (London: Heinemann Publishers, 1971).
[3] Tor Andrae, *Mohammed: The Man and His Faith* (New York: Harper Torchbooks, 1960), p. 31.

his home, could see it and its significance. The palaces in the cities of the Persian kings began to crack, those palaces for which Anushirwan had raised the roofs and made them symmetric. And fourteen of the highest pinnacles came crashing down. The Persian empire was broken because of terror of what would befall it and despoil it. The adored sacred fires in all the realms of the Persians were extinguished. All this happened when the full moon rose brightly and Muhammad's face appeared.[4]

BARRIERS

In her intimate exposition of the life of the Prophet, Annemarie Schimmel has documented with a wealth of detail this same theme of the unrivaled esteem the Prophet enjoys across the entire spectrum of believers. Given the role religious psychology has enjoyed in Western culture, beginning with St. Augustine and coming right down to Thomas Merton and C. S. Lewis, it would be fair to say that it is not so much subjective feelings that stump us as the accumulation of histori-cal detail, so that, whether with Augustine or with C. S. Lewis, we are inclined to spiritualize or metaphorize the simple facts of life. Consequently, religious and "historical" scholarship is steeped in moral sentiments, no less so than when we reduce description to questions of personal taste and individual feeling. The pro-cedure that allows us to read ourselves into historical events and personages is of a piece with our own project of self-realization rather than being a hard-nosed traffic with the facts as they are. For that reason, the Muslim attitude to the Prophet as one against whom Muslims measure themselves is several steps removed from the Western view of measuring the Prophet by our rules of taste and feeling. Nothing has caused greater misunderstanding with Muslims than our apparent inability—or unwillingness—to let the mountain of heroic individualism come to Muhammad. Instead, Muhammad must come to our mountain.

Reflecting on the Christian side, I am struck by how, for all our boast of the historical-critical method, we continue to be dominated by issues of myth, so that in the work of historical reconstruction, say, on the life of Jesus, we infer skepti-cism both from the uncertainty or inconclusiveness of evidence and from trust-worthy sources. If an account is supported by reliable evidence, or if we assume it is reliable because it seems hostile, as with the so-called *Satanic Verses* of the Qur'án, or the cleansing of the temple in Mark's gospel, we use it to determine what fits or does not fit, with the idea that mythological invention is at work much of the time. We feel that the Jesus of history whom we reconstruct from hard historical evidence comes down to nothing more than a tribal Jewish Jesus, bound by his context and as such of no relevance for later times. Alternatively, we en-counter in the gospels a Hellenized Christ, thickly coated with the imaginative inventiveness of his Greek Gentile followers, who were less interested in history

---

[4] Cited in Jan Knappert and Andrew Rippin, eds., *Textual Sources for the Study of Islam* (Manchester: Manchester University Press, 1986), pp. 67-68.

than in apologetics. So if we could establish the fact of the historical Jesus it would have no relevance, whereas the cosmic Christ of Greek philosophy is a rational construction with no basis in fact.

Thus the value we place on historical objectivity renders us tone deaf to the narrative character of stories whose historicity the original accounts would have had no intention of suggesting. So we take stories as evidence of historical improvisation, as evidence only of the penchant for invention and proof that religious actors lack a sense of historical realism, whereas we ought to see such stories as boundary markers that allow religious actors not only to make history but to explain it. Hence our concern that between history and myth, between reports and opinions, we should erect a steel barrier. We are convinced that what we have in religious texts is evidence of imaginative reworking of materials, and that is proof of failure of the historical sense in religious people. The imaginative medium is thus unscrambled with our modern tools of historical skepticism, with the awkward result that otherwise compelling historical figures like Clio and Cleopatra stumble credulously into the realm of myth. The real truth is that faith is fact packed with passion, not a vacuum into which fiction rushes.

BIOGRAPHY

When Muslims look to Muhammad as the clue to the meaning of their history, they challenge us to see in biography the true locus of historical purpose. Ever since Thucydides, Western scholars have found difficulty in taking biography seriously. As a genre in the modern West it straddles the twilight zone between retirement from active life and archival acquisition. For example, in his classic study of leading Victorian personalities, Lytton Strachey (1880-1932) began by an ironic observation that historians are disinclined to write about subjects about which they know too much, biography being one of these. Rather, he insists, for the historian ignorance is the first requisite, the ignorance which simplifies and clarifies, which selects and omits with placid perfection. It would explain why the religious subject is a rock of stumbling for the historian, because it contains at its core the claim to true and final knowledge! So Strachey chose a different path in proposing to write a biography of Victorians; over the vast ocean of historical knowledge he would lower down into it here and there a little bucket so that he could scoop up, not the entire content, but a rare specimen that is characteristic of the whole. The scholar of biography, Strachey affirmed, should expose, expound, and illustrate, not explain, object, and repudiate. The biographer has no business to be complimentary but to lay bare the facts of the case as he or she understands them, dispassionately, impartially, and without ulterior intentions. Strachey continued:

Human beings are too important to be treated as mere symptoms of the past. They have a value which is independent of any temporal processes—which is eternal, and must be felt for its own sake. The art of biography seems to have fallen on evil times in England. We have had, it is true, a few masterpieces, but we have never had, like the French, a great biographical tradition; we have had no Fontenelles and Condorcets, with their incomparable *éloges*, compressing into a few shining pages the manifold existences of men. With us, the most delicate and humane of all branches of the art of writing has been relegated to the journeymen of letters; we do not reflect that it is perhaps as difficult to write a good life as to live one.[5]

You do not have to be gullible to see that both the Qur'án and the Bible brim with personalities as bearers of world-shaking truth, those individuals who by their lives of faithfulness reveal to us why the universe came to be. Our modesty in these matters contrasts—and conflicts—with God's rule of having divine agency mediated by many channels, not the least of which is human agency, whatever the ambiguity of the human condition. We should concede a certain logical consistency in this. Our ability to distinguish between the true and the false is itself a human attribute, and if we were to overthrow that ability on the grounds that it is a subjective human attribute, then we would cripple the entire enterprise of being human. Even though in matters of religion we behave as if being human constitutes a disqualification, in the divine scheme we are given a role.

The attitude I took with me into the church on this matter was shaped by the view that social agents were the instruments of the divine righteousness, if only because the goal of divine righteousness is the securing of human happiness within the divine order. What I discovered was a certain distrust of persons except as social groups with interests. So with my attitude of society created under divine agency, I caused something of a scandal. My view of persons as channels of God's truth, as vessels and mediators of *barakah*, was discordant with the idea of God's truth being only mythical construction. In that scheme, truth as such is merely a function of the power to motivate and inspire. Thus the incarnation became a doctrine and not an individual, an idea rather than an event, and the church a mystical enclave rife with manipulation of the truth rather than an active society of saints and sinners, of the strong and the weak. Everywhere I looked I found evidence of the historicizing of religion, of the granulating and sifting of the historical kernel of religious life. Even when my teachers spoke of de-mythologizing, they were preoccupied with establishing myth as the primary mode of religion. It stripped religion completely of history, so that faith came to be predicated of "all things visible and invisible." I began to understand the widespread Muslim feeling that the West suffers from an ideological failure to see persons as bearers of *barakah*. Under those circumstances Muhammad should never have to come to the mountain of Western naturalism.

The Western intellectual project of understanding reality through normative categories invests mythological thinking with an autonomous, intrinsic value and relegates history to the humdrum world of surface events. It is no surprise that the so-called universal categories of abstract thought became culturally limiting in the sense that we felt that unless other cultures could think in our categories, they

---

[5] Lytton Strachey, *Eminent Victorians* (New York: Harcourt, Brace & Co., 1918), p. viii.

were excluded from sharing in our enterprise. It has been a barrier to cross-cultural understanding, so that the Muslim tradition and its solid sense of Muhammad's historical significance slips into a subcategory of Western classifications. Even in the irenic hands of Thomas Carlyle, for example, Muhammad is hero especially in the esthetic, imaginative sense, a Prophet of sensibility rather than a Prophet of God, though he is that, too. Muhammad as an esthetic category becomes a type in the genre of imaginative consciousness, a position he shares with countless others, including Byron, Coleridge, and even Cromwell, whatever common patches of creative impulse exist among them.

It would thus bring matters to a precise point to say that Christians have first to overcome their condescending attitude toward biography as such in order to see Muhammad as Muslims see him. Whatever uncertainties might exist on the first count, there is little doubt on the second about Muhammad's biographical preeminence in the hearts and minds of Muslims. Carlyle was right in this sense to fix on his human distinction. "They called him Prophet, you say? Why, he stood there face to face with them; bare, not enshrined in any mystery; visibly clouting his own cloak, cobbling his own shoes; fighting, counseling, ordering in the midst of them: they must have seen what kind of man he *was*, let him be *called* what you like! No emperor with his tiaras was obeyed as this man in a cloak of his own clouting." The very things that Christians find tedious and monotonous in the repetitive details of Muhammad's life Muslims find reason for confidence. Muhammad for them is not the thinker who produces abstract systems of thought, proving his case by logical demonstration. Rather, Muhammad is rooted in the very substance of time and space. His voice vibrates throughout the range of Muslim life and action, his outward manner and demeanor the very meaning of inward *barakah*. It is this *externality* of Muhammad, that is to say, his embodied presence, that demonstrates to Muslims the validity of the truth he proclaimed. Muhammad's historical concreteness is thus the close-knit fabric with which Muslims clothe the divine injunctions. Thus otherwise mundane acts like washing, cutting one's nails and hair, eating, marrying and raising a family, greeting people, selling and buying, and so forth, carry unique merit in the particular setting of the Prophet's life. He made *barakah* live.

Consequently, Muslims have available to them a rich source of biographical detail on the Prophet's life, the source we know as *hadíth*. Through its formal, stylized channel Muhammad's historical concreteness is conveyed in the copious flow of anecdote, episode, and reminiscence. Often the chains of transmission are so thick with names of witnesses and raconteurs that the substance of what is reported is disproportionately slight, causing us to wonder why a lone night-fly might be worth all the day-long elaborate industry of the spider's web. Yet it would be wrong to judge the *hadíth* solely by the rules of critical abundance. The *hadíth* presents Muhammad not just as one who spoke but as one who was also spoken for by others. We have in the *hadíth* not just one biography but innumerable biographies, or else biographical vignettes and cues, what the science of *hadíth* calls *'ilm al-rijal*. Men and women who would otherwise be inconsequential by the rules of historical grandeur arrive in our company as witnesses, or witnesses of the witnesses of Muhammad. The track on which biography proceeds depends, then, on the repeatability of biographical example, so that an idea or practice is attached to a tone, a face, and a gesture. The soundness of the chain of transmission hangs almost exclusively on the trustworthiness of the links of witnesses, with the slight danger of distortion occurring, either because an otherwise worthy-sounding account fails by its loose link or a spurious tradition slips through by being predicated of a recognized name. While clearly depending on the memory of real persons, biographical reminiscence may, therefore, complicate the historical record, leaving us uncertain about the extent of motivated intervention in the handing down of tradition. It is to this phenomenon that scholars like Wensinck, Goldziher, and Schacht have called our attention.

TRUTH AND ORDINARINESS

Nevertheless, as in the financial world, so here also counterfeits need the original to succeed, and it is above all the genuine article of Muhammad's life that has been both curb and incentive for over-imaginativeness. Muhammad so dominated his age that he became its symbol and ideal. He is presented in such tireless detail, depicted with such unforgettable repetition, his name is so highly revered in the devotional cycle, that concern with his biography animates the whole landscape of religious and historical understanding. On every detail of routine and personal style, alike on circumstances and persons, Muhammad alights as precept and principle.

If the pious disciples embellished Muhammad's biography they have not done so completely at the expense of the commonplace. That commonplace concerns the ordinary and natural character of his birth and upbringing, a character still preserved in the oldest records we possess, and one that, furthermore, survives in all mature reflections on his *sunnah.*

Virtually all Muslim authors on the subject stick more or less to the following outline. Muhammad was born in about 570 A.D., the exact date of his birth not being certain. His parents were Aminah and ᶜAbdallah. ᶜAbdallah, his father, died before Muhammad was born, and his mother when the child was six. Muhammad was raised by a wet nurse, Halimah. Muhammad was placed under his grandfather's care, ᶜAbdul Muttalib who died when Muhammad was eight. Then he was handed over to Abú Tálib, his uncle and the father of ᶜAli, the future fourth caliph. Thus, as súrah 93 points out, God found Muhammad an "orphan (*yatím*) and succored him, erring and guided him." Pious tradition went on to add a colorful flourish to the detail by regarding him as the *yatímah,* the pearl of priceless worth, as Annemarie Schimmel has pointed out.

As a young boy Muhammad engaged in trade, accompanying his uncle, Abú Tálib, in the Syrian caravan trade. On one such trip he encountered the monk Bahira, who recognized the seal of prophethood between the child's shoulders. Muslim accounts speak of Bahira testifying to Muhammad's future stature as the prophet foretold in John's gospel, the reference being to the "Comforter" that Jesus promised his own disciples (Jn 14:16-17, 26). That has become a source of much interest among Muslims and controversy with Christians. Muhammad was then aged twelve.

At age twenty-five Muhammad married Khadíjah at her instigation, the woman who had employed him in her caravan trade. The marriage was reward for Muhammad's honesty, though she was fifteen years his senior. She bore him four daughters and a son or two who died in infancy. Khadíjah was a tower of strength to Muhammad, putting the weight of wealth and experience behind him. Thus when Muhammad was going through a dark night of the soul, with great doubts gnawing at his resolve, it was Khadíjah who acted to steady his will and calm his nerve. He used to retire to the hills surrounding Mecca to meditate privately. That was the setting in which he received the call to prophethood.

Yet much ambiguity surrounds the actual details of the call. Two versions are combined in the standard account of Ibn Isháq (d. 768 A.D.). In one strand of the account Muhammad receives a vision at night in an unlit cave and is summoned to recite the words of the revelation, those being the opening words of súrah 96. This strand contains what some scholars believe to be a case of special pleading by those with an exegetical axe to grind, namely, the wish to promote súrah 96 to the first place of the Qur'án because the inaugural word of the súrah, in the imperative mood *iqra*, "recite," is a cognate of the verbal noun *Qur'án*, "recital." In the other strand, a vision comes to him in daylight, or at least when the "clear horizon" (of súrah 81:19) is glanced by the light of the rising sun as he stands on the open hills. This incident is described in súrah 53, the súrah with famous *satanic verses*. Among other things, the súrah speaks of a divine or celestial being who stood in the highest part of the horizon and approached to a distance of "two bows, or even closer," before revealing the matter to the Prophet.

Whether in the strand with the unlit cave or in that of the clear horizon, the accounts represent Muhammad as having a frightful time of it. "Sometimes the Revelation comes like the sound of a bell," he testified; "that is the most painful way. When it ceases I have remembered what was said. Sometimes it is an angel who talks to me like a human, and I remember what he says." Muhammad's reluctance to be a prophet, as expressed in the words, "It is only for the Messenger to deliver the manifest Message" (Arberry), or, "But the messenger hath no other charge than to convey (the message), plainly" (Pickthall) (Q. 24:53), echoes the words of Amos, "The Lord has spoken, who can but prophesy?" (Amos 3:8).

As closely examined by W. Montgomery Watt in his two-volume biography of the Prophet, the early preaching of Muhammad was taken up with the themes of resurrection and judgment, of a fierce eschatological eruption that would leave no one unanswerable, though faithful Muslims would abide its terror and receive the divine reward (cf. Q xlii:5). There is a strong eschatological seriousness, bordering on imminent crisis, about the Meccan phase of Muhammad's preaching, as the following selected passages make clear.

> Woe to every guilty impostor
> who hears the signs of God being recited to him,
> then perseveres in waxing proud, as if he has
> not heard them; so give him the good tidings of
> a painful chastisement.
> And when he knows anything of Our signs, he

takes them in mockery; those—for them await
   a humbling chastisement.
Behind them Gehenna; and that they have earned
shall not avail them aught, nor those they took
as protectors, apart from God; for them awaits
   a mighty chastisement.

   This is guidance;
and those who disbelieve in the signs of their
Lord, there awaits them a painful chastisement
   of wrath.
....
Or do those who commit evil deeds
think that We shall make them as those
who believe and do righteous deeds,
equal their living and their dying?
   How ill they judge!
God created the heavens and the earth
in truth, and that every soul may be
recompensed for what it has created;
   they shall not be wronged.
....
   They say,
'There is nothing but our present life;
we die, and we live, and nothing but
Time destroys us.' Of that they have
no knowledge; they merely conjecture.
And when Our signs are recited to them,
clear signs, their only argument is
that they say, 'Bring us our fathers,
   if you speak truly.'
      Say:
'God gives you life, then makes you die,

then He shall gather you to the Day
of Resurrection, wherein is no doubt,
   but most men do not know.'
                  (Arberry XLV, passim)

So let man consider of what he was created;
   he was created of gushing water
issuing between the loins and the breast-bones.
   Surely He is able to bring him back
upon the day when the secrets are tried,
   and he shall have no strength, no helper.

> By heaven of the returning rain,
> by earth splitting with verdure,
> surely it is a decisive word;
> it is no merriment.
> (Arberry, LXXXVI: 5ff.)

> No indeed; surely Man waxes insolent,
> for he thinks himself self-sufficient.
> Surely unto thy Lord is the Returning.
> (Arberry, XCVI: 6ff.)

> When the heaven is rent asunder
> and gives ear to its Lord, and is fitly disposed;
> when earth is stretched out
> and casts forth what is in it, and voids itself,
> and gives ear to its Lord, and is fitly disposed!

> O Man! Thou art labouring unto thy Lord laboriously,
> and thou shalt encounter Him.
> Then as for him who is given his book in his right hand,
> he shall surely receive an easy reckoning
> and he will return to his family joyfully.
> But as for him who is given his book behind his back,
> he shall call for destruction
> and he shall roast at a Blaze.
> (Arberry, LXXXIV: 1ff.)

Muhammad's eschatological emphasis, his insistence on deeds being judged on the Last Day, was a reaction to the biting sarcasm and material cynicism of the early Meccans, who ridiculed his message with a simple triune slogan, "We live, and we die, and we shall not be raised up," and its defiant unethical innuendo, so then let us eat, drink, and be merry (Is 22:13)!

> Said the Council of the unbelievers of his
> people,who cried lies to the encounter of
> the world to come, and to whom We have
> given ease in the present life, 'This is naught
> but a mortal like yourselves, who eats of
> what you eat and drinks of what you drink.
> If you obey a mortal like yourselves,
> then you will be losers.
> What, does he promise you that when you are
> dead, and become dust and bones, you shall
> be brought forth?
> Away, away

with that you are promised!
There is nothing but our present life;
we die, and we live, and we shall not be raised up.
He is naught but a man who has forged against
God a lie, and we will not believe him.'
(Arberry, XXIII: 34ff.)

They said, 'What, when we are dead
and become dust and bones, shall we be indeed raised up?
We and our fathers have been promised this
before; this is naught but the fairy-tales of the ancients.
(Arberry, XXIII: 84-85)

In the later revelations, especially those occurring at Medina, the tone shifts, not always all at once, to administrative questions and individual and collective guidelines, such as happens when religious protest has acquired the power to impose its will. Thus in one place in the Qur'án the community is given the outlines of an ethical charter regulating relations among them (Q. XVII:23-40), regulations dealing with the abolition of infanticide, proper sexual relations, treatment of orphans and property rights, keeping of promises, not bearing false witness, carrying oneself with humility ("Do not walk boisterously upon the earth; verily thou wilt not make a hole in the earth, nor yet reach the mountains in stature. The evil of all that has become to thy Lord distasteful." XVII:39. N. J. Dawood trans., pp. 229f.), and so on. At Medina also we have extended passages dealing with many of the familiar Old Testament prophets: Abraham, Moses, Solomon, David, Noah, Jonah, and Joseph, among others. Thus Medina as a Jewish settlement left its mark on the Prophet as on Islam.

At Mecca, where he had been a prophet without honor, Muhammad came into conflict with the leading citizens, who perceived him as a threat to the lucrative trade centered in the Ka'ba and as a social upstart. For about a decade, from 610 to 619, Muhammad continued to receive revelations until he was able to gather a fairly sizable number of followers. In 619 he lost Khadíjah through death, and in similar fashion his uncle, Abú Tálib. They were indispensable pillars of his movement as well as being sources of personal strength and inspiration. Their deaths affected him deeply, and besides, exposed him even more to his Meccan antagonists. In 621 Muhammad was approached by a party of sympathizers from Yathrib, an agricultural settlement to the north with a substantial Jewish population, straddling the sensitive artery that carried the caravan trade with Syria. These sympathizers appealed to him to come to Yathrib, not as a religious figure per se, but as a tribal *shaykh* to help mediate in their internal disputes, in effect, asking him to take over leadership of their community. With the circle of hostility narrowing around him in Mecca, Muhammad responded eagerly, if cautiously, to the Meccan overture; he did not want a premature leak of his Medinan plans lest he arouse Meccan reprisal. He sent some of his Meccan followers ahead of him while he made secret preparations to leave with Abú Bakr, an early convert and one destined to succeed the Prophet as caliph. Yathrib was to be renamed "the city of the Prophet," *madinatu-n-nabi,* shortened to Madina or Medina. The historical circumstance of the transfer to Medina being so propitious in retrospect has afforded lavish incentive for pious legend. One such legend recounts how after Muhammad and Abú Bakr had taken refuge in a cave en route to Medina, a spider spun its web and pigeons built their nests over it as evidence of miraculous intervention to shield the pair from the pursuing Meccans, a pursuit referred to in the Qur'án (súrah 9:40). Eventually Muhammad reached Medina in September 622. The Muslim party he had sent out had preceded him in the city, arriving there in June of the same year. The Islamic calendar observes June 622 as year one of the *hijrah,* that is, the emigration from Mecca, for although the Prophet was later in leaving Mecca, the decision to do so had been made. The *hijrah* has been canonized as Islam's birthday.

Soon after arriving in Medina Muhammad promulgated a constitution in an effort to govern the place. In the constitution he offered protection and security to the warring tribes living there, including a sizable Jewish community.

The Muslims introduced a new form of social stratification, one based not on blood and kin solidarity but on religion and obedience to the Prophet. At the top of the social order was the Prophet himself, followed by his companions (*asháb*), the ranks of emigrants (*muhájirún*), the Medinan helpers (*ansár*), the tributary populations, captives taken in razzias and similar sources, and those waiting to be subdued. "In Mecca Muhammad was a private citizen, in Medina the chief magistrate of a community. In Mecca he had to limit himself to more or less passive opposition to the existing order, in Medina he governed. In Mecca he had preached Islam, in Medina he was able to practise. The change necessarily affected the character, activities and doctrines of Muhammad and of Islam itself; the records pass from legend to history."[6] Such, in summary, were the delineations of the new Pax Islamica, so that at Medina Muhammad became both his own St. Paul and Constantine, a double role that left Islam a religion and a state.

Mecca continued to resist Muhammad, pushing him to respond with a political strategy of his own. So he could not rest till he had annexed it to his purpose. In 624 in a famous battle that took place at Badr near Medina, the Muslim forces, surprised and outnumbered, overcame enormous odds to break up the Meccan lines and put the enemy to flight. Badr was celebrated as a miraculous victory, the Qur'án referring to it as the time when God acted by the hands of the faithful Muslims to assure success. "Not you cast when you cast," it affirmed, "but God cast" (súrah 8:17). Badr joined the military instrument to the office of prophecy and set up the field commander as consecrated partner with the agent of the higher oracle.

Perhaps success had gone to the heads of the victors, for the next year saw them in another battle with the Meccans. That was at Mt. Uhud where that time the Muslims suffered serious losses. Some of the Prophet's best soldiers were lost

---

[6] Bernard Lewis, *The Arabs in History* (New York: Harper Torchbooks, 1966), p. 41.

in action, though he himself escaped with his life. He lost two teeth and sustained an injury on his left foot.

In 627 the Meccans tried again to storm Medina but were repulsed. The following year the Prophet decided to perform the *hajj*, pilgrimage, to the Ka'ba, which, since about 623 or 624, had replaced Jerusalem as the *qiblah*, the direction for the prescribed prayers of *salát*. Though he did not perform the *hajj* that year, he concluded a treaty with the now pacified Meccans, who recognized his right of access to the Ka'ba. It was only a matter of time before he took Mecca itself, which he did without contest in 630. He proceeded to clean out the Ka'ba of all its idols and sacred images and reconsecrated it to Muslim service. He then returned to Medina.

After Khadíjah died he married several times, including 'A'ísha, a young virgin and a favorite wife of his, widows of soldiers who had died in battle, and Zaynab, the ex-wife of his adopted son Zayd. A Coptic slave girl who was given to the Prophet bore him a son who died before he was two. His wives were respectfully called "the mothers of the faithful" (súrah 33:6). After his death they were allowed to remarry (33:53).

In 632 Muhammad again made the *hajj* to Mecca from Medina. It was his farewell pilgrimage, as it turned out. According to standard exegesis, he received confirmation of his mission on that occasion when God assured him: *inní akmaltu laka dínika islám dínan*, "I have perfected for you Islam your religion" (5:5). Muhammad died on 8 June 632 in 'A'ísha's apartments. 'A'ísha was then aged eighteen. His burial site was called *al-Rawdah*, "the green," the mausoleum in Medina which pilgrims visit, saying,

> I bear witness that thou art the Apostle of God. Thou hast conveyed the message. Thou hast fulfilled the trust. Thou hast counselled the community and enlightened the gloom, and shed glory on the darkness, and uttered words of wisdom.

Abú Bakr's assurance to the grief-stricken Muslims that although Muhammad was dead, yet God lives has served the cause more than he intended, for it is precisely in the assurance that God lives that the pious have found reason to observe the cult of the dead. If God whom we did not know and have not seen lives, how much more, then, should God's prophets and saints who have died but whom we have once known and seen! On that perennial foundation devout Muslims built an unshakable structure of spiritual vigilance, worship, devotion, and loyalty and promoted it across cultures and down the centuries. Thus in the great *shahádah*, the monotheist witness of the faithful, the name of the Prophet is joined to that of God, and Muhammad becomes the gateway to obtaining God's approval. Muslims might forgive anyone for taking the name of God lightly, but not so the name of Muhammad. We evade the Muslim sense of religious truth if we avoid the figure of the Prophet in the theological insistence that it is God alone who matters. Muhammad is the believer's guarantee that God has acted, justifying the call to witness, worship, devotion, and faithfulness. Muhammad's witness is God's ultimatum, is God's witness, the particular, historical form God has ordained for the divine message to be transmitted and received. God as see-through infinity is indistinguishable from self-enthronement, in effect, from exclusive human agency. A community that adopts a God without prophetic counsel must end up with religion as group self-worship and others as alien adjuncts. According to al-Ghazálí (1058-1111) and the other scholars of orthodoxy, prophecy is required for theistic faith, and Muhammad is God's provision for that. Muhammad is the asylum of the faithful from unbelief, and for his sake God allowed the scandal of unbelief a merciful if temporary reprieve. Muhammad is the human face of God's mercy and compassion, exalted alike in the hearts of the devout and in heaven, so that any attempt to reduce God to an abstract, infinite transcendence is to presume inexcusably on Muhammad's historical commission. Muslims feel that insofar as we are concerned as human beings, Muhammad is necessary and essential to participation in the divine scheme for human life. The Prophet is indispensable guarantor of Islam's particularity, for he it is who prevents Islam's being ground into an amorphous, inoffensive religious blend.

Muslim historian Abú Hayyán al-Tawhídí tersely summed up the historical achievement of Muhammad for Muslims thus: "You have seen . . . how their greatness dawned by the Call, their Call spread by religion, their religion became mighty by prophecy, their prophecy conquered by Holy Law, their Holy Law was buttressed by the Caliphate, their Caliphate prospered by religious and worldly policy" (cited in Lewis 1966, 49).

THE SPIRITUAL HERITAGE

Muhammad was called *uswa hasana* (33:21), "the beautiful model," his followers believing that God had sent him "as a mercy for the worlds" (*rahmatan li-l-'álamín*) and that God and his angels pronounce blessings on him (33:56). The words of the Qur'án might be those of Muhammad himself: "Lo, as for me, my Lord has guided me unto a straight path, a right religion, the community of Abraham, the upright, who was no idolater. Say: Lo, my worship and my sacrifice and my living and my dying are for God, Lord of the worlds" (súrah 6: 162). In passages redolent with his own disadvantaged, unhopeful beginning, the Qur'án offers the Prophet encouragement:

> Thy Lord has neither forsaken thee nor hates thee
> and the Last shall be better for thee than the First.
> Thy Lord shall give thee, and thou shalt be satisfied.

> Did He not find thee an orphan, and shelter thee?
> Did He not find thee erring, and guide thee?
> Did He not find thee needy, and suffice thee?
> (Arberry, XCIII: 3-9)

> Did We not expand thy breast for thee
> and lift from thee thy burden,

the burden that weighed down thy back?
Did We not exalt thy fame?

So truly with hardship comes ease,
truly with hardship comes ease.
So, when thou art empty, labour,
and let thy Lord be thy Quest.
(Arberry, XCIV: 2ff.)

Those and similar verses have been memorized, recited, and intoned by the faithful down the centuries as devotional encouragement as well as proof of God's tribute to the Prophet. Uncounted millions of Muslim children have learned and repeated those words in the first stages of Qur'án school, so that the Prophet's honor, his *barakah*, suffuses Islam's traditional educational system. If God favored the Prophet in spite of his crushing social and material handicaps, then we have assurance that God's favor will rest on all who place their trust in him and follow his guidance. When you learn that as a child, it influences, perhaps even inspires, your ethical life.

In the *shahádah*, Muhammad's name is invoked to give it its distinctive monotheist flavor. As Wilfred Smith has rightly observed, the reference to Muhammad in the *shahádah* is not so much a reference about him as an individual as such as about his role as the bearer of the revelation, so that Muhammad becomes in effect "an aspect of God's activity." It is the same idea that has permitted Muhammad to become the prescriptive rule for Muslim life and conduct down the ages.

A modern commentator has written, "For Muslims the moral and spiritual worth of the Prophet is not an abstraction or a supposition; it is a lived reality, and it is precisely this which proves its authenticity retrospectively." The founder of Islamic jurisprudence, al-Sháfi'í, had pioneered a revolutionary legal methodology by establishing the *sunnah* of the Prophet as a systematic canonical source. He built the immense structure of Islamic classical law on that single foundation, an achievement that has continued to affect all subsequent development of the law. At a less technical level, the words of al-Ghazálí illustrate what practical lessons might be drawn from what is judged authentic in the biography of Muhammad. He wrote in his magnum opus, the *al-Ihyá 'Ulúm al-Dín* (twentieth chapter):

Know now that the key to happiness is to follow the *sunna* and to imitate the Messenger of God in all his coming and going, his movements and rest, in his way of eating, his attitude, his sleep and his talk. I do not mean this in regard to religious observance, for there is no reason to neglect the traditions which were concerned with this aspect. I rather mean all the problems of custom and usage, for only by following them unrestricted succession is possible. God has said: 'Say: if you love God, follow me, and God will love you' (Sura 3:29), and He has said: 'What the messenger has brought—accept it, and what he has prohibited—refrain from it!' (Sura 59:7). That means, you have to sit while putting on trousers, and to stand when winding a turban, and to begin with the right foot when putting on shoes.[7]

CONCLUSIONS

It would be both unrealistic and facile to ask that Christians adopt the same attitude of biographical interest in the examples and precepts of prophets and saints that Muslims have toward the *sunnah* of Muhammad. There are, of course, many biographies and studies of the lives of saints in Christianity, one being *Butler's Lives of the Saints*, and another Jacobus de Voragine's *The Golden Legend: Readings on the Saints*, and Westerners who need practical help and guidance can still go to these biographies and studies. What I would ask is that a close consideration of the Muslim attitude to biography and narrative be allowed to challenge any lingering suspicion that lived reality can only be a subversion of the truth and a distraction from objective history. *Tradition* is a word with a bad odor in much of the West, and the idea that we are in any way beholden to past models is rejected in most quarters. But the question is: what value is religion without tradition and a model, and how can you have tradition if you exclude the lives and examples of those who exemplify it? It is as if you can have children without parents.

Second, we should be imaginative enough to appreciate what Muhammad means to Muslims rather than persisting with the delusion that if we remain adamant long enough in our repudiation, especially when supported with historical-critical claims, Muslim confidence will crumble. Whatever such an attitude might imply about the transitoriness of Muslim claims, stubbornness is not a single-edged weapon of religious combat. Both sides know well enough the coarse marks the crusader's chain mail cuts in each other's collective memory. Our proximity to each other in matters of the spirit as well as in physical coexistence requires us to cultivate a spirit of generosity toward each other. It does not require a sixth sense to see intolerance only begets its kind.

Third, in these twilight years of the twentieth century we would do well to learn from Muslims how religion and politics, church and state, the private and public have much to with each other. The fact that Muhammad combined in his own person the functions of St. Paul and Constantine gives Muslims an important premise of religious participation in the world. Beyond that Muslims seem in better tune with religion as a matter also for the public realm rather than only as a private subjective affair. There is no question here of a return to Christendom, with its oppressive territorial system that only knows coercion and the suppressing of difference as the way to deal with diversity. However, the modern Western status quo of religion as free speech without an objective foundation in truth is disastrous both in origin and in consequence. Standard Muslim sources are cor-

---

[7] For this particular passage see Kenneth Cragg, *The Call of the Minaret*, rev. ed. (Maryknoll, N.Y.: Orbis Books, 1985), p. 92.

rect that a state that would deserve public loyalty and respect cannot be neutral with regard to moral principles; the state must in that case either cooperate with religion, or coopt and enjoin it, or worse still, proscribe it. One type of Muslim response to this situation is to go for a temporal, theocratic, preemptive strike and adopt the state apparatus in the name of religion, though such a course might tempt the state to use religion for its own purpose. We must, therefore, find a solution that gets us beyond a disastrous Western status quo but short of the theocratic prescription of temporal Islam. The widespread postmodernist attitude that, since there are so many religions with a claim to truth, no one religion matters in the end, thus allowing us to ransack religions to suit our personal tastes, merely strengthens the status quo by driving religion from the public sphere into the private, with the weakening of religion going side by side with the growth of state power. So the Muslim criticism of religious privatization strikes at the heart of modern faith in the secular state as definitive of human destiny. There are, it goes without saying, immense problems in joining religion to politics, however warily it is done, but there would appear to be even greater dangers in driving an implacable wedge between them and encouraging a lopsided secular takeover of all domains of life. In the end, of course, even our secular triumphs over religion will turn to defeat without an acknowledgment of the religious purpose of human life. It remains the case as we know it that "man cannot live by bread alone" and that spiritual values are critical to responsible stewardship.

That was the theme of Vaclav Havel in his address on 21 January 1990, to the Senate of the United States during his official visit to Washington, D.C., though the American press and media omitted all such reference. In words that recall Muhammad's challenge to the Meccan materialism of his day, Havel challenged his audience: "The most dangerous enemy today is no longer the dark forces of totalitarianism, the various hostile and plotting mafias, but our own bad qualities. My presidential program is, therefore, to bring spirituality, moral responsibility, humaneness, and humility into politics and, in that respect, to make clear that there is something higher above us, that our deeds do not disappear into the black hole of time but are recorded somewhere and judged, that we have neither the right nor a reason to think we understand everything and that we can do everything." What Havel identifies as secular self-sufficiency Muslims attack as *shirk*, the false absolutes of human idolatry. It is time we realized that truth is not a matter of individual convenience.

And then, to bring the discussion into line with some Christian reflections, we in the West can learn a lot about ourselves as we attempt to understand how for Muslims Muhammad's life and example constitute the source and legitimation of reform: Islam was born in the Prophet's *hijrah*, even though Muslims also believe it was conceived in heaven. For its part, the church was born at Pentecost, whence it became a thoroughgoing Gentile movement. After Pentecost Christianity became a religious movement on the peripheries of Bethlehem and Jerusalem as Christian communities sprang up in Antioch, Ephesus, Philippi, Corinth, Thessalonika, Athens, Rome, Alexandria, and beyond. If the *hijrah* confirmed and preserved the Arabicness of Islam, and, within that, the indispensable universality of Mecca and Medina, Pentecost, by contrast, allowed the church to dispense altogether with the original Aramaic and Hebrew of Jesus' preaching, and, with that, Jerusalem as exclusive for orthodoxy, and to embrace languages and cultures hitherto considered alien to the law and the prophets. The *hijrah* ensconced Islam in the birthplace of Muhammad, and even Shi'ite separatism has not challenged that. Through the steady eye of the *hijrah* the camel of world Islam has been made to pass, however uneven or slow the pace of orthodox conformity. The *hijrah* has furnished the written charter for the reform of local Muslim practice, from Sinkiang in China to Sine-Saloum in Senegambia.

The opportunity for mutual instruction exists in the fact that Muslims and Christians have strengths and weaknesses which contrast with each other. The Arabicity of Islam, expressed in the nontranslatable Qur'án, enables the religion to enter local cultures in their religious heritage in order finally to transcend that heritage and give it a decisive Arabic-based, Meccan orientation. That Islam has more or less succeeded in this where it has succeeded at all amounts to a considerable achievement. That has been its strength. By contrast, the fact that at least in its modern expansion Christianity through vernacular translations of the Scriptures has consecrated the indigenous medium also attests to its strength in linking its spread to vernacular creativity. And therein lie also their respective weaknesses. By establishing vernacular translation into a principle of religious conversion, Christians unleashed all the consequences of local rivalry and schism, whereas by adhering to the rule of nontranslatability Muslims in effect disenfranchised the vernacular as a canonical medium and thus suppressed a unique and indispensable source of indigenous vitality.

Let me end, as I began, with a personal story. When I was a child, I learned that when you traveled to visit a relative elsewhere, you took with you a gift and that when you returned home you also brought a gift, so that, speaking symbolically, life gave you in return what you put into it, perhaps seventy times seven. It has relevance for interfaith relations. Speaking for the Christian side, we ought to affirm with as much confidence as is consistent with our checkered history the essentially Gentile character of the church, a character stamped upon Christianity by the Spirit itself. The Pentecostal insight continues to have revolutionary implications for interfaith as well as cross-cultural understanding. The fact of the matter is that the disciples were in no doubt that Gentile Antioch had no less exalted a place in God's scheme, that all hitherto taboo cultures and peoples stood fully and unconditionally admitted into the fellowship, that the native idioms, until then regarded as unworthy, were henceforth consecrated to bear the full and authentic message of God's forgiveness. All this revolutionary conception of religious truth was made possible by the suffering, death, and resurrection of Jesus Christ, the One who redeems persons and averts from their cultural worlds the curse of untouchability or triumphalism. The Christian difference with Muslims on this point must not be overlooked. The nontranslatability of the Qur'án does not deny the significance of language and culture, only that nontranslatability assigns to the untranslated Arabic medium an original, unalterable primacy, whereas Christian translatability concedes an identical significance for language and culture by the radically different procedure of mother-tongue adoption and consecration. Just as Muslims find it difficult to conceive of monotheist truth apart from Muhammad's unique and personal mediation, so Christians find it hard to conceive of a redeemed world without the culture-specific mediation of God's sacrificial act in Christ.

CHAPTER BIBLIOGRAPHY

'Abduh, Muhammad. *The Theology of Unity*. Translated by K. Cragg and I. Musa'ad. London, 1965.

Abu-l-Fazl, Mirza. *The Koran*. Bombay, 1955.

Adams, Charles J. *Reader's Guide to the Great Religions*. New York, 1965.

Ahmad, Khurshid. *Islam: Its Meaning and Message*. London, 1970.

Ahmad, Zahir. *Mohammad, Glimpses of the Prophet's Life and Times*. New Delhi, 1980.

'Ali, 'Abdallah Yusuf. *Fundamentals of Islam*. Geneva, 1929.

_____. *The Holy Qur'an*. 2 vols. Lahore, 1937/38.

_____. *The Message of Islam*. London, 1940.

_____. *The Personality of Muhammad*. Lahore, 1931.

'Ali, Hashim Amir. *The Student's Qur'an*. Hyderabad, 1959.

'Ali, Muhammad. *Manual of Hadith*. Lahore, n.d.

_____. *The Living Thoughts of the Prophet Muhammad*. London, 1947.

Amin, Osman. *Muhammad 'Abduh*. Washington, 1953.

Andrae, Tor. *Muhammad, the Man and His Faith*. Translated by T. Mentzel. New York, 1960.

Arberry, A. J. *The Holy Koran: An Introduction with Selections*. London, 1953.

_____. *The Koran Interpreted*. London, 1955; New York: Macmillan, 1969.

_____. *Revelation and Reason in Islam*. London: Allen & Unwin; New York, 1957.

Arnold, Thomas, and Guillaume, A. *The Legacy of Islam*. Oxford, 1931.

Asad, Muhammad. *The Message of the Qur'an*. Gibraltar, 1980.

Azad, Abu-l-Kalam. *Tarjuman al-Qur'an*. Translated by Syed Latif. 2 vols. Bombay, 1962.

'Azzam, 'Abd al-Rahman. *The Eternal Message of Muhammad*. New York: Mentor Books, 1965.

Bell, Richard. *Introduction to the Qur'an*. Edinburgh, 1963; rev. and enl. W. M. Watt, Edinburgh, 1970.

_____. *The Origin of Islam in Its Christian Environment*. London, 1926; repr. Frank Cass, 1968.

_____. *The Qur'an*, 2 vols. Edinburgh, 1937/39.

Bennabi, Malek. *Le Phénomène Coranique*. n.d.

Blachère, Regis. *Le Coran*. Paris, 1947.

_____. *Le Problème de Mahomet*. Paris, 1952.

Bosworth, C. E., ed. *The Legacy of Islam*. New edition. Oxford, 1970.

Burton, John. *The Collection of the Qur'án*. Cambridge, England, 1977.

Calverley, E. E. *Islam: An Introduction*. Cairo, 1958.

Cragg, Kenneth. *The Event of the Qur'an.* London, 1970.

_____. *The House of Islam.* 2d ed. Belmont, Cal., 1975.

_____. *The Mind of the Qur'an.* London, 1973.

_____, and R. Marston Speight. *Islam from Within.* Belmont, Cal. 1980.

Crollius, Ary A. R. *The Word in the Experience of Revelation in Qur'an and Hindu Scriptures.* Rome, 1974.

Dawood, N. J. *The Koran.* London: Penguin Books, 1956.

Donaldson, Dwight M. *The Shi'ite Religion.* London, 1933.

Engineer, Asghar A. *Origin and Development of Islam: An Essay on Its Socio-Economic Growth.* Bombay, 1980.

Esin, Emil. *Mecca and Medina.* London, 1963.

Fazlur, Rahman. *Islam.* London, 1961.

_____. *Major Themes of the Qur'an.* Minneapolis, 1980.

Foy, Whitfield. *Man's Religious Quest.* Part 8. London: Open University, 1978.

Gardet, Louis. *Connaître l'Islam.* Paris, 1958.

_____, and C. G. Anawati. *Introduction à la Théologie Musulmane.* Paris, 1948.

Gibb, H. A. R. *Muhammadanism: A Historical Survey.* New York, 1961.

_____, et al. *The Encyclopedia of Islam.* New edition. The Hague, from 1954.

Goldziher, Ignaz. *Etudes sur la Tradition Islamique.* Paris, 1952.

Grunebaum, G. E. von. *Modern Islam: The Search for Cultural Identity.* Berkeley, 1962.

Guillaume, Alfred. *The Traditions of Islam.* Oxford, 1924.

_____. *The Life of Muhammad.* Translated from Ibn Isháq's *Sírat Rasúl Alláh.* Oxford, 1955.

Hamidulláh, Muhammad. *Le Prophète de l 'Islam.* 2 vols. Paris, 1955.

_____. *The Battlefields of the Prophet Muhammad.* Woking, Surrey, 1957.

Haykal, Muhammad Husain. *Life of Muhammad.* Translated by A. Wessels. New York, 1976. *International Congress for the Study of the Qur'an.* Series 1. Canberra, 1982.

Iqbal, Muhammad. *The Reconstruction of Religious Thought in Islam* Lahore, 1944.

Izutsu, T. *God and Man in the Qur'an.* Tokyo, 1964.

_____. *Ethico-Religious Concepts in the Qur'an.* Montreal, 1966.

Jeffery, Arthur. *Islam: Muhammad and His Religion.* New York, 1958.

_____. *Reader in Islam.* The Hague, 1962.

Jomier, Jacques. *Bible et Coran.* Paris, 1959.

_____. *La Place du Coran dans la Vie Quotidienne en Egypte.* Tunis, 1952.

_____. *Le Commentaire Coranique du Manar.* Paris, 1955.

Khan, Muhammad Zafrullah. *Muhammad, Seal of the Prophets.* London, 1980.

Khwaja, Jamal. *Quest for Islam.* Bombay, 1977.

Lammens, Henri. *Islam, Beliefs and Institutions.* Translated by E. D. Ross. London, 1926. Reprinted London: Frank Cass, 1968.

Lane Poole, S. *Studies in a Mosque.* London, 1893.

Lewis, Bernard. *Islam from Muhammad to the Capture of Constantinople.* 2 vols. New York, 1974.

Lings, Martin. *Muhammad, His Life Based on Earliest Sources.* New Delhi, 1983.

Malik, Charles. *God and Man in Contemporary Islamic Thought.* Beirut, 1972.

Masson, D. *Le Coran et la Révélation Judéo-Chrétienne Comparée,* 2 vols. Paris, 1958.

Maudúdí, Abú-l-'Alá. *Islamic Law and Constitution.* Karachi, 1955.

_____. *Towards Understanding Islam.* Lahore, 1940.

McCarthy, Richard. *The Theology of Al-Ash'arí.* Beirut, 1953.

Muir, William. *Life of Mahomet,* 4 vols. London, 1858-61; new abr. ed., Edinburgh, 1923; rev. ed., New York, 1975.

Nadví, Abul Hasan. *Life of Muhammad.* Lucknow, n.d.

Numání, Shibh. *Muhammad.* Karachi, 1975.

Parrinder, Geoffrey. *Jesus in the Qur'an.* London, 1965.

Rahbar, Daud. *God of Justice, Ethical Doctrine of the Qur'an.* Leiden: E. J. Brill, 1960.

Rahnama, Zayn al-'Ábidín. *Payambar: The Messenger.* Translated by L. P. Elwell Sutton. Lahore, 1964.

Robinson, Francis. *Atlas of the Islamic World since 1500.* London, 1982.

Rodinson, Maxine. *Mohammed.* Translated by A. Carter. New edition. London: Penguin, 1971.

Sale, George. *The Koran.* Introductory essay and translation. Many editions since the eighteenth century.

Sarwar, H. G. *The Holy Qur'an.* Singapore, 1929.

_____. *Life of the Holy Prophet.* Lahore, 1937.

_____. *The Philosophy of the Qur'án.* Lahore, 1938.

Schuon, F. *Understanding Islam.* Translated by D. M. Matheson. London, 1963.

Sell, Edward. *The Faith of Islam.* 4th ed. London, 1920.

Smith, Jane. *An Historical and Semantic Study of the Term 'Islam' as Seen in a Sequence of Qur'an Commentaries.* Cambridge, Mass., 1975.

_____, and Y. Y. Haddad. *Islamic Understanding of Death and Resurrection.* Albany, 1981.

Stanton, H. U. W. *The Teaching of the Qur'án.* London, 1919.

Stewart, Desmond. *Mecca.* New York, 1980.

Swartz, Merlin. *Studies in Islam.* New York, 1980.

Sweetman, J. W. *Islam and Christian Theology.* London, part I, vol. 1, 1945; part I, vol. 2, 1947; part II, vol. 1, 1955.

Torrey, C. C. *Jewish Foundation of Islam.* New Haven, 1933.

Waardenburg, J. J. *L'Islam dans le Miroir de l'Occident.* The Hague, 1963.

Waddy, Charis. *The Muslim Mind.* New York, 1976.

_____. *Women in Muslim History.* New York, 1980.

Watt, W. Montgomery. *Companion to the Qur'an.* Edinburgh, 1968.

_____. *The Formative Period of Islamic Thought.* London, 1973.

_____. *Islamic Philosophy and Theology.* Edinburgh: Edinburgh University Press, 1962.

_____. *Muhammad at Mecca.* Oxford, 1953.

_____. *Muhammad at Medina.* Oxford, 1956.

_____. *Muhammad, Prophet and Statesman.* London, 1961.
Wensinck, A. J. *The Muslim Creed.* Cambridge, England, 1932; repr. Frank Cass, 1965.
_____. *Handbook of Early Muhammadan Tradition.* Leiden, 1960.
Westermarck, E. A. *Pagan Survivals in Mohammadan Civilization.* London, 1933.
Williams, J. A. *Islam.* London, 1961.

3

Religious Experience
Autonomy and Mutuality

Recounting an experience about his calling to the religious life, the Shehu describes how first God removed the veil from his sight and endowed him with spiritual gifts, more like *wáridát*, of insight and understanding. This was when he was thirty-six (in c.1790). The effect of what the Shehu himself describes as God's miraculous visitation was to confirm him in faith and intensify his sense of calling. Here are his own words:

> When I reached thirty-six years of age, God removed, the veil from my sight, and the dullness from my hearing and my smell, and the thickness from my taste, and the cramp from my two hands, and the restraint from my two feet, and the heaviness from my body. . . . That was a favour from God that He gives to whom He will. . . . Then I found written upon my fifth rib, on the right side, by the Pen of Power, "Praise be to God, Lord of the Created Worlds" ten times; and "O God, bless our Lord Muhammad, and the family of Muhammad, and give them peace" ten times; and "I beg forgiveness from the Glorious God" ten times; and I marvelled greatly at that.[1]

In this particular experience we are introduced in fact to a general theme of Muslim religious life, namely, the confession of faith in the *shahádah*, now cast in a deep devotional setting. The Shehu cultivated a regime of concentrated religious exercises, observing silence and withdrawing into the desert for prayer for a whole year. He was rewarded with a vision of the Prophet. On one occasion he undertook a fifteen-day retreat, and received a miraculous transfiguration when

---

[1] Cited in Mervyn Hiskett, *The Sword of Truth: The Life and Times of Shehu Usuman dan Fodio* (New York: Oxford University Press, 1973), pp. 64f.

he was taken to the throne of God. Malam (Ar. *mu'allim*, "teacher") Gidado, the contemporary biographer of the Shehu, gives the following account:

> Then the Lord of Creation said to him: "I put you in the retreat [*khalwah*] of al-Ash'arí, which is fifteen days, not the retreat of al-Junaid, which is forty days," and the Lord of creation gave him a *dhikr* [litany] and said to him: "Do not eat anything except what is required for bare sustenance during this period." He did this. When the period was complete the Lord of Creation led him to the Merciful and all the angels of the Merciful were present and the Shaikh, the pole of the Qadiriyya order, the Chosen One, was present— and the words that testify to the presence will come in due course—and the Shaikh 'Abd al-Qadir took our Shehu by the hand and sat him in front of him and said: "This man belongs to me," and for this reason the Shehu Usuman said in his *Qasida al-sudaniyya:* "Our intermediary to Muhammad is the Shaikh 'Abd al-Qadir" (Hiskett 1973, 65).

Thus did the Shehu receive formal confirmation for his historic work. His religious experiences up to this point in his life act only to recognize and strengthen his Muslim resolve; there is no departure from standard practice, no change of direction, no new initiative to speak of. Rather, the Shehu is drawn tighter into commitment he had earlier, and on less dramatic ground, entered into, namely, teaching, devotion, and moral guidance. For example, in speaking of his religious experiences at age thirty-six, he remarked on how those experiences enabled him to observe more scrupulously the code on dietary regulations rather than circumventing the code altogether. This seems such a typical feature of religious experience in mainstream Islam, the idea of supernatural experience reinforcing and not weakening the authority of the code.

There are, of course, exceptions, such as among the Mourides of Senegal, where the peasant throngs surrender their religious obligations and in turn vest all their faith in the *shuyúkh* of the brotherhood. For, they contend, when you are traveling in a train you do not carry a heavy load on your head: you set it down. The load is the religious code, the locomotive is the presiding *khalifah-general*, the carriages are the *shuyúkh*, and the passengers are the Mouride followers.[2] Yet, in this instance, it is not so much experience as trust in charismatic leadership that leads ordinary Mourides to lay down the demands of religion, a provocative move that brings them within firing range of reform-minded *'ulamá.*

EXPERIENCE AND STRUCTURE

Thus, to get back to religious experience, it acts in the instances we have thus far considered as a reinforcement of the canon, rather than as a challenge to it. The intensely subjective character of the experience is counterbalanced by

---

[2] Donal Cruise O'Brien, *The Mourides of Senegal* (Oxford: Clarendon Press, 1971), p. 152.

the authority of the objective canon which thus curbs any extremist or deviant tendencies. It leaves the authority of the religious code uncontested. There are, of course, numerous complex features in religious experience, including the extreme outlandish type in which seeming delirium is embellished with pious pretensions, and its converse, where the mundane is taken out of context and made into an elaborate source of the fantastic. In a credulous atmosphere, events that might be striking in their external coarseness, including fables and other imaginative inventions, are dragged into reality and dogmatically predicated of the exalted truth, with the eclectic appetite feeding the penchant. Fortunately, much of that, though heaven knows not all of it, dissolves from Islam's historical sense.

Nevertheless, it would be a serious error were we to make a sweeping generalization to the effect that all religious experience tends to charlatanry. That it is a slippery subject needs no emphasizing, but that is very different from saying that we should never recognize it as worthy of attention or that we should not scrutinize it with critical sympathy. Counterfeits only exploit the original, and, furthermore, the need to report and share will expose a personal hoard to common vetting. Clearly, then, religious experience, even when it has been obviously conditioned by practices conducive to it, may express enough of the sober realism of historical practice to command recognition of its common value.

Two elements in the Shehu's religious experiences may be relevant to the issue. One is that the religious experience may consecrate the person having it for the work of renewing the religion and securing greater adherence to religious teachings, and such a fact would represent a convergence between experience and structure. The second is that religious experience at a deeper level may be sought to correct or confirm the doubtful import of another religious experience; the message one receives in a dream or vision is unclear or represents too radical a departure from the norm not to require a retake. Therefore, further guidance is sought to resolve the matter decisively.

In the first case, the Shehu recounted what is essentially a vision of vocational service. He said at age forty, "God drew me to him," precisely how is not clear, and brought me into the company of the Apostle, the *ashâb*, the prophets and the saints who "welcomed me, and sat me down in their midst." Then 'Abd al-Qâdir al-Jílâní brought a green robe marked with the words of the *kalimah*, and a turban with the words, "He is God, the One," which he handed to the Apostle, who clasped them to his bosom before handing them over to Abú Bakr al-Siddiq, and so on down the line to 'Alí to Yúsúf and finally back to 'Abd al-Qâdir al-Jílâní, whom they appointed to act on their behalf. Then 'Abd al-Qâdir

> sat me down, and clothed me, and enturbaned me. Then he addressed me as "Imam of the saints" and commanded me to do what is approved of and forbade me to do what is disapproved of; and he girded me with the Sword of Truth (*sayf al-haqq*), to unsheathe it against the enemies of God. Then they commanded me with what they commanded me; and at the same time gave me leave to make this litany that is written upon my ribs widely known,

and promised me that whoever adhered to it, God would intercede for every one of his disciples (Hiskett 1973, 66).

That this experience is concerned with mobilizing the Qádiriyah *taríqah* as a reforming and renewing vehicle in Muslim Africa is obvious. It is designed to bring to the surface tendencies and attitudes of Islamic identity which might have been weakened from historical forces. Reform and renewal would make public virtue of religious profession, securing public sanction for individual acts of piety and obedience. It would also make the contrast with the compromising African heritage sharper. The experience is thus attached to the orthodox flagship.

The second element of religious experience as a corrective mechanism occurs also in the Shehu's biography, as it does widely in Muslim Africa. Religious experience might be compared, in the telling Shaker metaphor, to a tunnel: the deeper one gets into it the narrower it becomes, until finally one is out of range of recognizable landmarks and within range of the devil and wicked spirits. In that condition one is extremely vulnerable to the insinuations of the evil one and to straying. For Muslim religious masters the answer might be in other forms of experience that would contain corrective instruction. One of the most typical forms of such corrective experience is the lucid or perspicacious dream/vision (*ru'ya al-sálihah*), instructing the subject what course of action to follow. In this regard, the Shehu decided shortly after his mystical installation to leave Gobir on what would be a *hijrah*. However, before he carried out his plans 'Abd al-Qádir al-Jílání appeared to him in a vision to forbid the action. Eventually in 1803 or 1804 he was instructed, again in a vision, to leave Gobir for Gudu in north Nigeria, a move that opened the formal stage of the Islamic revolution that left a permanent mark on all Muslim West Africa.

If dreams and visions may restrain impulsive conduct, they may also jack up flagging resolve. The Shehu was once assured in a vision that the Prophet would come to greet him, about which he remained doubtful. He agreed, nevertheless, to submit the message to the test to prove its truthfulness, so he prayed for guidance. As a result, he claimed, the Prophet appeared to him "in circumstances that dispelled his doubts" (Hiskett 1973, 67).

Many people enter the tunnel experience of dreams and visions by using special religious exercises and devotions. *Khalwah*, religious retreat, is a standard device employed to induce dreams and visions for a special purpose, though an ill-prepared person might come out of *khalwah* confounded. Another highly popular practice is the *salát al-istikhárah*, more technical than *khalwah* but no less potent. Meaning literally "prayer of seeking guidance in a choice," *al-istikhárah* became the classic dream incubation method of Muslim reformers in Africa, the midnight calm before the day's storm. J. Spencer Trimingham, a pioneer scholar of Muslim Africa, claims that *al-istikhárah* was employed by virtually all Muslim reformers in Africa.[3] It occurs widely in Muslim literature. For example, Ibn

---

[3] J. Spencer Trimingham, *Islam in West Africa* (Oxford: Clarendon Press, 1959), pp. 122ff.; idem, *The Influence of Islam upon Africa* (Beirut: Librairie du Liban; London: Longman, 1968), p. 84.

Khaldún (1332-1406) wrote extensively about it and said he tried it to effect.[4] Ibn Battúta, the veteran Arab traveler who visited West Africa in 1325, also mentions the practice, saying he employed it with benefit.[5] What is crucial about *khalwah, al-istikhárah*, and other forms of religious retreat is that the experience acquired thereby should not become permanently peripheral but instead should be woven into the fabric of mainstream orthodoxy, and from there challenge deviant practice. The tunnel should guide what passes through it and bring it to the full scope of the light of day.

The special importance of dreams and visions as the culmination of Muslim religious experience strikes a somewhat discordant note in our own austere, skeptical age. Freud's impressive legacy about dreams as pathological symptoms has sundered them from their roots in religion, though dreams and visions occur in the Qur'án, and, for that matter, in the Bible, with great frequency. Even in Salman Rushdie's *Satanic Verses*, dreams occur as a distortion of reality, a position Mr. Rushdie himself vehemently defends. For example, in an open letter to Rajiv Gandhi, then Prime Minister of India, Rushdie complains that Muslim critics of his book fail to recognize how the offending parts of the novel hang on the dreams of sick persons and how, therefore, the book is far removed from reality, a defense that amounts to self-incrimination.[6] It is instructive to reflect on how dreams may function for us as an instrument of unreality, of escape and fantasy, whereas in both Islam and the Bible dreams are the polished horn of the spirit's eloquence.

AUTONOMY AND MUTUALITY

The central question we face about religious experience is whether, if it is too unique to share with others, it does not condemn us to silent isolation, and whether, if it is common enough, it may not flake into popular consumption, losing any uniquely experiential dimension at all. Furthermore, does not sharing itself open us to intrusion or even denial by others? The perils of the "shareability" of reli-

---

[4] Ibn Khaldún writes: "A Man is said to have done this after he had eaten but little and done *dhikr* exercises for several nights. A person appeared to him and said, 'I am your perfect nature.' A question was put to that person, and he gave the man the information he desired. With the help of these words, I have myself had remarkable dream visions, through which I learned things about myself that I wanted to know" (*Al-Muqaddimah: An Introduction to History*, 3 vols., tr. and ed. Franz Rosenthal [Princeton: Princeton University Press, 1968], vol.i, p. 213).

[5] Ibn Battúta, *Travels in Asia and Africa*, tr. and ed. H. A. R. Gibb (London: Routledge & Kegan Paul, 1929), p. 10.

[6] Rushdie writes that the sections of the book causing the most offense occur "in a dream, the fictional dream of a fictional character, an Indian movie star, and one who is losing his mind at that. How much further from history could one get?" In the very next breath, however, Rushdie concedes that he is in fact taking aim at historical Islam. "In this dream sequence," he concludes, "I have tried to offer my view of the phenomenon of revelation and the birth of a great world religion" (*The New York Times*, 19 October 1988).

gious experience, of making religious intimations "user-friendly," are thus obvious, for they open the door to an indistinct mush as the common essence of all religions. And, in similar fashion, if religious experience is so unique that it cannot be shared, does not that lead ultimately to its demise? If religious experience is some sort of elegiac bourn from which no traveler returns, so that it is irreversible, would that not leave the world to darkness and to us? Thus from the extreme flanks of religious experience as general essence or as a unique undisclosable phenomenon, we are led into either uncritical sameness or exclusive uniqueness. The closest we come to such uniqueness, for example, is glossolalia, that species of strange utterance impenetrable to understanding: in neat regular infusions glossolalia draws a shade over the light and leaves us in darkness. And it is to dispel such darkness that the Shehu and men of his ilk sought visions and received dreams.

We have, therefore, to ask whether sharing is possible as a middle course between introverted subjectivism and extroverted showmanship, and, if so, what its import might be for religious experience. An important part of the answer has to do with preserving religious particularity, so that distinctive teachings do not get lost in abstract syncretism or get sequestered by another tradition's particularity. We may put it this way: genuine religious experience carries with it proof of its origin, seal of its identity, and, if it is genuine, it will also express something of the general human quest for transforming truth and thus embrace by sympathy if not similarity what ordinarily remains implicit in its background assumptions and presuppositions. Identity speaks to particularity, and similarity to inclusiveness and pluralism. This situation should remind us that religion is a complex, dynamic force that is always including, excluding, uniting, and separating. This brings us to the anthropology of religious experience. While it is true that for Muslim reformers obedience and conformity to the code was a paramount motivation or goal, it is also the case that the reformers appealed to the norms of *maslahah*, the welfare and well-being of the people. Thus a certain sense of human community distinguished their religious work and experience, and they asked that their efforts be judged in that light, too.

THEORETICAL FORMULATIONS: PERSONAL AND INSTRUMENTAL RELIGION

That human community is the uniting strand in the intricate mesh of religious experience, not just in terms of the psychology of kindred feelings and emotional states, but in the layered moral dispositions and attitudes that attach themselves to the whole design. When the focus is on the self, the individual may get absorbed in moods of guilt, repentance, and release, and may thus constitute these as valid and sufficient religious effects. However, theist faith may submit those effects to the tests of truth, righteousness, and community. Religious experience may thus be sought, not simply for what we may attain by it, but for what it enables us to be and to do. Certainly in Muslim experience religion cannot completely be reduced to biochemical functions, for a reflex of the biceps is not of equal value to the posture of arms folded in penitent supplication. The jugular vein may bulge with excitement without any inkling that its subject is by comparison closer to his or her Maker (Qur'án 50:15). Bound in this creaturely coil, the devotee may nevertheless soar on wings of faith. A limiting, negative scheme of physical life will have thus evoked a positive scheme of spiritual freedom. Physical science is a tool or a toy; religion is relational. In the final analysis religious experience is the affirmation by the creature of the Creator, not giving or receiving anything that God does not already have, and thus receiving and giving only what God in his grace is disposed to give. And since ultimately what God gives is life, and the means for it, then through religious mediation we only receive and give that life, or the tokens for it. At its profoundest level, then, religious experience will bring us to the realization of self-giving as the only authentic form of giving, so that with regard to God as the source of life and being, we give nothing that is ours or that is not already God's. Hence self-abnegation constitutes the deepest level of personal religion, and through it the human spirit is refined into the precious thing God intends it to be. This sort of theological anthropology seems implicit in the religious basis of experience.

There is a second factor that takes us beyond the purely private world of individual feelings and emotions, although in this matter, too, a certain theological tendency can be detected. We may approach it by asking whether language as such exhausts the meaning and content of religious experience, or whether language, any language, is intrinsically inadequate to the truth to which it witnesses. The great Muslim mystics, such as Rumi and Ibn al-'Arabí, tended to take the view that truth transcends all language, but it would be incautious to represent that as typical.

By drawing in other comparative materials, from the Christian tradition and primal religious traditions, the following position can be stated. Religious language—or symbols—may be defined on three levels. On the first level, religious language operates *elliptically* by representing religious experience in terms of instrumental effects rather than by calling attention to the nature and qualities of God. Almost in the Thomist sense, God is encountered at this level through the effects God produces in the material and phenomenal world. Religion at this level is *instrumental*, with the idea of a personal God somewhat faint in the background. Such instrumental ideas end up emphasizing results, consequences, and strategies toward religion, so that sharing any experience involves a certain degree of manipulation, bargain, packaging, and marketing. This is the "user-friendly" approach that media evangelists have refined into a booming industry in the United States.

The second level is in the neo-Wittgenstinian sense of the primacy of context wherein religious language may be compared to a stream: it takes on the color of the terrain over which it flows without completely merging with it. We might call this the *symbolic* use of language and understand it as the way language and symbols, while not representing God in themselves, become in certain specific contexts and to certain specific persons God, or the idea of God. For example, the sounds and tones of the Arabic Qur'án represent to Muslims the very truth of God, even though those characteristics of the language do not have that meaning for other native-born Arabs who are non-Muslim. Nor, in fact, do the characteristics of the language so considered carry the same weight even for Muslims outside the special context of the Arabic Qur'án. Christians have taken this notion to its logical conclusion by denying to any one language the status of revealed truth, so that the truth of the *One* God is expressed in the *many* forms of human speech. Religious experience at this level does not presuppose a uniform language or culture, since the diversity of situations and contexts as well as the variety of backgrounds and experiences will produce a commensurate variety of forms and symbols.

The Muslim attitude to the Arabic of the Qur'án introduces the third level of the use of religious language, and that is as a *figure of identity*. At this level the proximity of language or symbol to the thing spoken about or thus represented is so exact of the truth that an equivalent relationship is said to exist. This is the position with regard to the Arabic Qur'án in Islam and to Jesus Christ in orthodox Christianity. It is also the case in certain primal religious traditions. For example, in his classic description of the religion of the ancient Ainu of Hokkaido, Japan, John Batchelor tells how the bear is regarded as a divinity that is raised as a cub and sacrificed when full grown.[7] Its worshipers then eat the flesh to effect the identity that they believe exists between them and their deity.[8] Yet the circularity of terms here, being quite obvious, set the Ainu apart; they sacrifice to the divinity what is in itself divine, and they themselves stand at the end and receive what they thus sacrifice. The paradox of this is that religious experience, completely lacking in any of the ingredients of piacular intention or self-abnegation, subsides, if it rises at all, in group projection, not in the differentiation of individual consciousness. It takes *instrumental* elements from the elliptical domain and transposes them into figures of identity. Sharing experience at this stage is predicated on assimilating into the original medium itself.

Figures of identity, whether in their negative or positive effects, tend to an absolutized or idealized conception of religious forms. Thus, on the negative side, they promote an exclusive view of the medium through which we experience religion, and, on the positive side, they support a normative inclusiveness such as might be expressed in monistic systems and other theosophic or advaitic claims. On one level distinctions are reduced to a form that assumes a universal exclusive mode, and on the other they are invested, all of them, with a universal inclusive quality.

These three forms of religious language, the *elliptical*, the *symbolic*, and *figures of identity* combine to cut deep but distinct channels for the streams of religious experience. It is interesting to reflect that William James, in his classic work, *The Varieties of Religious Experience* (his Gifford Lectures) was extremely critical of the tendency to absolutize the language and symbols of religious conversion, especially when the cases in question refer to stages of adolescent development.[9] Obviously biological changes and rhythms, when they also assume psy-

---

[7] John Batchelor, *The Ainu and Their Folk-lore* (London: The Religious Tract Society, 1901), pp. 479-96.

[8] Joseph Kitagawa assesses John Batchelor's unique materials, "The Ainu Bear Festival (Iyomante)," *History of Religion* 1, no.1 (Summer, 1961): 95-151.

[9] William James, *The Varieties of Religious Experience* (New York: New American Library, 1958), p. 164.

chological forms, need not crystallize into spiritual types to recognize their role in religious experience. The very rule of relativization that James sought to rivet on so-called conversion experience exists in eloquent form with *elliptical* and *symbolic* kinds of religious experience. In their ideal conceptions, *elliptical* experience may bring individuals or groups to an existential awareness, while *symbolic* experience may call attention to the structures required to establish and nurture habits of conformity. With *figures of identity*, by contrast, we might produce an ideology consistent with it, namely, a prescriptive rigidity that perceives in the absolute equivalence of symbol and the thing thus symbolized a corresponding guarantee of access, or even monopoly of truth and virtue.

CONCLUSIONS

I began with Muslim examples, and I should conclude with a Muslim reference that also draws upon some Christian parallels. My reference this time is to the black nationalist militant Malcolm X, who was assassinated in February, 1965, before he was forty, having earlier converted to Islam through the Black Muslims. In his autobiography Malcolm X describes his conversion in language that expresses a profound religious experience. He speaks of that experience as a dramatic change from guilt and moral twistedness to truth as personal challenge. In terms of the theoretical formulations just considered, Malcolm X, making his first acquaintance with Islam through its dietary prohibitions against pork, comes finally to an existential experience of prescriptive religion. Of that experience he writes as follows:

Many a time I have looked back, trying to assess, just for myself, my first reaction to all this. Every instinct of the ghetto jungle streets, every hustling fox and criminal wolf instinct in me, which would have scoffed at and rejected anything else, was struck dumb. It was as though all of that life was back there without any remaining effect, or influence. I remember how, sometime later, reading the Bible in the Norfolk Prison Colony Library, I came upon, then I read, over and over, how Paul on the road to Damascus, upon hearing the voice of Christ, was so smitten that he was knocked off his horse, in a daze. I do not now, and I did not then, liken myself to Paul. But I do understand his experience. . . . I have since learned—helping me to understand what then began to happen within me—that the truth can be quickly received, or received at all, only by the sinner who knows and admits that he is guilty of having sinned much. Stated another way: only guilt admitted accepts truth. . . . The very enormity of my previous life's guilt prepared me to accept the truth. Not for weeks yet would I deal with the direct, personal application to myself, as a black man, of the truth. It still was like a blinding light.[10]

---

[10] Malcolm X, *The Autobiography*, with the assistance of Alex Haley (London: Penguin Books, 1968), pp. 257f.

Elaborating on his experience, Malcolm X said he was compelled to revise certain fundamental ideas he had imbibed about the cultural and racial criteria of truth and virtue. This ethical transformation he also likens to a religious experience, thus identifying the sort of religious anthropology that shapes language and thought. For Malcolm X, Islam's inclusive anthropology stood in profound conflict with his experience of the racial exclusiveness of Western Christianity, with the effect that what he deduced about God from Christian racism crippled him from being capable of any spontaneous gracious response. On a visit to Mecca on pilgrimage, and out of range of Western racial stereotypes, Malcolm X suffered a reversal of his long-held attitudes. Commenting on the generous hospitality of his Arab host in Jeddah, Malcolm came to this unsettling reckoning:

I was speechless at the man's attitude, and at my own physical feeling of no difference between us as human beings. I had heard for years of Muslim hospitality, but no one couldn't quite imagine such warmth. . . . There had before been in my emotions such an impulse to pray—and I did, prostrating myself on the living-room rug. Nothing in either of my two careers as a black man in America had served to give me any idealistic tendencies. My instincts automatically examined the reasons, the motives, of anyone who did anything they didn't have to do for me. Always in my life, if it was any white person, I could see a selfish motive. But there in that hotel that morning. . . . was one of the few times I had been so awed that I was totally without resistance (Malcolm X 1968, 445f.).

Malcolm suggests that Islam had harmonized for him the *One* and the *Many*, bringing together *One* God and the *many* nations and races of the world who find in God a common humanity. He spoke of Islam having "proved the power of the One God." At Mecca itself, after he had completed the pilgrimage obligation and kissed the black stone of the Ka'ba, he testified:

I understood it better now than I had before. In the Holy World, away from America's race problem, was the first time I ever had been able to think clearly about the basic divisions of white people in America, and how their attitudes and their motives related to, and affected Negroes. In my thirty-nine years on this earth, the Holy City of Mecca had been the first time I had ever stood before the Creator of All and felt like a complete human being (Malcolm X 1968, 482).

It says something both for the autonomy and mutuality of religious experience that, in spite of bitter lessons to make individuals feel hemmed in an impenetrable tunnel, Malcolm X should in that position go on to discover a basic underlying connectedness in genuine human encounter, finding that sharing helps to deepen religious experience rather than draining it. The established fact of racism does not combine well with the bitterness it naturally induces, which is its irony. It requires moral strength to undergo racism and still commit oneself to projects of forgiveness and reconciliation as the remedy. Malcolm seems to have found that moral strength in Islam, and so he wished to share it with the world, especially the world of his oppression. He succeeded in extricating himself from racial bitterness, and, through the bonds of his newfound humanity, he contributed toward the possibility of global human interconnectedness. That interconnectedness is still some way short of universal fellowship, but it contributes to it. In that way, Malcolm may serve as an example to encourage mutual bridge-building. In thus sharing his story, Malcolm poses the ethical challenge of overcoming the obstacles created by the long history of religion collaborating with racism and discriminatory practices.

CHAPTER BIBLIOGRAPHY

Augustine. *Confessions*. New York: Image Books/Doubleday and Anchor, 1960.

Batchelor, John. *The Ainu and their Folk-lore*. London: The Religious Tract Society, 1901.

Battúta, Ibn. *Travels in Asia and Africa*. Translated and edited by H. A. R. Gibb. London: Routledge & Kegan Paul, 1929; repr. 1957.

Camps, Arnulf. "The Prayers for Peace at Assisi, October 27, 1986: What Was Shared?" In Jerald D. Gort, Hendrik M. Vroom, Rein Fernhout, and Anton Wessels, eds. *On Sharing Religious Experience: Possibilities of Interfaith Mutuality*. Amsterdam, 1992.

Daiber, Hans. "Abú Hatim ar-Razi (10th century A.D.) on the Unity and Diversity of Religions." In Jerald D. Gort, et al., eds. *Dialogue and Syncretism: An Interdisciplinary Approach*. Amsterdam: Editions Rodopi; Grand Rapids: William B. Eerdmans, 1989.

_____. "Sharing Religious Experience as a Problem in Early Islamic Mysticism." In Jerald D. Gort, Hendrik M. Vroom, Rein Fernhout, and Anton Wessels, eds. *On Sharing Religious Experience: Possibilities of Interfaith Mutuality*. Amsterdam, 1992.

Droogers, André. "Meaning, Power and the Sharing of Religious Experience: An Anthropology of Religion [sic] Point of View." In Jerald D. Gort, Hendrik M. Vroom, Rein Fernhout, and Anton Wessels, eds. *On Sharing Religious Experience: Possibilities of Interfaith Mutuality*. Amsterdam, 1992.

Fahd, Toufic. *La Divination Arabe: Etudes Religieuses, Sociologiques et Folklorique sur la Milieu Natif de l'Islam*. Leiden: E. J. Brill, 1966.

Fernhout, Rein. "Can Faith in the 'Inspiration' of Holy Scripture Be Shared?" In Jerald D. Gort, Hendrik M. Vroom, Rein Fernhout, and Anton Wessels, eds. *On Sharing Religious Experience: Possibilities of Interfaith Mutuality*. Amsterdam, 1992.

Gort, Jerald D. "Liberative Ecumenism: Gateway to the Sharing of Religious Experience Today." In Jerald D. Gort, Hendrik M. Vroom, Rein Fernhout, and Anton Wessels, eds. *On Sharing Religious Experience: Possibilities of Interfaith Mutuality*. Amsterdam, 1992. Editions Rodopi, Grand Rapids, Michigan: William B. Eerdmans Publishing Company, 1992.

Hiskett, Mervyn. *The Sword of Truth: The Life and Times of Shehu Usuman dan Fodio*. New York: Oxford University Press, 1973.

James, William. *Varieties of Religious Experience*. New York: Mentor Books, 1958.

Khaldún, Ibn. *Al-Muqaddimah: An Introduction to History*. 3 vols. Translated by Franz Rosenthal. Princeton: Princeton University Press, 1968.

Kitagawa, Joseph. "Ainu Bear Festival (Iyomante)." *History of Religion* 1, no. 1 (Summer, 1961).

Lewis, C. S. *Surprised by Joy*. London: Collins, 1975.

Malcolm X (with Alex Haley). *Autobiography*. London: Penguin Books, 1968.

Oberhammer, Gerhard. "Hermeneutics of Religious Experience." In Jerald D. Gort, Hendrik M. Vroom, Rein Fernhout, and Anton Wessels, eds. *On Sharing Religious Experience: Possibilities of Interfaith Mutuality*. Amsterdam, 1992.

O'Brien, Donal Cruise. *The Mourides of Senegal*. Oxford: Clarendon Press, 1971.

Smith, Wilfred C. *The Faith of Other Men*. New York: Harper Torchbooks, 1963.

_____. *The Meaning and End of Religion: A New Approach to the Religious Traditions of Mankind*. New York: Mentor Books, 1963.

_____. *Questions of Religious Truth*. London: Victor Gollancz Ltd., 1967.

_____. "Can Believers Share the Qur'an and the Bible as Word of God?" In Jerald D. Gort, Hendrik M. Vroom, Rein Fernhout, and Anton Wessels, eds. *On Sharing Religious Experience: Possibilities of Interfaith Mutuality*. Amsterdam, 1992.

Strolz, Walter. "The Incomparability of God as Biblical Experience of Faith." In Jerald D. Gort, Hendrik M. Vroom, Rein Fernhout, and Anton Wessels, eds. *On Sharing Religious Experience: Possibilities of Interfaith Mutuality*. Amsterdam, 1992.

Trimingham, J. Spencer. *A History of Islam in West Africa*. London: Oxford University Press, 1962.

_____. *The Influence of Islam upon Africa*. Beirut: Librairie du Liban; London: Longman Publishers, 1968.

_____. *Islam in West Africa*. Oxford: Clarendon Press, 1959.

Vroom, Hendrik M. "Sharing Religious Experience: Recapitulation, Comments and Questions." In Jerald D. Gort, Hendrik M. Vroom, Rein Fernhout, and Anton Wessels, eds. *On Sharing Religious Experience: Possibilities of Interfaith Mutuality*. Amsterdam, 1992.

Wessels, Anton. "The Experience of the Prophet Mohammed." In Jerald D. Gort, Hendrik M. Vroom, Rein Fernhout, and Anton Wessels, eds. *On Sharing Religious Experience: Possibilities of Interfaith Mutuality*. Amsterdam, 1992.

Zaehner, R. C. *Hindu and Muslim Mysticism*. New York: Schocken Books, 1972.

_____. *Mysticism, Sacred and Profane: An Inquiry into Some Varieties of Praeternatural Experience*. London: Oxford University Press, 1973.

_____. *At Sundry Times: An Essay in the Comparison of Religions*. London, 1958.

_____. *The Teaching of the Magi*. London: Oxford University Press, 1956.

4

Christian-Muslim Encounter in Freetown in the Nineteenth Century

Implications for Interfaith Engagement

The Muslim Africans' experience of interreligious encounter assumed its most focused and articulate expression in dialogue with Christian Africans. This is illustrated in a debate staged in Freetown in 1888 on Islam and Christianity, with the motion: "Is Christianity or Islam best suited to promote the true interests of the Negro race?" The debate was inspired by the publication a year earlier of Dr. Edward Blyden's book *Christianity, Islam and the Negro Race*, and it generated a great deal of public interest and was faithfully reported in a local paper, *The Artisan*, beginning with the issue of 24 November 1888 and ending with that of Wednesday, 17 April 1889. It is likely that Dr. Blyden was himself in the audience—or at least personally aware of the debate. With a few minor omissions *The Artisan* reproduced the full text of the proceedings. I intend in this chapter, first, to describe the setting and form of the debate; second, to report its substance; third, to place it in the social and historical context of nineteenth-century Freetown; and, finally, to draw out points of relevance and interest for current thinking and discussion about interreligious relations. I shall offer a critical appraisal of the significance of Dr. Blyden for interreligious relations in Africa and their implications for the public good, examining Blyden's legacy against the background of the apogee of European colonialism and contrasting it with the situation today. The coming of political independence raised the issue of religion and cultural identity, that is, whether, and how, faith can be totally nationalized without loss of its core. I conclude with that theme.

THE FORM AND SETTING OF THE DEBATE

The proceedings were conducted in the manner of a formal parliamentary debate in which the speakers do not refer to each other by name and in which the motion is advocated and contested by the principal speakers on each side. The subject is introduced by a formal motion, and the speakers act on the topic at issue by moving or opposing it. One side presents its arguments, and its case may be argued by two or three principal advocates and by a limited number of speakers from those present. Then the other side answers. The principal speakers, their supporters and those present constitute the "house," and the house is led by the chairman (the speaker), through whom the debaters address the meeting. The chairman is expected to maintain strict neutrality and is empowered to intervene in the course of the debate either on a point of order or to control the discussion. The chairman is timekeeper and impartial referee, or is supposed to be. At the end of the debate the principal protagonists are asked to sum up for their respective sides. They are not allowed to introduce new evidence or arguments in their summing up. The chairman then reminds the house of the motion before it, briefly summarizes the discussions, and asks the house to decide for one side or the other on the basis of the evidence adduced. After a division and counting of the votes, the chairman announces the results and may conclude the meeting with a personal vote of thanks. From the moment the motion is formally put to the declaration of the votes everybody in the house is bound by the rules of debate.

The parliamentary style of the proceedings considerably minimizes the risk of the debate turning into a harangue or a one-sided tirade or degenerating into polemic or mutual recrimination. In spite of the august terms of such a debate, we get a glimpse into areas of genuine appreciation as well as difficulty between the two religions.

The Artisan, which carried the story of the debate, does not, unfortunately, tell us anything about where it was held, who precisely the participants were, or the background from which they came. We are left to glean some of this information from the presentation before the house. Some of the people there would have been English, probably with connections with the Church Missionary Society (CMS) theological college, Fourah Bay College. At least one of the speakers, the principal speaker opening the debate for Islam, was a woman. Perhaps the majority of the speakers were Sierra Leonean Christians, including the chairman. We also gather from the way the debate was conducted that Muslims did not play an active part, if they were present at all. It says something for the form in which the debate was cast that an issue like that could be considered in great detail without recourse to attempts at genuine representation. However, the character of a parliamentary debate is designed to avert one-sidedness and to prevent the audience from upsetting the course of the proceedings. That is why it is crucial to have an impartial speaker preside over the proceedings and ensure that the forms of parliamentary etiquette are duly observed. Such conventions allowed for interreligious exchange without the risk of fanaticism. Thus even if we get a partial picture of interreligious encounter between Islam and Christianity, that picture is instructive and may, therefore, serve as a guide of the way in which the two sides stood in each other's estimate. Christians and Muslims entertained the ideas they did of each other because of deep theological affinity supported by real social and historical experience, all of which would make religious exclusiveness unappealing. The debate needs, therefore, to be judged within such a propitious context. Furthermore, to say this is to encourage us to see what important ecumenical lessons we can draw from it, because the debate touches on themes that are of pertinent interest, and because such local experience provides the impetus and credibility for ecumenical solidarity. By the standards of the time as well by the polarized attitudes of today, it was a remarkable event deserving of careful study.

THE ISSUES

What then were the main issues discussed in the debate? The fact that it was an unusual event appears to have exercised a powerful influence on the house and the chairman who, in introducing the opening speaker for Islam, revealed his mental unease. He thought that if Islam was better "then, the sooner the fact is recognized the better: if it be not so, it is time that those interested in Christianity laid aside their apathy and refute an assertion fraught with such perilous consequences not only to the religion of Christ but to the welfare of their country and their people."[1] The pro-Christian bias of that statement came close to robbing the chairman of the neutral eminence with which his office is invested. Later on he slipped further down the procedural bypath when he stated that the principal speaker for the motion was going to fulfill her formal duty of speaking on behalf of Islam but that she did not believe the good things she would be saying about Islam. It became clear at this point that the speakers would have to save the debate from degenerating into an exercise in dogmatic bigotry and doctrinaire hostility to which the chairman seems to have been inviting them. In the main the speakers can be said to have succeeded, although in his summing up the chairman felt that the fuels of religious antagonism had not been sufficiently fed and he decided to make up for lost opportunity.

There were six speakers for Islam and eleven speakers for Christianity, but the second speaker for the Muslim side was not reported. This glaring numerical imbalance did not, fortunately, correspond to the qualitative value of the views presented by the two sides. The Muslim side, however, appears less in earnest and not a little defensive, and as a result emerged less convincing, while the Christian side, perhaps overwhelmed by a sense of representational superiority and lured by the pleasing prospects of easy conquest, lunged into the attack with self-acclaim and approval.

The speakers dwelled upon the merits of the two great religious systems, but the Muslim side was less inclined to stress doctrinal and theological questions, which were the major preoccupation of speakers on the Christian side. The Muslim side presented evidence to support the view that Islam can be seen to have made a more permanent impression upon African life while Christianity remained superficial to black culture. The Christian riposte did not try to answer this point

---

[1] Supplement to *The Artisan*, vol. IV (Saturday, 24 November 1888), p. 4.

directly but rather moved the discussion toward an examination of the theological claims of the two religions. It scored heavily in this area, thanks to current doctrinal prejudice against Islam. This difference in approach tended to give the debate a certain unevenness and even elusiveness. The sparks which flew in the discussion came mostly from the Christian side, where they were generated by a double desire to attack Islam and to defend Christianity, whereas the Muslim side was content with making claims for Islam.

Some of the points which emerged are worth discussing here more fully. The Muslim side can be divided into two sections, one emphasizing the value of Islam as a religious system and the other discussing its practical beneficial effects on African life. A peculiarity of the evidence presented from the Muslim side was the prominence given to Christian writers on Islam, something which the Christian side did not have. Was this because Muslims had been slow to develop sufficient interest in Christianity to study it with the sympathy and expertise with which many Christians had tried to approach Islam? The first aspect of the Muslim evidence dwelled at some length on the fact that people were being gradually and inevitably awakened to the realization that all religions had something to teach about truth, that no religion was exclusively good or exclusively bad, and that any religion that had a real and continued hold on a large body of humanity must satisfy a real spiritual need and was so far good.[2] This view was immediately challenged by the third speaker on the grounds that it verged on a sell-out of the Christian truth. For the Muslim side two authorities were quoted at length, both of them Christians, namely, Dr. Edward Wilmot Blyden, the great Pan-Negro patriot who lived and worked in Freetown, and the Anglican clergyman Canon Isaac Taylor, canon of York and rector of Settingham, Yorkshire, England. Both these men treated the question of the impact of Islam on African life in the social and personal spheres. This was the second aspect of their arguments, to which we must now turn.

Dr. Blyden, because of his Christian credentials, was termed "an untainted witness" on behalf of Islam. He was quoted in the debate as saying in his renowned book *Christianity, Islam and the Negro Race* that Islam contributed far more to the advancement of the Negro race than its great rival. Three specific points were raised in connection with Dr. Blyden. The first was that Islam, according to him, had introduced to the Negro race an ideology of struggle to try to overcome the world of primal religious worship and replace it with a monotheist system. The second was that African Muslims were introduced through Islam into a universal community with a wide distribution and a long articulate history, and this was bound to improve the condition of the Negro race. The third point is connected with the second. It stressed that Islam introduced religious literature which chronicled the exploits of distinguished Negroes in the early history of the religion (Dr. Blyden may have been thinking of people like Bilál ibn Ribáh, the freed slave and personal attendant of Muhammad), and this literature was widely disseminated in Muslim Africa. Blyden is reported as saying that in one village he

---

[2] R. Bosworth Smith, *Mohammed and Mohammedanism*, 2d ed. (London: Smith and Elder, 1876), p. 63.

personally knew (probably in Sierra Leone[3]) there was material like this composed in Egypt or Nubia. The children in the Qur'án school studied this "so that Mohammedan youths from the books they read have a far better opportunity of becoming acquainted with the great men of their race than the Christian youth and therefore of acquiring deeper self-respect and an earnest attachment to a religion in which their own people performed such achievements."[4] On the question of the theological status of Islam in relation to Christianity, Dr. Blyden was willing to see it as a kindred faith, although the debaters were anxious to make the point that it was still an inferior religion, a genuine light but one which only reflected the glory of the greater sunlight of the cross.[5]

The views of Canon Taylor as presented at the debate coincide at some points with Dr. Blyden's. According to Canon Taylor, Islam was not an anti-Christian faith but "a republication of the faith of Abraham and Moses with Christian elements."[6] Islam for Canon Taylor was, as the seventh speaker pointed out, "a divinely appointed work" and there was nothing "in it antagonistic to Christianity." Indeed, from the Christian point of view Islam was closer in affinity than, say, Judaism, for "it recognizes the miracles, the teaching and the Messiahship of Jesus Christ." On the basis of such a close relationship Christians needed to cultivate Islam as an ally, and even if some deep theological differences remained such points of divergence should challenge Christians to try to strengthen rather than subvert the faith of Muslims. Christians who sincerely harbored doubts about Islam and its divinely appointed role in history should ponder the words of Gamaliel with special reference to Islam: "If this counsel or this work be of men, it will come to nought: but if it be of God, ye cannot overthrow it; lest haply ye be found even to fight against God" (Acts 5:38-39, *KJV*). The import of that verse is that an Islam that has proved itself capable of commanding the faith and allegiance of multitudes of people over more than a millennium, and has, in the bargain, successfully resisted Christian attempts at conversion, merits consideration as existing by divine intention. It cannot be but the will of God that Islam should be, and should be let to be.

The Muslim side concentrated for the remainder of the time on the arguments of Canon Taylor, and these divided themselves into two broad categories. In the

---

[3] Sierra Leone in this context means the hinterland of the territory rather than the more restricted area around the colony of Freetown. Dr. Blyden was the recipient of a number of titles, among them Professor in the College of Liberia, Secretary of State for Liberia, Minister Plenipotentiary of the Republic of Liberia at the Court of St. James, Fellow of the American Philological Association, Corresponding Member of the society of Science and Letters, Bengal, and Vice-President of the American Colonization Society. For the life of Blyden see H. R. Lynch, *Edward Wilmot Blyden: Pan-Negro Patriot* (New York: Oxford University Press, 1967).

[4] According to *The Artisan*, vol. IV, no. 2 (Wednesday, 30 January 1889), the fourth speaker quoted this material.

[5] Dr. Blyden's own words encourage the adoption of this view.

[6] Canon Taylor was quoted *in extenso* by the sixth speaker from a document which appears to have been in general circulation, for other speakers referred to it as well as to the circumstances in which it was produced. The seventh speaker specifically referred to the Jewish parallels.

first place, Islamic ethics and morality were described as having had a beneficial effect on individuals and communities. Second, Islam had deeply penetrated African societies and affected the material culture in a permanent and widespread fashion. It is worth taking up these two themes in turn.

The debate paid close attention to the question of Islamic ethics and morality with a view to deciding whether in the interaction between Islam and African societies it was possible to discover and measure the genuine contribution Islam made to communal welfare and personal improvement. The focal point of discussion was the contrasting attitudes of Islam and Christianity toward alcoholic beverages, considered in this context as a social evil. Islam banned the consumption (some authorities would also include the sale) of wines and alcoholic beverages (Qur'án 5:92), and this contributed greatly to the preservation of society and individual worth. The spread of Christianity, on the other hand, had closely followed the channels of European trade and commerce, and with this went a steady inflow of spirits with a rise in attendant social problems. By contrast, Islam spread primarily through its appeal as a distinctive social system with practical instructions as well as a supernatural religious system.[7] One speaker in particular linked the phenomenon of drunkenness with the Christian presence.[8] Islam, for its part, not only encouraged temperance and sobriety but made these a requirement of sound faith.

On the second theme, the practical effect of Islam on the material culture, a somewhat romantic and unrealistic picture was being painted, fed probably by Christian impatience with the slow numerical growth of the church. Canon Taylor's comments on this aspect of the problem were discovered later in the meeting to have come from a passage lifted straight out of a book without due acknowledgment, and this was seized on eagerly by the speakers from the other side. The evidence presented at the meeting is discussed here because of its contemporary value and current interest and not because of its intrinsic factual merits. According to Canon Taylor, quoting from R. Bosworth Smith's *Mohammed and Mohammedanism*, the introduction of Islam had led to the eradication of numerous evil practices in African societies, including devil-worship, fetishism, cannibalism, immodest dances, gambling, unchastity, and witchcraft. In their place Islam had introduced a stiff code of ethics and personal morality: respectable dress, cleanliness, law and order, a constituted social order, abstinence, hospitality, industriousness, and discipline. In addition, the sixth speaker said, according to Canon Taylor the evils of polygamy and slavery were controlled.[9] In a statement

---

[7] These views were advanced by Canon Taylor, relying on secondhand sources, chiefly R. Bosworth Smith.

[8] The eighth speaker was here echoing the words of Canon Taylor as quoted by the sixth speaker.

[9] It is difficult to understand what is meant here. In the West African context polygamy and slavery were closely interrelated. Slave masters, anxious to boost their family stock, would usually add slave women as concubines to their household. Although the legal limit for the number of wives a man may keep is four (Qur'án IV:3) there is no limit on the number of concubines he may have. See Ibn abí Zayd Al-Qayrawání, *La Risálah: ou épître sur les éléments du dogme et de la loi de l'Islam selon le rite malikite*, ed. and tr. L. Bercher (Algier 1945), p. 178; Neil B. E. Baillie, *A Digest of Moohummudan Law* (1869-75; reprinted Lahore: Premier Book House, 1974), p. 367; Fisher and Fisher, *Slavery and Muslim Society in Africa* (New York, 1971; London: Christopher Hurst Pub., 1971).

that tried to credit Islam with what the church had sought to achieve in Africa, Canon Taylor was quoted by the sixth speaker in the debate as saying, "Islam, above all, is the most powerful total abstinence association in the world, whereas the expansion of European trade means the extension of drunkenness and vice and the degradation of the people." This statement may be contrasted with the record of Christian social criticism in movements such as Methodism and the numerous movements of temperance and pacifism, as well as missionary conflicts with slave traders and Western liquor and arms merchants.

At any rate the Christian rebuttal to this opening gambit was swift and, in the eyes of the audience, effective. Since so much prominence was given to evidence culled from Dr. Edward Blyden and Canon Taylor, it was felt important by the Christian side to challenge the value of this evidence. Canon Taylor was summarily dismissed as a man parading in borrowed plumes, so to speak. He had poached the ideas of R. Bosworth Smith whom he quoted verbatim without acknowledging this in his script.[10] Thus Canon Taylor was arraigned before the house as a counterfeit scholar whose evidence, relied on so greatly by the other side, could not be seriously entertained since it did not represent his own experience or work. This was of course a question of form and procedure, but on its basis the Christian side began a detailed demolition of the factual basis of Canon Taylor's account, and we shall turn to this aspect presently. With regard to Dr. Blyden two things were said: first, that he himself, although a devoted and respected student of Islam, was nevertheless a convinced and practicing Negro Christian, and his unquestioned eminence was eloquent tribute to Christianity's influence on the Negro race. Second, the eleventh speaker said, Dr. Blyden in his writings was arguing from expediency rather than from principle. Putting together the testimony of the advocates of Islam it was possible, according to the presentation of the eleventh speaker, to detect an inherent contradiction. Dr. Blyden and Canon Taylor contended in their writings that Islam was a preliminary and preparation for Christianity,[11] and yet others like R. Bosworth Smith and Sir William Muir, that great nineteenth-century Islamicist, stressed that the barrier that Islam interposed between men and Christianity was insuperable. Canon Taylor himself admitted this, the eleventh speaker claimed, when he asserted that adherence to Islam by Africans effectively closed the door against reverting to Paganism or to Christianity.

It may be profitable now to try to develop two themes of special interest to the debate. The sponsors of the motion quoted evidence to prove that not only was Islam better suited to Africa, but also that it was making more progress than Christianity in gaining converts. Canon Taylor, dilating upon the alleged beneficial effects of Islam on Africa, cited figures to show how everywhere that Islam came into competition with Christianity the influence of the latter waned as a conse-

---

[10] The ninth speaker cited pages 42 and 4 of R. Bosworth Smith's book as the original source of Canon Taylor's material. It was also pointed out in the debate that R. Bosworth Smith himself had challenged Canon Taylor before the latter was obliged to admit his source (*The Artisan*, vol. IV, no. 3 [6 March 1889]).

[11] Blyden's words quoted to this effect are: "Whatever it may be in other lands, in Africa the work of Islam is preliminary and preparatory."

quence; more people embraced Islam than Christianity, and the trend was so consistent that there was no doubt which of the two great missionary religions was likely to come out stronger.

One of the Christian spokesmen addressed himself specifically to this question. He had, he said, in his possession a paper by Sir William Wilson which was read before the Indian section of the Society of Arts in London on the Religions of India. This paper was delivered on 24 February 1888 and subsequently published in the London *Times* the following day. Since Canon Taylor had claimed that Christianity faced more bleak prospects in India than Islam, this could be answered by statistics. In Sir William's paper, the tenth speaker said, it was stated that there was a rapid and proportionate increase among native Christians which was unparalleled among the other religions, including Islam. The census officer for Bengal said, according to Sir William, that no conversions to Islam on a significant scale had taken place since 1872. Another census officer for the North West Province gave similar testimony. The general population increase in the nine years preceding 1881 was at the rate of 10.89%, in which the Muslims increased at the rate of 10.96%, the Hindus below 13.64%, and Christians of all races at the rate of 40.71%, and Indian Christians at the rate of 64.07%. It is not clear in this whether the figures applied to the North West Province only or to all India. Whatever the case may be, as bare statistics these figures are meaningless. Why should a predominantly Hindu country record any conversion rate of people to Hinduism? Furthermore, why should a high rate of Christian conversion—64%—necessarily correspond to a high number of Christians? An Indian state which had, for instance, two thousand Christians out of the total population could show an increase of 60% by a small upward fluctuation without this producing a significant change. But for the purposes of the debate this material was useful ammunition, and it was used to maximum advantage.

As regards the claim of Canon Taylor that Islam was marching victoriously in Sierra Leone and sweeping all before it, including a precarious Christianity, this was stoutly denied. But the Christian spokesmen did not produce any evidence to back up their denial and seem to have been content to allow the matter to resolve itself on the favorable grounds of the Indian comparison. Neither side appreciated that Islam in Africa was to face the combined pressures of a potent Paganism (African religions) and a vigorous self-confident Christianity, a challenge which was extended by the intrusion of secular and secularizing forces.

A second theme concerns the suitability of Islam to African needs. Those who saw Islam as an instrument of progress in Africa had painted in glowing hues its achievements on behalf of the African convert. Canon Taylor, probably quoting R. Bosworth Smith, argued that Islam "is eminently adapted to be a civilizing and elevating religion for barbarous tribes." What this implies is that although Islam was not a very high kind of religion, it was nevertheless suited to the stunted genius of the Negro not merely as a stage along the way to Christianity but as a religion in its own right. This was vigorously challenged by the ninth speaker, who said such views were "not very flattering to the *amour propre* of these . . . who believe in the capabilities of the African." The same speaker went on to ask: "Is the Negro such an outcast on the face of the earth that he must not even aspire to fellowship in the religion of Jesus? Did this policy commend itself to Christ and His Apostles?" He went on to quote 1 Corinthians 1:2-29, to cite the example of Simon the Cyrenean bearing the cross of Jesus (Mk 15:21), and to point out that Africa had furnished the church with some of the most outstanding early Church Fathers. If Canon Taylor and others acknowledged Islam to be an imperfect faith, however akin to Christianity, then why should the African be excluded from seeking that higher faith, and with it advancement in the church?

This is a question of some importance, for it relates to current debate in missiological circles about the status of the churches in Africa. Should they be encouraged to delve deeper into sources of African religious life and to that extent be left to their own devices? Or may Christian Africa, with its own idiom and accent, represent a further evolution of a religion that made the breakthrough from Palestine to Greece and Rome? Should that fact mitigate the anxiety so commonly expressed in the West about outlandish or heretical innovations in Christian Africa? Would a reconstituted Christian Africa offer a bridge to a declining Western church? For a variety of reasons some people have suggested a moratorium, some complete autonomy, others flexible association, and still others a perpetuation of old ties. Whatever the option, the question of the validity of Christianity in Africa would seem to rest on the special conditions of pluralism, linguistic diversity, and interethnic encounter as the crucible of faith and practice on the continent.

A sensitive issue was being tackled by the debate at this stage. Prejudice against Islam in Victorian as in later times was being covertly perpetuated in the guise of tolerance, even paternalistic indulgence, for islamized Africa. This apparently tolerant attitude also concealed a corresponding prejudice against black Africans. It was with exposing these attitudes that some of the main speakers were concerned. When Islam established a stronghold in African societies this was seen as laudable and proof of its intrinsic merit. On the other hand, when Christianity was enthusiastically adopted by Africans this was sharply criticized as evidence of unthinking imitation by Africans. A different scale of judgment was being applied to an identical process of religious change. There is no need to go into this here, but it may be observed that the renewed interest of Europeans in African independent and revivalist churches, quite apart from the importance of these churches as bearers and transmitters of Christianity in independent Africa, does not necessarily signify a genuine advance on the continuing prejudice toward christianized Africa. It will not be until the West can take seriously the flourishing of its own Christian heritage in its transformed African version that we can speak confidently of Europe overcoming its cultural prejudice and paternalism.[12]

An important contribution to the discussion of the promise and potential of African religious ideas and practice for Christianity has been the classic study by John V. Taylor (one-time Bishop of Winchester) entitled *The Primal Vision*. The works of people like Harry Sawyerr, Christian Baëta, John Mbiti, and Bolaji Idowu,

---

[12] Two excellent studies are H. W. Turner, *African Independent Church*, 2 vols. (London, 1967), and John D. Y. Peel, *Aladura: A Religious Movement among the Yoruba* (London: Oxford University Press for the International African Institute, 1968).

and, in anthropology, of Sir Edward Evans-Pritchard, Godfrey Lienhardt, and Victor Turner, among others, have given greater meaning and content to this discussion.[13] It is increasingly recognized that the question of accepting (or rejecting) the Christian message is being resolved against a variety of backgrounds, and this must necessarily give the process a certain richness of language and complexity of worship and liturgical life. If God is Spirit (Jn 4:24) then the attempt by Africans to conceive of God in the spirit of traditional forms of worship and prayer is a valid step in the process of establishing new forms of community and identity. There is both fulfilment and challenge in that process, and Christian life and practice would reveal that tension in all its diversity. Whatever the final outcome, African Christianity would stand squarely in the historic tradition of the transmission and appropriation of the message, with the crucial, unprecedented difference that Africans themselves would be the architects of the cause.

Even at this relatively early stage of faith formation, Christian Africa gives every indication of vital life and vigorous quest, resolved to make a solid connection between the New Israel of the Scriptures and the old Africa of the ancestors. Some scholars have argued that such religious convergence is natural and inevitable, requiring no foreign stimulus or mediation, because the small-scale sedentary traditions of Africa had in any case begun to break up and to release in people on the move an aching longing for a universal monotheism such as Christianity or Islam. Whether that is really so or is an argument made *ex post facto*, the fact remains that Africa has responded in strikingly different ways to Christianity and Islam, or at any rate has responded to the two religions by mobilizing different facets of its indigenous traditions. For example, Africa has responded to Christianity by mobilizing mother-tongue languages and the ethnic-cultural forces they enshrine, whereas Islam has succeeded through the appeal of a non-translatable Qur'án and its ritual formulas. Consequently, it may be no more than historical optimism that leads us to impute a uniform, unilinear monotheist culmination to the process normally at work in polytheist Africa.[14]

From here on the debate veered away more and more from the substantive motion, with speakers plunging into unedifying depths of malice and slander. It would not serve any useful purpose here to try to reproduce the range of innuendo and aspersion. A certain rigidity fixed itself upon the house as speakers fell back on theological rhetoric and cultural caricature. The character of Muhammad was unfavorably compared to that of Jesus. The Qur'án as the Holy Book of Islam

---

[13] E. Bolaji Idowu, *Olodumaré, God in Yoruba Belief* (London: Longman, 1962); C. G. Baëta, *Prophetism in Ghana* (London, 1961); John Mbiti, *New Testament Eschatology in an African Background* (London: Cambridge University Press, 1971); Harry Sawyerr, *God: Ancestor or Creator* (London, 1970).

[14] R. Horton, "African Conversion," *Africa* [Journal of the International African Institute], XLI, no. 2 (April 1971). Horton advances the theses that "acceptance of Islam and Christianity is due as much to development of the traditional cosmology in response to *other* features of the modern situation as it is to the activities of the missionaries" and that Islam and Christianity act merely as catalysts in this process (pp. 103, 105). A reply to Horton can be found in Humphrey J. Fisher, "Conversion Reconsidered: Some Historical Aspects or Religious Conversion in Black Africa," *Africa*, XLIII, no. 1 (January 1973).

was shown in bad light as a work of slight aesthetic merit and a compilation of incoherent fragments. Its divine status was denied by the familiar technique of lifting out seemingly compromising passages, particularly the so-called Satanic verses (Qur'án, LIII:19-20)[15] and couching partisanship with the logic of learned discourse. The quite valid Muslim jurisprudential rule of setting aside an earlier verse of the Qur'án by reference to a later one when the two are similar or deal with the same subject—called the doctrine of *naskh*, that is, abrogation (Qur'án II:100)—was seized on as proof of the Qur'án's unreliability, a cunning device, it was alleged, which sought to gain for Muhammad what he deservedly failed to obtain through infallible revelation. The miracle stories in the Qur'án and Muhammad's alleged encounters with jinns in the valley of Nakhlah (Qur'án XLVI:28-31; LXXII:1-2) were further evidence of deliberate fabrication that must inevitably detract from the revelatory status of the Qur'án. That criticism is a variation of the one St. Thomas Aquinas made in his *Summa contra Gentiles*, book 1, chapter 6, that whereas many signs and evidences attest to Christianity's superiority, no such exalted corroboration exists for Islam, although it seems a little inconsistent, then, to go on, as the sainted doctor did, to place Christian teaching on natural law foundations and say it appeals rationally to educated, cultured and mature people. Nevertheless, that kind of attack on the Qur'án was intended to impugn the motives of the Prophet and to discredit Islam, questioning its value in achieving any worthwhile benefits for Africa.

THE MEANING OF THE DEBATE AND ITS RELEVANCE TODAY

Certain lessons can be drawn from this debate, which may help us in understanding the present relationship between Christians and Muslims in this part of Africa. Almost at the same time as the debate a meeting was organized between Christians and Muslims in Freetown, in which representative spokesmen from both sides addressed the need for closer collaboration. The meeting, widely reported in *The Sierra Leone Weekly News* of 9 January 1889 and in the issue of the same weekly three days later, was termed a "new feature" and in another place a "novel gathering." It was held at the Methodist High School between Christian Creoles and Muslim Creoles from Fula Town and Fourah Bay, both areas in the East End of Freetown. At this meeting Abayomi-Cole, a Christian clergyman with connections with the American Wesleyan Mission, gave a talk on Olorun, the High God of Yoruba religion. Abayomi-Cole addressed the meeting in Yoruba, which was the common language of both the Christian and Muslim members of the audience. He declared that "the redemption of Africa depends on all irrespective of religion [and that] all minor differences should sink to dust . . . and all should unite for the salvation of Africa and leave the event to God who has made all men of one blood."[16] Muhammad Sanusi, an Arabic letter-writer for the government and a teacher of Arabic at Fourah Bay College, positions which he owed

[15] See also W. M. Watt, *Muhammad at Mecca* (London, 1953; repr. 1965), pp. 101-9.
[16] *Sierra Leone Weekly News*, V (9 January 1889), 19, 5, cited in Peterson, *Province of Freedom* (London, 1969), pp. 247-48.

to the strenuous exertions of Dr. Blyden, also addressed the meeting. He praised Blyden's achievements, particularly for teaching Muslims about Christianity and Christians about Islam and said that both Muslims and Christians of Sierra Leone were one race. An Association was formed, called the Creole Association, which met in April, 1889. Abayomi-Cole addressed this gathering again, followed by the *imám*, i.e., prayer leader, of Fula Town, Almami Amara, who told the meeting of between 7,000 and 10,000 that the Association wanted peace and to prevent "too much quarrel." Ahmed Alhadi, a Muslim who was to emerge into greater prominence later, was active in the defense of Creole interests and solidarity. He edited and produced a pamphlet, *The Re-emancipation of the Colony of Sierra Leone*, with the support of Dr. Bankole Bright (d. 1958), an important Creole political figure.

The interaction between the Christian and Muslim Creoles (the latter are better known as Akus or Okus) took place against a background of intense factionalism and "too much quarrel" which had become serious enough to require concerted attempts at finding an amicable solution. These attempts never succeeded and a barrier of suspicion and prejudice continued to separate the two sides.

This is a remarkable state of affairs, that people of the same racial stock should find themselves estranged by seemingly religious factors. The historical reasons behind this apparent anomaly may go some way toward explaining the situation. Sierra Leone has had a unique history as a Christian colony, with religion at the center of it. From the beginning official British policy was to encourage Christian expansion and consolidation, and, in contrast, to discourage Muslim activity. For a time certain restrictions were imposed on Muslims, including the destruction of Muslim places of worship. Zoning was introduced, called the Parish scheme, to control Muslim immigration into Freetown, and laws were passed to forbid Muslim religious activity among settled Christians in places like Gloucester, Regent, Hastings, and Waterloo. This forced the emigration of Muslims already settled in these villages just outside Freetown to areas in the East End of Freetown. After about 1870, largely through the indefatigable efforts of Dr. Blyden, official policy underwent a volte-face and some encouragement was given to Muslims. Although a certain social and economic stigma continued to attach to Muslims, there was no political bar. To take advantage of opportunities in Sierra Leone Muslims enrolled in Christian-controlled schools where they could not register under their Muslim names. Many such Muslims carried two names as a consequence, a Christian name by which they were recognized at school and a baptismal name by which they were known at home. This continued until very recent times, and in some Christian-controlled schools it is still the practice. Usually these Muslim children were lodged with Christian Creole families as guardians who gave them "house names" as a condition of their wardship. It should be said that Muslim families also provided for a change of name for Christian children, showing the importance both sides attached to names and naming. Such multiple names were normally kept by choice, leading at times to colorful juxtaposition.

Christian educational policy conformed to this pattern of naming and reinforced it. Earlier in the twentieth century Muslim primary schools, called Madrasas, were established in Freetown to cater for Muslim children. It was the first scheme of its kind in West Africa. Fees were introduced. The CMS, afraid of being squeezed out in its traditional stronghold, responded by founding the CMS Mohammedan School, and, just to make sure, abolished all fees in order to undersell the competition.[17] The Muslim question had qualified for interreligious involvement. Yet the competition excited other ambitions. A CMS representative once declared, a little enigmatically, that the CMS "would conquer Port Loko (a Muslim stronghold) or die" (Proudfoot and Wilson 1960, 90). When the government set up the Model School explicitly for Muslims, the Christian teachers in the school, it is alleged, arranged to give most of the places to the children of Christian parents (ibid.). Saddled from the outset by such onerous disadvantages the Muslims, turning in on themselves, became wracked by internal divisions and ethnic antagonism. Yet, in spite of the potential for interreligious mischief, Christian-Muslim relations never fractured into overt political hostility. However, ethnic solidarity, as that between Christian and Muslim Yorubas, was challenged by religious competition which, however, remained largely peaceful.

The situation we have inherited today is the result of past policy and attitudes, and the burden this imposes is one that government alone cannot and should not be expected to carry. A good measure of it must be borne by interreligious initiatives and involvement in society, perhaps through a scheme of collaboration in educational planning and the development of alternative nongovernmental schemes. The positive backing that the efforts of Dr. Blyden received from both church and state shows that even at that time radical change was possible, although it is ironic that Dr. Blyden, in spite of his impeccable credentials, should find himself bitterly opposed by some of the very Muslims whose cause he had tried unstintingly to advance.[18]

The debate was torn between the two sides, corresponding also to the religious division, namely, the emphasis on social and ethical themes by the Muslim side and concern with great theological issues on the Christian side. The confidence shown by the Christian side indicated that the Christians enjoyed a far greater proportion of the resources in society. However, such glaring inequality has drastically changed since that time, and overt discrimination against Muslims has largely ceased. With the coming of political independence in 1961, and more recently with the generous inflow of petro-dollars from oil-enriched Arab states, the fear of being swamped by an active Christian proselytization movement has been mercifully overcome. Nevertheless, residual mistrust still persists, and if the suspicion that history has inflicted on both Christians and Muslims is not to continue to grow, concrete steps are necessary to move people forward. Can religious leaders together and separately act before the opportunity is lost? That was the unspoken wish of the participants at the debate.

---

[17] Leslie Proudfoot and H. S. Wilson, "Muslim Attitudes to Education in Sierra Leone," *The Muslim World*, vol. 50, no. 1 (January 1960), p. 90.

[18] The man who led the opposition against Dr. Blyden was the Muslim leader Legally Savage. See Leslie Proudfoot, "An Aku Factional Fight in East Freetown," *Sierra Leone Bulletin of Religion*, vol. 4, no. 2 (December 1962), p. 76.

THE DEBATE AND THE RELIGIOUS RULES OF ENGAGEMENT

Nineteenth-century Freetown was dominated by the personality of Dr. Blyden, and the debate was testimony to his brilliant intellectual career and commitment to interreligious engagement. He had almost single-handedly raised the subject to a higher level and cleared the atmosphere of much negative stereotyping. Rarely has Blyden been credited with a part in what amounted to a revolution in the modern Christian attitude toward Islam and Muslims, with having contributed significantly to moving Christians from their medieval fear and distortion of Islam to the terms and realities of shared experience in society. Yet his effect on official and public policy toward Islam and Muslims was nothing short of radical. He helped to shift energy from abstract academic debate to living issues, bringing the fruits of study and understanding to bear on practical concerns in the Muslim community. If he erred on the side of romanticizing Islam, that was because he carried so little of the dead-weight prejudice that dragged down so many of his contemporaries. However, in terms of developments in Africa, Blyden's vision had a profound pertinence. His lasting legacy was to convince Christian African elites that Islam is part and parcel of Africa, that it has a vital contribution to make to the cause of the nationalist awakening, that the pattern of Christian involvement in Africa is anticipated to a significant degree in Muslim Africa, and that the ancient antagonisms between cross and crescent are woefully out of place on the continent. Consequently, Christian Africans may draw close to Muslim Africans without fear of compromise.

That can be effected on the cultural level where Islam's nonsacerdotal, lay character lends itself to broader involvement by ordinary Christians. The task facing Africa, Blyden believed, was of a Pan-African nature, stemming as it does from the general and widespread imposition of European colonial rule and its ideology of racial superiority of whites over blacks. Blyden accused the white colonial powers of a complete disregard of the sensibilities of Africans and a total disinterest in cultivating what he called "the well-spring of a nobler life within" the African soul. All that left Africans supine victims of an unsympathetic apparatus of political and commercial machinery, mere stubble in the unbending path of Europe's juggernaut. Islam, Blyden felt, offered the possibility of a Pan-African ideology necessary in the legitimate struggle to repudiate white racism and overcome its psychological effects.

It does not discredit Blyden to point out that his public policy agenda of the time was developed first and then attached to Islam, so that his view of the historical usefulness of the religion was conditioned by the provocative forces of the high imperial age. Islam evoked for him an unassailable counterpoint to the otherwise dominant Western idiom, though he minimized thereby Islam's opposition to African religions and corresponding indigenous institutions. Yet, as I said, his unusual procedure should not blind us to the fact that he tried valiantly to bring religious allegiance to bear on pressing historical and political issues and to commend Muslims and Christians to a common task and mutual responsibility. Perhaps in the light of the odds against him, we might in the end wish to forgive Blyden for his tendency to romanticize Islam and to promote it as part of the great stirring spirit of the age—similar to Thomas Carlyle's heroic interpretation of the Prophet Muhammad as a kind of Napoleonic superman in a tricolor turban.

Such considerations bring us inevitably into the relation between religion and contemporary issues in public life. Both Muslim and Christian Africans are the heirs to the unitary national secular state as the legacy of an Enlightenment West, a state that by definition views itself as the superior arbiter of human destiny, with religion consigned to an inferior position. While Blyden could take it for granted that religion played a role in contemporary issues, we live in an age that splits religion and political culture and regards religious persons as marginal or irrelevant to public issues. However, it should be stressed that in much of Africa religion has continued to play a critical, sometimes an incendiary, role in mass movements, from Muslim radicalism in Algeria, the Sudan, and Nigeria to Christian liberation in South Africa. However, Blyden's example of taking the initiative and providing intellectual leadership is one that could do with repeating in our otherwise very different circumstances.

CONCLUSIONS

There are implications in all this for interreligious relations in society and public life. Contact between people and across ethnic divisions has been a normal, ordinary fact of existence for Africans. The normal pattern is for ethnic solidarity to receive priority over other considerations, but in some significant cases people have related to each other on the basis of mutual interest, common belief, and common need. This makes it difficult to strip religion and marginalize it. People who are in any case drawn together by the natural ties of family, clan, tribe, language, and occupation also find enduring solidarity in religion and are able, for example, to appreciate their similarities as well as differences in the generous light of the Creator's beneficence. In the West religion is a sub-compartment of life and is defined in the light of secular values, rather than secular values being defined in the searching light of religion. Even in as sympathetic an observer as Blyden we find evidence of this Western viewpoint in his desire to prove religion credible by contemporary concerns rather than by acknowledgment of religion's transcendent claims. In few other areas of life is the West's intellectual dominance so great as in the secular overthrow of religion. Blyden conceded that when he called on religion to endorse a secular agenda. Yet, in the Africa of his day, religion flourished like wild nature itself; all institutions, structures, and personalities of any consequence were permeated by it. Religion was the primary category for knowing and living. The Christian presence in this situation has led, or has begun the process of leading, to deeper engagement with issues of personal and social identity in Scripture, tradition, and history, and with questions of individual transformation and cultural fulfillment. Much of that has taken place in the context of lively awareness of the African religious worldview. In the absence of such deep involvement Christians would be tempted to draw artificial boundaries and be limited to superficial reflection. Communities in such threshold situations have been unsparingly confronted with the political and social realities of their time and place, as Adrian Hastings has eloquently pointed out.[19] Such historical imperatives have prevented Christianity, or Islam, from being turned into a bastion of pietist escapism. The responsibilities of national citizenship, for example, have demanded commitment far deeper than the rules of jingoist nationalism and economic self-interest. For religion, citizenship has had to be purified by self-denial and nationalism by penitence, a sentiment much discussed in Muslim and Christian religious sources. Blyden is a salutary lesson for all these reasons, though we would not follow his lead in the cavalier treatment he gave, or alleged Islam to have given, to African primal religions. On that point, Christianity, or at least non-Western African forms of it, has a better chance of making fruitful contact with indigenous religions than scriptural Islam, an issue discussed in Chapter 1 above.

In that spirit, Christianity and Islam in Africa have not been separated from the public or material sphere, with the consequence that both religions have continued to be important in the lives of Africans now facing mounting pressures in the modern world. Consequently, the public policy dimension of religious practice has been important in the reception and appropriation of the Christian and Muslim traditions, although we need now to pay greater attention to this dimension in view of new and urgent challenges. I shall attempt a preliminary exploration of this theme in later chapters.

Beyond that there is the cross-cultural frontier of religious transmission. That cross-cultural front has had abiding pertinence for the new forms of religious identity emerging on the continent, and it is indispensable to understand that. It has, however, not been enough that the African reception and expression of faith be grounded in indigenous forms and idioms, with social and communal exigencies exerting a powerful influence on the outcome, but it has been important that such appropriation not amount to a take-over of the message. The intimate connection between religion and culture has already created enormous strains as well as opportunities in several parts of Muslim and Christian Africa where the established status quo has come under pressure. It would be easy for the shifting landscape of social and political identity, shaken from the collision with modernity, to recompose itself with recourse to the tribal and ethnic fault line, with the missionary urge of the new religions sublimated into a chosen people dogma. It would not be reasonable or adequate to deal with this problem without confronting the question of religion and culture, especially religion as cultural triumphalism and its converse of culture as messianic destiny, the kind of political monism by which ethnic insecurity has traditionally sought to immunize itself against the feared virus of global exposure.

One hopeful way forward is reaffirming the cross-cultural and comparative nature of religious practice in Africa, for recognition of the multiple frontiers and levels of religious identity will restrain the urge to make exclusive virtue of one cultural idiom. Often the most destructive thing that can happen—even among people who think they have a tacit agreement to agree to disagree—is that one

---

[19] Adrian Hastings, *A History of African Christianity: 1950-1975* (Cambridge: Cambridge University Press, 1979).

party is completely ignorant of what the other believes or does not believe, so that what one might assume to be the other person's side is in fact no such thing at all. Such an imaginary projection is allied to the sort of xenophobia that a monocultural view of the world breeds. The decentering that is needed to break down the walls of isolation and to open us to the full potential of global human community will only come from a plurality of cultural idioms and a willingness to translate across the cultural divide. I have argued here and elsewhere that the African dimension of interreligious and cross-cultural encounter provides fresh and exciting resources for moving forward with encouragement into the future.

Christian African experience could on this basis contribute to an enriching, deepening understanding of the language of mutual responsibility and service as well as the phenomenon of interreligious penetration and contact through which historical relations have evolved. The Freetown 1888 debate showed that both communities were attuned to the changes affecting the continent, and although a new situation was arising, everyone concerned realized the old assurances would be inadequate, even counter-productive. However, leaders at the time lacked the requisite training to grasp the opportunities for interreligious conversation, though the debate showed that some were making a gallant effort. Our own age has no more reason for complacency in view of undiminishing woeful mutual ignorance and other signs of mutual unresponsiveness. However unsteady the hand of friendship and mutual acknowledgment extended at the debate, the participants and their audience demonstrated an interest and a willingness to explore each other's tradition. It is doubtful whether less is demanded of us in our search today for global ecumenical solidarity.

CHAPTER BIBLIOGRAPHY

Artisan, The. Freetown.

Blyden, Edward W. *Christianity, Islam and the Negro Race.* London 1887; repr. Edinburgh: Edinburgh University Press, 1967.

Digest of Moohummudan Law: Containing the Doctrines of the Hanifeea Code of Jurisprudence. Edited and translated by Neil B. E. Baillie. 1869-75; reprinted Lahore: Premier Book House, 1974.

Fisher, Humphrey J. "Conversion Reconsidered: Some Historical Aspects or Religious Conversion in Black Africa," in *Africa* [Journal of the International African Institute] XLIII, no. 1 (January 1973).

_____, and A. G. B. Fisher. *Slavery and Muslim Society in Africa.* London: Christopher Hurst Publishers, 1971.

Hastings, Adrian. *A History of African Christianity: 1950-1975.* Cambridge: Cambridge University Press, 1979.

Horton, Robin. "African Conversion." *Africa* [Journal of the International African Institute] XLI, no. 2 (April 1971).

Idowu, E. Bolaji. *Olodumaré, God in Yoruba Belief.* London: Longman, 1962.

Lynch, H. R. *Edward Wilmot Blyden: Pan-Negro Patriot.* New York: Oxford University Press, 1967.

Mbiti, John S. *New Testament Eschatology in an African Background.* London: Cambridge University Press, 1971.

Peel, John D. Y. *Aladura: A Religious Movement among the Yoruba.* London: Oxford University Press for the International African Institute, 1968.

Peterson, John. *Province of Freedom.* London, 1969.

Proudfoot, Leslie. "An Aku Factional Fight in East Freetown," *Sierra Leone Bulletin of Religion,* vol. 4, no. 2 (1962).

Proudfoot, Leslie, and Wilson, H. S. "Muslim Attitudes to Education in Sierra Leone," *Muslim World,* vol. 50, no. 1 (1960).

Qayrawání, Ibn Abí Zayd al-. *La Risálah: ou épitre sue les éléments du dogme et de la loi de l'Islam selon le rite malikte.* Edited and translated by Léon Bercher. Algiers: Éditions Jules Carbonel, 1952. English edition: Joseph Kenny, ed. and tr. *The Risálah.* Minna, Nigeria: The Islamic Educational Trust, 1992.

Sierra Leone Weekly News [Freetown] (January 1889).

Smith, R. Bosworth. *Mohammed and Mohammedanism.* 2d edition. London: Smith and Elder Co., 1876.

Taylor, John V. *The Primal Vision.* London: SCM, 1963.

5

Religion and Politics
A Comparative Religious Critique

The modern West in its dramatic intrusion in Africa and elsewhere has been the bearer of two massive but uneven influences, one secular and the other religious. The secular influence has expressed itself in the autonomy of the national state, and the religious in the organization and extension of the missionary movement. Both influences have left enduring legacies: a secular elite that maintains and is in turn maintained by the machinery of state bureaucracy, and ecclesiastical jurisdictions that minister to the flocks. The uneven quality of these influences arises from the fact that state bureaucracy has primacy over the religious domain, with national sovereignty superior to ecclesiastical jurisdiction. This is the post-Enlightenment secular legacy that has competed with religion for the allegiance of Africans. It is with the development and consequences of this uneven legacy, and with its novel character, that this chapter is concerned.

Although relatively recently introduced in Africa, the secular national state has had a deep effect on African society. We should, therefore, examine its roots in the West in order to have a sense of the scale of the changes required by its establishment in Africa. As a dogmatic concept, the national secular state is in part the legacy of Machiavelli and Bodin. In *The Prince*, published in 1515, Machiavelli establishes an absolute executive sovereignty as the supreme form of the state, whose purpose is unity and order. Bodin, in his *République*, published in 1577, creates a state with uncontested power over citizens and subjects, itself free of the constraints of the laws it enacts. The roots of the modern Western secular state and of the science of instrumental politics may be traced to these two authors and their historical contemporaries.[1]

Western political influence has not been confined to Western society but has penetrated other societies. As Lord Hailey remarked in his monumental study of

---

[1] For a summary of the views of Machiavelli and Bodin in the context of the modern national state, see Sir Ernest Barker, *Principles of Social and Political Theory* (Oxford: Clarendon Press, 1951), pp. 13ff.

African conditions under colonial rule, "It is the singular fate of Africa that so many of its countries should be subject to the political control of one or other of the European Powers," though Lord Hailey took no notice of the nationalist movements that were active at his writing and which were questioning the basis of his confident assertions.[2] The existing state boundaries of Africa, for example, were created by Western colonial powers and inherited by the independent governments. These boundaries still provide the context of state jurisdiction in modern Africa, and, indeed, of religious identity.

Through the artificial colonial creation of tribes as an amalgamation of ethnic groups and of nations as the fusion of tribes, states were established as the vehicle by which Africans could enter the twentieth century. The whole political apparatus of colonial and nationalist politics in Africa required the setting aside of Africa's own history, of its precolonial heritage, and a blind charge into a future of material fulfilment. In the context of the doctrine of the state as the machinery of progress and modernization, the denial of Africa's history, the charge of a dark, primitive continent without landmarks, produced the dialectics of progress versus tradition, of science against magic, with the vanguards of enlightenment ranged against the puppets of feudal privilege. The new discourse had the effect of compromising the modern African elites, who were absorbed into the Western political heritage though they lacked any meaningful roots in it or, as Awolowo of Nigeria admitted,[3] in their own societies. They were in close enough proximity to colonialism to be drawn willy-nilly into the colonial orbit. However, precisely because of the relatively superficial nature of the assimilation of these new African elites and because they did not participate in the informed debate that should accompany the rise of national states, these elites became ineffective modernist brokers to their people. That provoked a crisis in the relations between state and society in view of which we should scrutinize inherited political institutions and ideas. It is a process of reappraisal in which Muslims, too, have joined.

In his detailed discussion of the colonial context of church-state relations in Africa, Holger Hansen of Copenhagen, for example, described how the Berlin Congress of February 1885, which partitioned Africa among the colonial powers, stipulated freedom of religion and state neutrality as the appropriate framework for Western overlordship.[4] However, when applied to Africa, the European formulation of the relation of religion and politics revealed glaring anomalies, the most significant being the lack of indigenous parallels to the Christian presuppositions of a laic state. Nevertheless, the colonial powers found a remedy in the several missionary organizations that were entering or had entered Africa, and so these organizations were allowed to operate with the blessing of the state but without the state prescribing belief or enjoining practice. This was not the same as

---

[2] Lord Hailey, *An African Survey: Revised 1956* (Oxford: Clarendon Press, 1957), p. 145.

[3] See Basil Davidson, *The Black Man's Burden: Africa and the Curse of the Nation State* (London: James Currey, 1992), p. 107.

[4] Holger Bernt Hansen, *Mission, Church and State in a Colonial Setting: Uganda: 1890-1925* (London: Heinemann, 1984), pp. 25ff.

state indifference to religion for the obvious reason that religious affiliation often carried political implications. For example, if a local ruler, let us say, converted to Catholicism, should his land and territories be incorporated into a Catholic missionary sphere or should they be broken up and offered to Baptists, Anglicans, Presbyterians and others as well? Should the state afford similar protection and guarantees to Muslims? Apparently, at the Berlin Congress the German chancellor, Prince Otto von Bismarck, retreated from his original statement about the new colonial powers "favoring and aiding all religions" when Turkey, a Muslim state and a signatory to the convention, insisted that Muslim missionaries be included (Hansen 1984, 26).

Typically, the concordat was the instrument that prescribed for church-state relations, assuring mutual benefit without harmful side effects; Muslims, however, were insufficiently reared in the habit of separation to accept that arrangement. In the new colonial empires the policy was adopted to protect and contain Christian missions, and to do so on strictly impartial grounds so far as institutional religious interests are concerned. The question of freedom of religion was thus interpreted to mean the right of institutional mission agencies and churches to establish themselves rather than freedom of religion as an individual personal matter without state involvement, though in Muslim areas the state would act as protector. Consequently, shades of territoriality survived in the policy of institutional religious spheres of influence. This distinction had implications for administrative practice. The state would be neutral or indifferent insofar as the *content* of religious belief was concerned, but when it came to acts and deeds, it would be active and participate in the work of religious agencies. Whether such state interest restricts or helps religious agencies is another question; for example, does close co-operation in education and family life also mean control and dependence? Furthermore, if the state imagined that Christianity would play to a unitary idea of church and state, it was mistaken; denominations were proof that there was no monolithic Christianity and that church membership did not imply inclusion in a unified European religious community. In the course of time, a diverse African Christianity would emerge as the personal faith of individuals scattered among the tribes, however persistent collective ethnic loyalties might be.

In the general African view, religion and society are connected, even if not synonymous. Thus the Enlightenment distinction between religion as private belief or as a subject fit only for study, on the one hand, and, on the other hand, religion as public practice, had no analogue in the radically different conditions of Africa, although educated African elites endorsed it. In contrast, missionaries were not too much out of step with African opinion on this matter. To the natural question, What is a Christian society?, missionaries answered in terms of what was familiar to them: Victorian conformist morality and ethics mobilized behind a sympathetic colonial state. After all, the rule of good manners of Victorian sensibility sets only such standards as it can enforce, whatever the risk of cultural interference.

Thus to most missionaries, such as Robert Laws of Livingstonia in 1880, Robert Moffat of Kuruman, or the agents of the Blantyre mission, a Christian society was a desideratum, especially where Christian colonies of freed slaves could be set up to that end under white suzerainty. Yet the idea of such a society as a foreign political enclave, protected by European colonial power from without and governed by rules and regulations imposed by missionaries from within, was deemed an obstacle by the missionaries themselves rather than a help to the service of the kind of gospel that thrives from personal initiative.[5] In consequence, the special circumstances of Africa made such unthinking cultural transference all but impossible.

Let us pursue the subject and assess the religious aspect of the presence of the Western political heritage in Africa in three parts: the first, using some African examples, will examine the nature of the relationship between religion and politics, in particular, what religious interest there might be in political affairs and whether such interest is compatible with religious autonomy; the second will expound the Islamic formulation of the issue in terms of the rightful integration as well as proper separation of religion and politics; and, finally, the third will offer some reflections on the religious case for the inadequacy of the national state to serve as an absolute moral arbiter of human relations. The conclusion will be that the current ferment in religious circles in Africa and elsewhere in the Muslim world provides a useful context for reexamining standard Western suppositions on the principle of separation of church and state. We should therefore turn our critical eye back on the West and reassess what its successful expansion abroad has brought to other societies.[6]

A thread that will run throughout this discussion is that both national loyalty and religious loyalty appeal to, and have their source in, a commitment that is in the final analysis spiritual, so that an exclusive political bid for that commitment throws a gauntlet to the religious interest in the matter. In response, religious people may seek umbrage under "holy nationalism"[7] to give religion a chance, even if that should provoke a debate on the issue.[8] Such a debate may open the state to moral scrutiny and therefore to a qualification of its absolute claims. In view of such complex issues, we may argue that religion, in its critical realism about human nature, has a role in public affairs as well as in social life. This argument can be extended by taking due cognizance of developments in Muslim thought that shows a divergence from Western political practice.

---

[5] M. W. Waldman, "The Church of Scotland Mission at Blantyre, Nyasaland: Its Political Implications," *Bulletin of the Society of African Church History*, 2/4 (1968), pp. 299-310.

[6] See Max Stackhouse, "Politics and Religion," *Encyclopedia of Religion*, vol. 11, ed. Mircea Eliade (New York: Macmillan, 1987), pp. 408-23.

[7] The phrase occurs in Conor Cruise O'Brien, *God Land: Reflections on Religion and Politics* (Cambridge: Harvard University Press, 1987).

[8] Among others, says Ninian Smart, the Christian or Buddhist "will have a certain ultimate skepticism about patriotism." The reason is that the nation state "has nothing truly transcendent," except, of course, a universal imperial urge. See Peter H. Merkl and Ninian Smart, eds., *Religion and Politics in the Modern World* (New York: New York University Press, 1985), p. 27.

ON ORIGIN AND TENSION

Any analysis of the impact of the secular state in Africa will result in two conclusions. One is the fact that national, linguistic, or ethnic identity does not coincide with the boundaries of the state. Similarly, the state as presently constituted is unable to cope with the resulting complex political, economic, and military order. This has encouraged the creation of coalitions, alliances, and pacts between and across nations, including membership in international organizations. The other conclusion is that religious questions often go beyond national state jurisdiction, and, given the persistence of religion as a force for change and identity (or, on the negative side, as a force for obduracy and intractability), the modern national state often encounters religion in the course of seeking or constructing popular endorsement.

A potentially dangerous imbalance inheres in the relationship between religion and the national state, such as when ethnic nationalism is forged from the hard crust of ethnic custom and transmuted into the state instrument, and when the state in turn represents the unity of ethnic triumph and moral destiny. Under the right conditions, including when religion has been thoroughly domesticated as cultural identity, the ethnic state can become the opiate of the people, an intoxicating infusion of sentiments of national transcendence in defiance of logic and history. Our failure to recognize or understand the distinction rather than the antipathy between church and state tips the scales on the side of the sacralized ethnic state.

The crux of the case being presented in this chapter may be stated as follows: those who have followed Machiavelli and Bodin in arming the sovereignty of the state in full panoply have also dissolved the separation of church and state by awarding authority to the state in religious matters. At the same time, the state, by being so absolutized, challenges religion in its own sphere. By proceeding on one front it must, in fact, proceed on another, much in the manner of the traditional square dance: moving three or four steps to the right anticipates as many steps to the left. In one pattern of political "absolutization" we elicit a contrasting pattern of religious "relativization." In Africa such gyrations have characterized much of the scene. In addition, it is clear that the absolutized state incurs a double jeopardy: it cripples the instrumental function of authority and infects religious motivation with tactical rewards. Thus has the versatile state stumbled on its own inflexible contradiction.

The conditions for the absolutization of political norms have their source in the theory of sovereignty. "Sovereignty," says Sir Ernest Barker, "is unlimited and illimitable" (Barker 1951, 60). As the definition of sovereignty expanded over time, it came to be applied to human relations in the notion of the liberator-state, which may intervene to protect social groups from interfering with the principle of the free agency of their members. Marsiglio of Padua, a medieval writer who straddled the world of the Middle Ages and early modern Europe and as such was a precursor of Bodin, "asserted the primacy of law-making over all other expressions of state power; he insisted on the indivisibility of ultimate legislative authority."[9] Although it is clear that Marsiglio did not develop his ideas into a coherent theory of sovereignty, his emphasis on the formal right of the ruler to make laws provides support for the Machiavellian executive sovereign.

Two important elements may be said to persist in medieval writings about political authority, at least in writings about the medieval world in the advanced stages of its development.[10] One is the role assigned to reason and natural law, and the other is the concept of political obligation, especially how, if at all, dissent fits in with such obligation. The ruler is assumed to be beholden to norms of reason and justice, but in fact the circularity of thought involved makes those norms attributes of the sovereign. What is given with the right hand is taken with the left. It was the veteran ideologue Abbé Sieyès who, as guiding spirit of the French Revolution, made the national state assume an implacable doctrinaire posture when he wrote in 1789: "The nation exists before all, it is the origin of everything. Its will is always legal, it is the law itself."[11] Who or what the nation is makes a difference here. Thus when the Abbé Sieyès's injunction is fused with Rousseau's "general will" to become in effect the popular will, it entrenches an uncompromising nation state dogma that typically ignites into chosen-people activism once it is whipped up with racial or national fervor. Thus is spawned from both the left and right a veritable Leviathan that consumes all its opponents and rivals, the church included.

Given the benefit of hindsight, we may say the national state in its long and forceful expansion in Africa and elsewhere has thrived from its incestuous appetite and now appears to have reached the limits of its development. Consequently, we have reached a point where the task is to define the limits of the national state in terms of the new international order, human rights, social pluralism, and religious freedom—old questions, perhaps, but cast in a new light by unprecedented modern developments. The culture of political sacralization to which, say, Muslim theocratic demands seem to lend support, is appealing to a state that wants to bolster itself with metaphysical norms. However, when properly directed, current religious ferment in the Third World may be mobilized to check the excesses of the predatory state, as has happened in Ghana under Acheampong and in South Africa, with religion able to demonstrate, in however tentative or precarious a fashion, the limited nature of political sovereignty.

The secular, rational state thus conceived is not just the victim but an active protagonist in the religious controversy concerning its will and purpose. By absolutizing itself the state claims not only the power to organize life and command the obedience of men and women but to be itself what H. Richard Niebuhr

---

[9] Ewart Lewis, *Medieval Political Ideas,* 2 vols. (New York: Cooper Square Publishers, 1974), vol. 1, p. 30.
[10] See Charles H. McIlwain, "Mediæval Institutions in the Modern World," in Karl H. Dannenfeldt, ed., *The Renaissance: Medieval or Modern?* Problems in European Civilization series (Boston: D. C. Heath, 1959), pp. 29-34.
[11] Cited in Conor Cruise O'Brien, "The Wrath of Ages: Nationalism's Primordial Roots," *Foreign Affairs* (November/December, 1993), p. 143.

calls "the value-center," consecrating its operative dealings with the henotheist faith of national loyalty.[12] It is a short step from there to the next, when the state becomes, in the words of ancient sacred monarchies, "the shadow of God on earth," followed by a third step in which the state makes obligation a matter exclusively of its control.

Not content to restrain and arbitrate but committed to prescribe faith of a moral kind and conformity of an absolute nature, the omnipotent state in Africa has opened for itself a wide channel of power. Ideological advocates of the state who had used their theories to combat religious dangers have now inherited in the omnipotent state far worse hazards, only now magistrates have upstaged mullahs and commissars cardinals. With that change the state has attained a radical arbitrary posture for which a suitable motto might be, If the state loses the confidence of the people, it shall dissolve the people and elect another. The idea of political stability is interchanged with that of the continuity of the state, bringing closer the day when, as Gladstone once described it, we have "the negation of God erected into a system of government."

My basic contention here is not born of a facile romanticism for a stateless society and a Rousseauistic innocence but rather of the conviction that the omnipotent state in Africa has been its own undoing, that it is riddled with fundamental contradictions. Such a state promotes a political metaphysics in place of religion. Dietrich Bonhoeffer used to complain that the modern world in which the church tries to minister has outgrown the metaphysical religious outlook of the Bible—"God as the working hypothesis" has been superseded in a "world come of age."[13] In fact, however, religious metaphysics has been replaced with political metaphysics, with political messianism the creed in which people place their trust. Thus, the otherwise natural convoy of religion and politics has been reduced to capture by the state, with citizenship its hostage.

In many countries in Africa the capture of religion by the state was signaled by formal agreements. The Missionary Concordat of 1940 and the Statute of 1941, for example, created privileges for the Roman Catholic Church in Portuguese Angola and Mozambique along the lines of the 1926 Missionary Accord. Under the terms of the Concordat the Portuguese state recognized the Catholic church as an official institution to promote the national and colonial aims of the state in the overseas territories, with financial provision for the church to that end. Cardinal Carejeira of Lisbon announced on national radio in May 1940 that the Concordat returned Portugal to its spiritual roots and would commence a process of inward national renewal and vigorous outward colonial expansion. Although Carejeira insisted that the Concordat did not create a state church, Antonio Salazar, the president of Portugal, was more candid, saying that the church would be subject to the higher requirements of national interest and public order, that the clergy would be "guaranteed" patriotic education, and that

---

[12] See H. Richard Niebuhr, *Radical Monotheism and Western Culture* (New York: Harper and Brothers, 1960).

[13] Dietrich Bonhoeffer, *Letters and Papers from Prison*, reprint (London: SCM, 1971), pp. 381, 286, 326.

the state would be a party in the selection of the highest ecclesiastical authorities.[14] With particular reference to Africa, Salazar saw the Concordat as the completion of the Colonial Act, whose purpose was to nationalize missionary work and harmonize it with colonial policy. In his address to the National Assembly in Lisbon, Salazar was in a heady mood about church and state as one harmonious ideal. "We return," he said effusively, "with the force and vigor of a reborn state to one of the greatest springs of our national life and, without abandoning our contemporary period with its material progress and the victories of civilization, we are in the upper spheres of spirituality—the same as eight hundred years ago" (Henderson 1992, 253-54). Salazar was the impetus in the tidal wave of Portuguese immigration into Africa, which by 1974 numbered 350,000 in Angola and 200,000 in Mozambique, all of which bloated Portugal's Christendom pretensions. Thus Salazar's version of Christendom rested on the colonial project as a unilateral construct, without any recourse to Africans. Portugal's future greatness would be the echo of historic Christendom, and the African colonies, though without exact parallels in the cohesive territoriality of classical Christendom, would nevertheless fit or be made to fit into an archetypal religious scheme. In this, as in so much else, Salazar was wrong, and the consequent unrest in Portugal's African empire, combined with progressive forces in the expanding European Community, would undermine organic stability at home.

In retrospect, Salazar's colonial religious flirtations seem like rhetorical diversions when compared to the stripping that awaited the church in an independent Angola or Mozambique. On 11 November 1975 Angola declared its independence from Portugal amid a fractured armed liberation movement and the shreds of a divided society. The new MPLA government adopted Marxist-Leninism under a centralized party machinery as the vanguard of the revolution. Political militancy was at once declared the corrective to religion, a position that placed the party on a war path with the church. In December 1977 the official organs of the government announced that Catholics and Protestants did not qualify to become members of the party or the government. There was widespread harassment of religion, including the confiscation of property and the forcible taking of children from their parents for indoctrination. When the Catholic church responded on 21 January 1978 to the situation, with Vatican Radio denouncing the discriminatory measures against the church, the party answered back with charges of lies and conspiracy against the church. The secretary of the Party Central Committee, Lúcio Lara, cut to the chase with a long-running attack on the church, emphasizing its foreignness to Angola and thus by implication its traitorous character. To the church's criticism about imposing on Angolan society a foreign-born ideology like Marxism-Leninism, Lara answered that Christ was not born in Angola either, thus exonerating the imported primacy of Marxism by the strategy of the proscribed foreignness of the church (Henderson 1992, 357). He warned opponents that government had provided itself with the means to consider "as illegal and

---

[14] Lawrence W. Henderson, *The Church in Angola: A River of Many Currents* (Cleveland: The Pilgrim Press, 1992), p. 253.

therefore [as] punishable any activity which places faith or religious belief in opposition to the revolutionary transformation of society."[15] The government moved against religious schools, taking them over and instituting a program of scientific socialism to shut down all access to Angola's long and distinguished religious history, beginning with King Afonso I (ruled 1506-1543).

The attacks on the church, and their tediously elaborate justifications in the theory of party supremacy, have led more than one commentator to conclude that Marxist-Leninism is actually a religion, even a church, and that it is competing with Catholicism or Protestantism for primacy. This is unconvincing, and confuses—and rewards—political ideology with what it has plundered from religion. Thus the MPLA government produced what it called the Ten Principles of the Pioneers, deliberately modelled on the Ten Commandments, and in case that was not obvious, ransacked the New Testament to identify a parallel set of what the party called Ten Commandments for Christian Youth.[16] The propaganda catechism of the MPLA government was an amalgam of expedient platitudes, and its wish to be compared to Scripture as a matter simply of comparing texts only proved forgery. The resemblance admits the difference. How else can we explain the hostility with which the government regarded religion? Thus in the torture and deaths of priests, sisters, and pastors, we have a pattern inscribed with the grim logic of political vengeance. It is small comfort to tell the religious faithful, who witnessed and survived these acts, that surveillance and repression were directed at them on account of their kinship with the agents of political control. In the typical instance of a religious party saying the Rosary and meditating on the sorrowful mysteries while under attack, we have not kin bonding but a state vendetta. A leading Protestant churchman was constrained to observe that while he himself would offer conciliation and cooperation, what the government required of religion was that it should remain a target for suppression (Henderson 1992, 354). Thus did the secular ideological state overturn the popular basis of Catholic piety to assert political monism. Politics as religion redeems no more than religion as politics.

The Christendom view of religion, in which church and state formed a unified though flawed institution, was at work in other parts of Africa, too. In Ethiopia Emperor Haile Selassie was crowned on 2 November 1930 in the cathedral in Addis Ababa, and the Ethiopian Constitution formally recognized "the person of the Emperor as sacred, his dignity . . . inviolable and his power indisputable." In the 1955 Revised Constitution, after the Ethiopian Orthodox church was declared the established church with state backing, the emperor and the patriarch had thrones side by side in the cathedral in Addis Ababa, a value-added formula that was rooted in Ethiopia's national origin. The emperor was given the right of approval in the election and appointment of senior church officials and the right of attendance at Holy Synod meetings with veto power over decisions there. Archbishop Basileyos, on his ordination and at his elevation to the patriarchate, swore an oath of loyalty to the emperor. He was given a place on the Council of Regency and on

---

[15] *Jornal de Angola*, 5 February 1978. Cited in Henderson 1992, 357.
[16] *Jornal de Angola*, 22 February 1976.

the Crown Council. Thus did the Revised Constitution effect the state take-over of the church and made the fit between government and religion exact. The Penal Code of 1957 recognized the festivals of the Ethiopian church as national holidays, and the Civil Code of 1960 gave legal sanction to the church with respect to its dioceses, monasteries, and parishes.

These measures may also be seen as the "gelding of God" or as the church's forfeiture of its maiden honor at the hands of an aggressive state. In our analysis of what happened in Ethiopia or Portugal, we should note that religion may become a state idea by the devious path of the state becoming a religious idea. Thus did the normal state boundaries expand to incorporate the church as a quasi-department of government. Religion, in turn, became mixed up with the shifting fortunes of political expediency, allying itself with people useful for short-term gain only and repulsing others whose long-term principles might cohere with those of religion but whose particular stand at the time made them oppose the state. For example, in 1960 there was an abortive left-wing coup in Addis Ababa led by Germame Neway, who called for a program of nationalization of land, including land belonging to the church. After the coup was quelled, the church responded by declaring the coup leaders and supporters antireligious traitors. The church could not foresee the political storm that would engulf it after September 1974, when the emperor was overthrown in a Marxist coup.[17]

Following dramatic political changes in these states from the mid-1970s on, the governments of Angola and Mozambique and of Ethiopia swiftly moved to abolish preferment and to enact freedom of religion. Elsewhere in Africa it was a period of stormy relations as churches maneuvered for autonomy: in Ghana, there was the fateful confrontation of the church with the regime of General Acheampong; in Uganda, the clash between the churches and General Idi Amin led to the murder of Archbishop Lanani Luwum in 1977; and in Liberia, the coup d'état in 1980 of the late President Doe installed a military government that chose to make an example of the pastor-politicians who had ruled Liberia from the very beginning of the republic.[18] Similar tensions have existed in Zaire, Nigeria, the Sudan, Zambia, and Kenya. For example, in the tense atmosphere following the abortive coup attempt of August 1982, the churches in Kenya decided to respond to government attempts to introduce political indoctrination in schools. In September 1983 the churches published a document entitled "Love, Peace, and Unity: A Christian View of Politics in Kenya," which stated that the churches should be true to their prophetic calling rather than merely do the state's bidding.

From all these complex situations we may draw the following observation: in the final analysis, it comes to the same thing whether religion is a state idea or the state is a religious idea. However church and state may be combined, an identical fate awaits them, for the reason that the mixing of church and state stakes every-

---

[17] See Andargachew Tiruneh, *The Ethiopian Revolution: 1974-1985* (Cambridge: Cambridge University Press, 1993; reprinted 1995).

[18] See David M. Gitari, "The Church's Witness to the Living God: Seeking Just Political, Social, and Economic Structures in Contemporary Africa," *Transformation: An International Dialogue on Evangelical Social Ethics* 5 (2) (April/June 1988).

thing on the temporal ground. The risk is that both sectors will get caught with tangled signals, that unrest will spread evenly between them even if unrest has only one or other origin. Each is hoist with the other's petard.

On another level, we may note that the call for political mobilization in Africa has made wide use of religious symbols, whether or not such symbols have received official sanction. This has led to a hybrid politico-religious culture, making familiar such phrases as "national redemption," "economic salvation," "political justification," "national regeneration," "seeking first the political kingdom," "sanctity of the state," "the supreme law of the state," and so forth. In a move calculated to muzzle the civil service, President Kwame Nkrumah of Ghana declared in 1962 that a civil servant "who sells information concerning his work is worse than a traitor and incurs an eternal curse upon his head."[19] The "eternal curse" was a code for political stigmatization, a fate carrying a serious threat. Nkrumah was on occasion more explicit, as when his Young Pioneers Movement adopted the Lord's Prayer for a political catechism, substituting political vocabulary for religion. He intended the political takeover of religion as a matter of universal logic, not simply a question of settling local scores. His effect on contemporary African youth, including the present writer, is hard to measure, so enormous was it.

In the hands of leaders of his ilk, then, the state assumed metaphysical connotations, with the single-party state becoming a monotheist secular absolute. Such a state is ideologically intolerant of pluralism, which excites all the bitter passion and iconoclastic fury monotheist crusaders reserve for polytheists and brings a connection of religion and politics to the controversial stage of state seizure. As a result, political life became divisive, with African leaders promoting themselves as anointed messianic champions.[20] One of the most successful contemporary figures of political messianism is General Mobutu of Zaire, who refers to himself as "the Father and god of the nation" (*The New York Times*, 14 April 1990). His face is everywhere.

His photograph hangs in every office in his realm. His ministers wear gold pins with tiny photographs of him on the lapels of their tailored pin-striped suits. He names streets, football stadiums, hospitals, and universities after himself. . . . He insists on being called "doctor" or "conqueror" or "teacher" or "the big elephant" or "the number-one peasant" or "the wise old man" or "the natural miracle" or "the most popular leader in the world." His every pronouncement is reported on the front page. . . . He bans all political parties except the one he controls. He rigs elections. He emasculates the courts. He cows the press. He stifles academia. He goes to church.[21]

---

[19] Cited in Trevor Jones, *Ghana's First Republic: The Pursuit of the Political Kingdom* (London: Methuen, 1976), p. 52.

[20] Echoes of this theme occur in David E. Apter, "Political Religion in the New Nations," in *Old Societies and New States: The Quest for Modernity in Asia and Africa*, ed. Clifford Geertz (New York: Free Press, 1963).

[21] See Blaine Harden, *Africa: Dispatches from a Fragile Continent* (New York: W. W. Norton, 1990); see also Thomas Callaghy, *The State-Society Struggle: Zaire in Comparative Perspective* (New York: Columbia University Press, 1984).

The rhetoric of state power, however, is nearly in inverse proportion to the influence it exerts. In much of Africa political rhetoric has aroused feelings and expectations far in excess of realizable goals. People have responded with withdrawal, which leaders have alleged to be apathy resulting from colonial alienation. As messianic slogans have turned incandescent in the darkness, the bedazzled populations have also turned skeptical. Farmers, peasants, and workers in the mines and on the roads, rivers, and railways have bucked the system by holding back or falling to the highest bidder. Productivity has collapsed and with it state revenues. Parastatals have entered the scene and have combined economic incentives with political rewards to reverse the process, though the adopted measures have failed abysmally, with people seeing them as versions of state excess.

The assault of the state on its citizens has left people with a return to traditional values, however defined, as a last resort. However, even there the state has pursued the people, arrogating the right to define those values and to appropriate them for itself. Hence Mobutu's call for "African authenticity," including the dropping of European names and the adopting of African ones. Socialist doctrine in other parts of the continent has been assortedly upholstered in colorful communitarian values and stiffened with oriental lessons,[22] mostly "lean-to" ideas jacked up by party activists. A spiritual reaction has followed in which church leaders, backed by the rank and file, have taken up the cudgels. In response, the state has pretended that political obligation is a matter of its exclusive control, a state of mind requiring surrender and submission. It is as a state of mind that the churches have opposed the state bureaucracy.

As African and other political leaders have been quick to realize, religion and politics are intimately connected: they affect each other, draw on each other's insights, and make an identical appeal to trust and loyalty. "United or opposed to each other," writes Peter Merkl, "virulent nationism and religious myths have been major political factors in modern history" (Merkl and Smart 1985, 1). Yet we appear to have inherited in Africa a Manichaean ideal, with the state as the embodiment of truth and goodness—a dichotomy that breeds political divisiveness. It allows political leaders when it suits their interests to give religion an enclave, voluntary status, a secondary value vis-á-vis the primary truth-center of political action, although from the religious point of view "enclavement" may promote a superior sense of liminal separation. A notion has grown that politics impinge on religion in a superior way: that the state as the superior and ultimate

---

[22] In imitation of China, Malagassy President Didier Ratsiraka adopted what he called a Red Book (*Boky Mena*) program of state-directed policies in August 1975, marked by populist radical rhetoric. Its linchpin was the notion of *fokonolona*, the traditional village community *soi-disant*, but now conceived in agrarian revolutionary terms as a territorial collectivity. The rural economy, supplying 80 percent of the country's export earnings, was shattered as a consequence, with the disaster being blamed on "compradore bourgeoisie." Ratsiraka resorted to secret-police tactics to combat disaffection; the Catholic church, however, stood its ground. See Mervyn Brown, *Madagascar Rediscovered: From Early Times to Independence* (Hamden, CT: Archon Books, 1979); see also "The Church and Christians in Madagascar Today," *Pro Mundi Vita Dossiers,* Africa Dossier 6 (July-August 1978).

representation of human reality will survive the demise of religion and, meanwhile, must actively work toward that end. The state has seized on its instrumental capability to press its right to limitless power. Consequently, in several well-known instances, religious people have responded with a counter-challenge, viewing the claims of political metaphysics as vestiges of genuine religious metaphysics. It is this religious case that receives eloquent treatment in the Islamic tradition, and to that we now turn.

THE ISLAMIC RELIGIOUS AND POLITICAL FERMENT

Representative Muslim scholars treat the issue of religion and politics without the sanguine notion that the public and private domains require separate and exclusive understanding. The Muslim counter-argument, now the topic in media and print reports,[23] is symptomatic of the widespread disenchantment with the national state as a moral absolute. Early Muslim nationalists, however, had to run the gauntlet of orthodox suspicions that they were encouraging the usurping tendencies of the modern state. Thus it was that in the constitutional debates preceding the establishment of the state of Pakistan, Muhammad 'Alí Jinnah, a founding father of Pakistan and a leading voice in the Constituent Assembly, in 1947 declared support for a secular, nonreligious basis for the new nation. "You may belong to any religion or creed or caste—that has nothing to do with the business of the state. . . . You will find," he added provocatively, "that in the course of time Hindus [will] cease to be Hindus and Muslims cease to be Muslims, not in the religious sense because that is the personal faith of each individual, but in a political sense as citizens of the State."[24] In a prophetic outburst against religious caviling, Jinnah insisted that "Pakistan is not going to be a Theocratic State ruled by priests with a divine mission."[25]

Yet the religious sentiment that legitimated the entire project of a separate state for Indian Muslims was only inflamed by Jinnah's assertions. Speaking to the same issue on a different occasion, Sádiq al-Mahdí, a veteran of Sudanese politics and more than once Sudan's prime minister, implicitly answered Jinnah's contention: "The concepts of secularism, humanism, nationalism, materialism, and rationalism which are all based on partial truths, became deities in their own right; one-eyed superbeings. They are responsible for the present Euro-American spiritual crisis. The partial truths in all these powerful ideas can be satisfied by Islam."[26] As

---

[23] The late Ayátulláh Khumayní of Iran, for instance, was quoted as saying that Muslims have been robbed of their heritage through the connivance of the West (see A. Rippin and J. Knappert, eds., *Textual Sources on Islam* [Manchester: Manchester University Press, 1986], pp. 191-92).

[24] Cited in E. I. J. Rosenthal, *Islam and the Modern National State* (Cambridge: Cambridge University Press, 1965), p. 212.

[25] Ibid. See also Kenneth Cragg, *Counsels in Contemporary Islam* (Edinburgh: Edinburgh University Press, 1965), pp. 21ff.

[26] G. H. Jansen, *Militant Islam* (London: Pan Books, 1979), pp. 126-27; see also Cragg 1965, pp. 115ff.; and Rosenthal 1965, pp. 138, 206.

this and other statements clearly suggest, the great ferment in the Muslim world today is proof of the riveting appeal of religion and politics for ordinary people. As Kenneth Cragg writes: "The renewed and effective politicization of Islam is the most important single fact of the new century."[27] This politicization is at the level of the rank-and-file faithful and includes an overscrupulous populist reaction to the perceived religious menace of Europe and North America, regions that are also now home to significant Muslim communities.

Classical Islamic sources deny any strict distinction between religion and politics. The caliph (*khalifah*), the earthly sovereign, as the Prophet's successor, is one charged with the "power to bind and to loosen," and is furthermore commanded to restrain people from bloodshed and to ensure their welfare in this world and in the future life.[28] Following the demise of the caliphate, the reformulation of Muslim political thought shifted the weight of opinion to the maintenance of the *Sharí'ah*, the religious code, as the prerequisite of a viable community life. In the modern world of national states this reformulation has been practiced at the grass-roots level, where it has introduced an ideology of populist legitimacy. This would suggest a shift in favor of the civil community, with the state representing rather than replacing popular appeal. Unlike the caliphate, the *Sharí'ah* is every believer's responsibility and comes within the terms of duties mandated not by the state but by the religious code. Since the *Sharí'ah* involves duties and obligations deemed incumbent on rank-and-file Muslims without respect to nationality, its introduction into ordinary life restricts state jurisdiction over the obedience of citizens whose "peoplehood" now has a primary religious basis to it. It explains why in several cases, it was the mullahs, imáms, and other *Sharí'ah* officials who led the movement to discredit the national state. As the Shehu, a famous African Muslim reformer, put it, "Most people are ignorant of the sharí'ah, and it is obligatory [therefore] that there should be, in every mosque and quarter in the town, a *faqíh* [religious scholar] teaching the people their religion."[29] Thus did religious teachings acquire political significance.

In one sense Islam broke with the Aristotelian idea of "the good of the state [being] manifestly a greater and more perfect good" by making the "highest good" a religious one: a person's last end is happiness in God, and that is as much a pursuit as it is "the gift of God." Knowledge of existing things helps in practical pursuits of many kinds, but perfection in the ethical life defines the higher happiness (*sa'ádah*) (Rosenthal 1958, 13ff.). The state itself is held to these norms. In another sense, however, Islam has extended the Aristotelian idea by positing the *ummah*, the religious community, as the indispensable foundation of human civilization. Aristotle's assertion, following Plato, that the human being is a "political being" is now expanded in the Muslim view that the human being is created for

---

[27] Kenneth Cragg, *The Call of the Minaret,* rev. ed. (Maryknoll, NY: Orbis Books, 1985), p. 8; see also Cragg 1965.

[28] See E. I. J. Rosenthal, *Political Thought in Medieval Islam* (Cambridge: Cambridge University Press, 1958), pp. 21–61.

[29] Isma'íl A. B. Balogun, tr. and ed., *The Life and Works of 'Uthmán dan Fodio* (Lagos: Islamic Publications Bureau, 1975), p. 74.

religious solidarity. Either way, whether it concerns the greater good of the state or the true end of human life, the religious foundation for the human enterprise is secured. In that sense Islam rejects the rigid separation of religion and politics to assert its stake in both realms.

Nevertheless, mainstream thought still supports at least a notional separation of religion and politics for eminently religious reasons. One general approach is the distinction Muslims draw between doctrinal stipulations and historical circumstances, between the external formulations of the jurists and the inner reality of life. As Gibb stressed, "Between the real content of Muslim thought and its juristic expression there is a certain dislocation,"[30] preventing us from being able to infer the reality from the outer form. Doctrinal formulation is not so much a historical transcript as a legal device serving a procedural and partial end. If we take this approach, then we may say that *Shari'ah* supremacy is in terms of its juristic custody, of its being in the rightful possession of the guild of qualified jurists, rather than in terms of its comprehensive implementation.[31] In other words, it is the recognition of the proper sphere of *Shari'ah* authority, not its sectarian application.

However, there is the other side to that view. While doctrinal formulation compresses the diverse reality into a rigid mold, as Gibb describes it, it also serves notice that religious thought will not be "bound by outward formulae. It exerts a constant pressure, whose influence is to be seen in the unobtrusive reshaping of theory which, beneath an outward inflexibility, characterizes all branches of speculative activity in Islam, where Islam has remained a living organism" (Gibb 1962, 149).

If this distinction between formal doctrine and the content of life is valid, it opens the way for affirmation of the religious sphere as nonidentical, though connected, with the political sphere. Religious activity is too bound up with everyday contingency to fit into the neat lines of formal doctrine, so that temporal Islam errs in seeking such a fit, and yet at the same time in its "everydayness" religion cannot be robbed of political significance either. The classical Muslim scholar Sufyán Thaurí, referred to in the next chapter, emphasized this double theme by counseling religious scholars to maintain a prudent distance from political rulers who, in their turn, should seek wise counsel from religious scholars. Sufyán Thaurí intends to say that actions of political expedience must be qualified by moral norms, but moral norms must not be qualified by political expedience. Muslim scholars have argued, for example, that coercion is unworthy of religious integrity, basing this view on a verse from the Qur'án to the effect that "there is no compulsion in religion" (*lá ikráha fí-l-dín*) (Qur'án, II:256). Thus, a prescriptive religious state conflicts with that scriptural injunction and, at another level, with the high ethical purpose of human felicity. In such a state many people undoubtedly would choose to join or remain in the religious fold for very sound religious

[30] H. A. R. Gibb, *Studies on the Civilization of Islam*, ed. Stanford J. Shaw and William R. Polk (London: Routledge & Kegan Paul, 1962), pp. 148f.
[31] See W. Montgomery Watt, *Islamic Political Thought: The Basic Concepts* (Edinburgh: Edinburgh University Press, 1968), pp. 102-3.

reasons, but others would do so for reasons that would be very bad from a religious point of view: fear of reprisal, hope of gain, or the force of blackmail—motives fatal to the spiritual pursuit. Similarly, such a state would make it impossible to treat minorities and other nonconformists, religious or other, with anything but expedient cynicism. Even the state cannot survive for long if it were to make repression its only justification, for then repression would become the political means as well as the moral end of human conduct. Yet if means and end are thus interchanged, expediency and moral truth would fuse and result in tyranny. Therefore, church and state should be separated not only for practical mundane reasons but also for exalted religious ones.

The question of equal treatment for non-Muslims in an Islamic state has had a long and detailed examination, although attempts to assure critics that classical Islamic resources offer full guarantees have not been entirely persuasive.[32] Privileges conferred on minority groups in a prescriptive religious state soon carry the stigma of exclusion, with statutory safeguards becoming nothing better than inquisitional staging posts—society's handy valve for disgorging unassimilated elements in times of crisis. Even the majority under those circumstances would feel sucked in by the momentum of the engine of oppression directed at minority groups. Intolerance has few scruples about discriminating between the stigmatized and the canonized. It will play the game both ways. This situation, therefore, forces us back to the sacred logic of distinguishing between religion and politics.

A Muslim writer who devoted considerable attention to this matter was Ibn Khaldún (d. 1406), and, given his importance for the subject, we should look at his life and work to determine what impact they had on his views on religion and politics.

Abú Zayd 'Abd al-Rahmán Ibn Khaldún was born in Tunis in 1332, of a family from the Hadramaut in south Arabia. Early in the Muslim conquest of Spain, the Ibn Khaldún family moved there and became established in Seville. There the family served a succession of Muslim dynasties, rising eventually to a position of influence and power. In the mid-thirteenth century, following the attempts of the Christian reconquest of Spain, the family left Seville and came to Ceuta in North Africa. Ibn Khaldún's grandfather became the minister of finance in the Muslim administration in Tunis. Ibn Khaldún's father was a soldier and administrator but changed careers to study law, theology, and letters. He died of the Black Death in 1349, when Ibn Khaldún was seventeen.

Ibn Khaldún's education followed the traditional Islamic model: learning the Qur'án by rote, followed by study of grammar, philology, poetry, traditions of the Prophet, law, and history. At age twenty he entered public life as secretary to the sultan of Fez, Morocco. This period coincided with the collapse of the Almohad dynasty in North Africa and the ensuing turmoil. Losing his appointment, Ibn

---

[32] In the debates on the creation of an Islamic Constitution for Pakistan, Congressman B. K. Datta observed in this connection that in such a state "minorities [have] an inferior status. The nation would remain communally divided into two houses, the minorities tasting neither democracy, nor freedom, nor equality, nor social justice, but being merely tolerated" (see Rosenthal 1958, 210).

Khaldún left for Spain in 1362 to enter the service of the king of Granada, who sent him on an embassy to Pedro, nicknamed the Cruel, king of Castile. His talents were appreciated by the Christian king, and Ibn Khaldún was offered employment and restoration of his ancestral property, which he declined. Instead, he accepted a fiefdom granted him by the sultan of Granada and decided to settle there, bringing his family for the purpose. It turned out to be a brief interlude, for we find him shortly thereafter leaving Spain for reasons of political prudence and returning to North Africa, where he obtained employment as prime minister in the court of the sultan of Bourgie, Algeria. In the next several years Ibn Khaldún's life was entangled in the complex web of political intrigue, plot, counter-plot, diplomatic wrangle, and military skirmish. By 1375 he had had enough of this turbulent life and, with his family, retired to a castle near Oran, Algeria, to begin work on his magnum opus, *The Prolegomena to Universal History*. In the course of writing that work he looked for documentation in Tunis, where the active, cosmopolitan ambiance appealed to his temperament, and so he decided to move back there. His popularity and authority in the city, however, aroused the jealousy of the scholars and courtiers and left him looking for an alternative place to live. He decided in 1382 to go on the pilgrimage to Mecca, taking a ship to Alexandria and thence making his way to Cairo.

Cairo also appealed to Ibn Khaldún's cosmopolitan nature and moved him to lyrical praise. Of the city he wrote, "What one sees in dreams surpasses reality, but all that one could dream of Cairo falls short of the truth." Not surprisingly, when the Mameluke sultan offered him the post of chief justice, Ibn Khaldún needed little persuading, putting off his pilgrimage.

His task as chief justice involved some drastic housecleaning, sweeping away the corruption that had clogged the city and suffocated the courts. As he described it, he was committed to "the pursuit of justice and right, and the rejection of outside influence." In revenge, his enemies instigated a commission of inquiry into his tenure, and although no charges leveled against him were upheld, the inquiry stirred up sufficient agitation to affect his usefulness for the patronage-minded rulers. Just at this time he lost his family in a shipwreck between Tunis and Egypt, and that dealt the last blow to any remaining hopes for regrouping. He felt disconsolate, and he pined for relief from the office that had brought him such public opprobrium. He felt his prayers answered when the sultan requested his resignation, which he accordingly tendered. In 1387 he resumed his interrupted pilgrimage to Mecca and then returned to Egypt, intending to lead a quiet life.

However, it was not to be. In 1400/01 the sultan took him and a group of leading jurists and scholars to Damascus to undertake delicate negotiations with the Tartar conqueror Tamarlane, who was reputedly impressed enough with the Ibn Khaldún's abilities to offer him a position. Ibn Khaldún declined the dubious honor but took advantage of the offer to collect valuable historical information on Mongol and Tartar history and rehearse with Tamarlane some Maghribi history.

Ibn Khaldún's meeting with Tamarlane was a highly charged affair. In his testimony of it, Ibn Khaldún spoke of having to steer a course by his wits, gingerly picking his way through the minefield of subtle and oblique tests to his loyalty and motives.[33] Ibn Khaldún was able to escape the Tartar sacking of Damascus, rescuing many of the important nobles of the city before returning to Egypt. As a reward for his services he was once again appointed chief justice. Shortly thereafter he died in 1406 at age seventy-four. He was buried in a Sufi cemetery in the city.

Ibn Khaldún was able to draw on his vast practical experience of public life and his meticulous scholarly investigations to delineate the relationship between political affairs and religious life. It was an advantage to him that he could thus combine practical knowledge and intellectual acumen to explore this important theme. Reflecting that double experience, he cautioned against the uncritical mixing of religion and worldly affairs lest, in his words, we

patch our worldly affairs by tearing our religion to pieces. Thus, neither our religion lasts nor (the worldly affairs) we have been patching.[34]

For Ibn Khaldún, religion is entangled at numerous levels with society, from having an established position at the center to being an uncoopted force. Thus religion has two senses; it is either a social ornament or a ruling ideology, useful or necessary.

The great insight of Ibn Khaldún consists in giving secular justification for the development of political institutions. However much he deferred formally to religion, he was an astute enough scholar to recognize theocratic claims as simplistic and lacking in historical realism. In essence, Ibn Khaldún argues that political society is founded on group cohesion, what he terms *solidarity* (*'asabiyáh*). He takes the prudent step of appealing to a *hadíth* from the Prophet, who is reputed to have said, "Learn your genealogies to know who are your near of kin." Aware of other traditions that have the Prophet abolishing kinship, Ibn Khaldún redeems himself by turning to the same source to find that the Prophet intended us to understand that "kinship only serves a function when blood ties lead to actual cooperation and mutual aid in danger—other degrees of kinship being insignificant."[35] In continuing with the defense of kinship, Ibn Khaldún asserts that the Prophet did not intend to neglect group solidarity but merely to inculcate its relative merit as a worldly arrangement vis-à-vis the higher obedience centered in revelation. In all this, Ibn Khaldún's project was the radical one of discerning sociological laws in collective historical institutions and hierarchies and in removing from all serious analysis any appeal to dogma. It is important to cite his own words on this point. According to him, rulership as such is not divine but is the outgrowth of social development. This is so because rulership

---

[33] See "Al-Ta'rif bi-ibn Khaldún" ("Information Concerning Ibn Khaldún) excerpt in James Kritzeck, ed., *Anthology of Islamic Literature* (New York: A Meridian Book of the New American Library, 1964), "Conversations with Tamarlane," tr. Walter J. Fischel, pp. 281-84.

[34] A verse attributed to Abú al-'Atáhiyah and cited by Ibn Khaldún, *Al-Muqaddimah*, i, 427.

[35] Charles Issawi, *An Arab Philosophy of History* (London: George Allen & Unwin, 1963), p. 104.

is the natural end to which social solidarity leads. And this transformation is not a matter of choice but a necessary consequence of the natural order and disposition of things. . . . For no laws, religions, or institutions can be effective unless a cohesive group enforce and impose them and without solidarity they cannot be established. Social solidarity is, therefore, indispensable if a nation is to play the role which God has chosen for it. . . . For unless religious laws derive their sanctions from social solidarity they will remain totally ineffective" (Issawi 1963, 137).

The importance Ibn Khaldún attaches to *'asabiyáh* brings the concept into deep affinity with modern notions of nationalism in which a people, fired by sentiments of kin identity enclosed within stable territorial boundaries, establishes an effective community for the purpose. Such a community transcends the individual and expresses itself in the collective will to command; to prescribe for the present and future; and to judge, reward, and punish. Ibn Khaldún says that kind of social solidarity is identical with the spiritual community. Therefore, "no religious movement can succeed unless based on solidarity" (Issawi 1963, 133). Solidarity is the backbone of religion as it is of the state.

Such views have implications for political legitimacy, too, as Ibn Khaldún noted. He was at pains to point out that effective leadership is a matter not of revealed truth but of pragmatic competence. Good leaders are determined by the quality of their rule as seen by their subjects rather than by the purity of the ideals to which they subscribe. Governments are the just deserts of the societies in which they are found. Ibn Khaldún contends, "If such rulership is good and beneficial, it will serve the interests of the subjects. If it is bad and unfair, it will be harmful to them and cause their destruction" (*Al-Muqaddimah*, vol. i, 328-29). Ibn Khaldún, writing here as a scholar, is not primarily concerned with spelling out the practical institutional arrangements by which harm may be determined and remedied,[36] but his insights would be compatible with our modern notions of democratic political liberalism, constitutional accountability and participation. However, a theoretical limitation in his views is his failing to make the safety of citizens—what we speak of as human rights—a fundamental qualification of political obligation and state sovereignty. Be that as it may, he pioneered a methodology in which political society is sundered from any comprehensive doctrinal mooring and set amid a pluralist social and historical context.

What is surprising in all this is how, within his explanatory scheme, Ibn Khaldún could maintain religion as revealed truth. Two brief explanations may be offered. One is that Ibn Khaldún is concerned with the civil status of "man," that is, with human beings as members of the political community (when they enter into business and action), rather than as moral agents under God (when they are a subject of truth affirmation). The civil community is by its nature contingent, built as it is on intersecting plural interests, on the dynamic alliance of group solidarity and

---

[36] In an unflattering observation, Ibn Khaldún remarked on the unsuitability of intellectuals for political office. The intellectual life is afflicted with the same tendency for abstraction and idealization that affect the religious life (*Al-Muqaddimah*, i, 382f.).

interest which would be effective in an instrumental, expedient sense, however inadequate in terms of any comprehensive moral norm. In this understanding the primary focus of historical study should be rational human interests that can be ordered and mobilized by a system of incentives, sanctions, and similar behavioral measures, without implying that historical study completes and exhausts the truth of being human. I am inclined to this view as the more important to Ibn Khaldún.

However, another explanation is offered by Sir Hamilton Gibb. According to Gibb, Ibn Khaldún used religion in two ways. The first is religion in the true or absolute sense, "when the whole will of man is governed by his religious conviction and his animal nature is held in check. Opposed to this is 'acquired religion,' a secondhand and relatively feeble thing, which saps his manhood and fails to control his animal impulses" (Gibb 1962, 166-75, 171). Gibb is convinced that religion in the first sense continued to occupy a central place in Ibn Khaldún's thought, as follows: Statistically, human communities are disinclined to follow revealed truth for the conduct of affairs, and given this fact Ibn Khaldún would say that human society is locked into a grim cycle of rise and fall, "conditioned by the 'natural' and inevitable consequences of the predominance of its animal instincts. In this sense," Gibb avers, Ibn Khaldún's "pessimism has a moral and religious, not a sociological, basis" (Gibb 1962, 174). This may be related to Weber's assessment that Islam is almost by itself among the world religions in offering a practical orientation to political and worldly affairs.[37] We should repeat, however, that Ibn Khaldún's theory of history received its most cogent and explicit development from the preponderance of fact and practice, thereby implying the downgrading of theological speculation in favor of empirical observation. In his methodology, he was a pragmatist first and a moralist last, and so it is still a valid question about where religion stands after the dust has settled. If Gibb is right about Ibn Khaldún's *moral and religious pessimism* in contrast to his confident historical extrapolations, then we may say that his pessimism has its root in his idea of religion as a state enterprise, a theological limitation that cramped his historical view.

Ibn Khaldún understood religion as political dogma, and that is evidently at odds with the kind of confident historical positivism he was pioneering, for in that scheme religion is not necessary to the understanding of historical change, although religion must be in view of what Ibn Khaldún claims for it. Thus, by the time he returned to religion, Ibn Khaldún had gone far enough to show he could get on without it, though he seems unprepared for that. Religion, he thinks, can be important only as political *ummah* rather than as personal faith based on persuasion and choice. His methodology requires no providence for historical understanding or consummation. He is disconcerted by this, and accordingly rouses himself and hurries back to religion to find he can only make rhetorical and anecdotal use of it. So he muses ruefully to himself about flawed human capacity as

---

[37] Max Weber, *The Sociology of Religion*, tr. Ephraim Fischoff (Boston: Beacon Press, 1963), p. 263.

the reason for religion not being as decisive in human affairs as it deserves. But what he saves of religion by that tactic is still too little too late, for religious rhetoric now slips into pessimism about humanity's animal impulses. Little did he realize that such a polarity of the human and divine denies any possibility of a vital contact point between history and providence. The historical record, filled with evidence of feeble animal impulses rather than with evidence of truth affirmation, predominates over divine primacy in faith and conduct, as material will predominates over spiritual ideal.

Thus Ibn Khaldún's otherwise penetrating insight fails near its religious elevation, for, to amend Emerson, while allowing an influx of divinity into his mind with his historical generalization, he flinched when it came to making the purpose of divinity congruent in terms of effects with the human striving for freedom and goodness, which affects the political realm without politics being driven into a theocratic shell. He secured the social levers of political change and felt with the same motion he must proceed against the enjoined pivot of religious truth. In spite of its brilliant originality, then, his schema, with its basis in the power of social scale, is too determinist to accede to any viable theory of political life grounded in spiritual truth.

THE STATE: SOURCE OR INSTRUMENT?
CHRISTIAN RUMINATIONS

The august counsels of Muslims demand an analogous response from Christians and others concerning the state.[38] The Islamic attitude indicates that the accepted principle of separation of church and state should come under close scrutiny.

In Western Christian thought, the fresh appraisal of the interconnection of religion and politics goes back to the origins of the modern state. Sir Thomas More (d. 1535) in *Utopia*, responded to the challenges of the "new economics" by speaking to the moral issues raised by the changes. To do this, he turned to the Sermon on the Mount and suggested that the interests of the worldly kingdom are not disconnected from those of the heavenly kingdom, an insight he deepened by closely reading St. Augustine's *City of God.* More felt that God's claims on us should oblige us to establish a City of Man such that God would be pleased to dwell within it.[39]

In his monumental work *Of the Laws of the Ecclesiastical Polity*, Richard Hooker (d. 1600) made the first ambitious attempt to make the civil compact

---

[38] Ninian Smart writes that the Christian or Buddhist, among others, "will have a certain ultimate scepticism about patriotism," for the reason that the nation-state "has nothing truly transcendent," except, of course, when it adopts a universal imperial destiny (Merkl and Smart 1985, 27).

[39] Alistair Fox, *Thomas More: History and Providence* (New Haven: Yale University Press, 1983).

parallel to the religious community. In Hooker's scheme the state may safely be entrusted with the ecclesiastical polity, and he adduced reasons to that end. Hooker was a religious radical but a theological moderate. He accepted the rational law, or the light of reason/nature, as no less authoritative than divine injunction, but he rejected the antinomian strains of Puritan thought with its relentless anti-Catholic tendencies. Hooker would have nothing to do with the Barthianism of the Puritans, the theology that set a God of inscrutable will over against the "accursed nature of Man," as that dialectic creates a simultaneous extremism of the "right" and of the "left": ask of any institution whether it is of God, in which case you will fall down and worship it, or whether it is of man, then you attack and destroy it. Unlike the majority of Puritans, Hooker was not searching for the true church and could never have prayed with John Donne, "Show me deare Christ, thy spouse."[40] His view of church and state is conditioned by his premise of Christianity as a "religion of the provinces," as Edward Gibbon would call it,[41] that is to say, as a religion that assimilates the characteristics of national cultures.[42] Such pluralism was important to Hooker's thesis that the church belongs equally to this world and the next, which enabled him to secure natural law alongside Scripture as a necessary juridical source. Furthermore, Hooker, unlike the extreme Puritans, acknowledged and affirmed those who, because they were considered heretics, idolaters, or otherwise wicked, might for that reason be excluded from the "sound" part of the church. Hooker believed that churches were "rather like diverse families than like divers [*sic*] servants of one family," so that no "one certain form" of polity need be common to them all (Lewis 1954, 455).

All ages have their shibboleths, powerful generalizations that exert their influence beneath the surface of thought. Our age is no exception. The principle of the separation of powers, formulated in vastly different historical contexts, has become the implacable doctrine of instrumental science. In extreme form the doctrine denies the connection between the moral and the expedient and between means and ends. It goes further, however, by making separation the grounds for hostility between church and state. Yet many scholars in the West are critical of

---

[40] Cited in C. S. Lewis, *English Literature in the Sixteenth Century*, in *Oxford History of English Literature* (London and New York: Oxford University Press, 1954), p. 454. For an abridged edition of Richard Hooker's work, see *Of the Laws of Ecclesiastical Polity*, ed. A. S. McGrade and Brian Vickers (New York: St. Martin's Press, 1975).
[41] See Edward Gibbon, *The Decline and Fall of the Roman Empire*, 3 vols. (New York: Modern Library, n.d.), especially chapters 14 and 15 of volume 1.
[42] Mojola Agbebi, a leader in the African Church movement in Lagos, Nigeria, made some acute observations on how the successful assimilation of Christianity into English life and culture justifies a corresponding process in Nigeria. The authors of the Anglican Book of Common Prayer, he notes, supported the view that "every country should use such ceremonies as they shall think best to setting forth of God's honor and glory," and consequently deny that they "prescribe anything but to their own people only." See his inaugural sermon preached in 1902 and reproduced in J. Ayo Langley, ed., *Ideologies of Liberation in Black Africa: 1856-1970* (London: Rex Collings, 1979), pp. 72-77.

such an interpretation, a criticism echoed in practice throughout Africa, including Muslim Africa.

In this regard, the words of the American philosopher William Ernest Hocking are apt. In *The Coming World Civilization* he writes, "We rely on the political community to do its part in the making of men, but first of all to furnish the conditions under which men can make themselves."[43] But he goes on to say that "the state, purely as secular, comes to be regarded as capable of civilizing the human being, and in doing so of remaking him, training his will, moralizing him" (Hocking 1956, 2). Yet the political community is seriously handicapped in enabling human beings to mature fully as moral agents. We need another realm for that. Hocking argues:

> Human nature has indeed another mirror, and therewith another source of self-training. It is often the religious community—let us call it in all its forms "the church"—which has promised to give the human individual the most complete view of his destiny and of himself. It projects that destiny beyond the range of human history. . . . It provides standards of self-judgment not alone in terms of behavior, as does the law, but also in terms of motive and principle—of the inner man which the state cannot reach (Hocking 1956, 2).

Hocking contends we are unwilling to see the state as a partial mirror of truth, being inclined instead to concur when the state

> regards itself as the more reliable interpreter of human nature—dealing as it does solely with verifiable experience—and as a sufficient interpreter. . . . Outside the Marxist orbit, the prevalent disposition of the secular state in recent years has been less to combat the church than to carry on a slow empirical demonstration of the state's full equivalence in picturing the attainable good life, and its superior pertinence to actual issues. As this demonstration gains force the expectation grows that it will be the church, not the state, that will wither away (Hocking 1956, 3).

William Esuman-Gwira Sekyi (1892-1956) of Ghana, also known as Kobina Sekyi, expressed the continuity between religion and political affairs. Writing in 1925, Sekyi quoted an Akan proverb as follows, *Oman si ho na posuban sim* ("The company fence stands only so long as the state exists"). He comments: "Our ancestors were above all things a religious people, with whom religion was no mere matter of form or weekly ceremony. Religion with our ancestors was interwoven with the whole fabric of their daily life; and therefore when the company system was established among them it was not without its religious con-

---

[43] William Ernest Hocking, *The Coming World Civilization* (New York: Harper, 1956), p. 1.

comitants."[44] Sekyi affirmed that religious loyalty was fundamental for state effectiveness without implying religion has only analogous value. Another wise saying of the Akan is, *Aban wo twuw n'dazi; wo nnsua no* ("Governments, too often heavily weighted with power, are to be pulled along the ground but not to be carried").[45] This suggests a need for a radical reappraisal of the church-state theme that goes beyond instrumental codes for public and personal conduct.

SUMMARY AND CONCLUSIONS

In new environments, transplanted phenomena tend to sit awkwardly; they flatter themselves by exaggerating their own strengths and minimizing those of the host environment, when in fact the reverse is often the case. In the process, however, these transplanted ideas and institutions bring to focus something of their essential character. The secular state in its expansion abroad has assumed this exaggeration and thus revealed, even in its triumphs, basic limitations in its nature. In the context of religion in Africa, in particular Islam, we find gaps in the operation of the national state, raising questions about its effectiveness. The proximity of religion and politics in practical situations discounts any rigid separation of the two, although by the same token an important distinction needs to be drawn between politics as instrumental and expedient and religion as a heritage of normative injunctions, lest the state become above all sanctified and the church merely expedient in its teachings. Ideally, there are as sound religious grounds just as there are pragmatic ones for not confusing religion and politics, though in practice it is risky to attempt splitting the two. Cross-cultural and interreligious issues and reflections in Africa and among Muslims may help shed light on the relation of religion and politics and thus help deepen our grasp of vital ground in the encounter between the two.

CHAPTER BIBLIOGRAPHY

Apter, David E. "Political Religion in the New Nations." In *Old Societies and New States: The Quest for Modernity in Asia and Africa.* Edited by Clifford Geertz. New York: Free Press, 1963.
Balogun, Isma'íl A. B., tr. and ed. *The Life and Works of 'Uthmán dan Fodio.* Lagos: Islamic Publications Bureau, 1975.
Barker, Sir Ernest. *Principles of Social and Political Theory.* Oxford: Clarendon Press, 1951.
Bartels, F. L. *The Roots of Ghana Methodism.* Accra: Methodist Book Depot; London: Cambridge University Press, 1965.

---

[44] Kobina Sekyi, *The Parting of the Ways*, reprinted in Langley 1979, 251-52.
[45] Cited in F. L. Bartels, *The Roots of Ghana Methodism* (Accra: Methodist Book Depot; London: Cambridge University Press, 1965), pp. 241-42.

Bonhoeffer, Dietrich. *Letters and Papers from Prison.* London: SCM, 1971. Reprinted.

Brown, Mervyn. *Madagascar Rediscovered: From Early Times to Independence.* Hamden, CT: Archon Books, 1979.

Callaghy, Thomas. *The State-Society Struggle: Zaire in Comparative Perspective.* New York: Columbia University Press, 1984.

Cragg, Kenneth. *The Call of the Minaret.* Revised ed. Maryknoll, NY: Orbis Books, 1985.

_____. *Counsels in Contemporary Islam.* Edinburgh: Edinburgh University Press, 1965.

Davidson, Basil. *The Black Man's Burden: Africa and the Curse of the Nation State.* London: James Currey, 1992.

Gibb, H. A. R. *Studies on the Civilization of Islam.* Collected essays. Edited by Stanford J. Shaw and William R. Polk. London: Routledge & Kegan Paul, 1962.

Gibbon, Edward. *The Decline and Fall of the Roman Empire.* 3 vols. New York: Modern Library, n.d.

Gitari, David M. "The Church's Witness to the Living God: Seeking Just Political, Social, and Economic Structures in Contemporary Africa," *Transformation: An International Dialogue on Evangelical Social Ethics* 5 (2) (April/June 1988).

_____. "The Church and Politics in Kenya," *Transformation: An International Evangelical Dialogue on Mission and Ethics* (July/September 1991).

Hailey, Lord. *An African Survey: Revised 1956.* Oxford: Clarendon Press, 1957.

Harden, Blaine. *Africa: Dispatches from a Fragile Continent.* New York: W. W. Norton, 1990.

Hastings, Adrian. *The Church in Africa: 1450-1950.* Oxford: Clarendon Press, 1994.

Hansen, Holger Bernt. *Mission, Church and State in a Colonial Setting: Uganda: 1890-1925.* London: Heinemann, 1984.

Hocking, William Ernest. *The Coming World Civilization.* New York: Harper, 1956.

Hodgkin, Thomas. "The Fact of Islamic History (II): Islam in West Africa," *Africa South,* vol. 2, no. 3 (1958): 88-99.

_____. "Islam and National Movements in West Africa," *Journal of African History,* vol. 3, no. 2 (1962).

_____. "Islam, History and Politics," *Journal of Modern African Studies,* vol. 1, no. 1 (1963).

Huntingdon, Samuel P. "The Clash of Civilizations?," *Foreign Affairs* (Summer 1993).

Issawi, Charles. *An Arab Philosophy of History.* London: George Allen & Unwin, 1963.

Jansen, G. H. *Militant Islam.* London: Pan Books, 1979.

Jones, Trevor. *Ghana's First Republic: The Pursuit of the Political Kingdom.* London: Methuen, 1976.

Kastfelt, Niels. *Religion and Politics in Nigeria: A Study of Middle Belt Christianity.* London: British Academic Press, 1994.

Kerr, Malcolm. *The Arab Cold War: Gamal 'Abd al-Nasir and His Rivals: 1958-1970.* 3d edition. London: Oxford University Press for the Royal Institute of International Affairs, 1971.

Langley, J. Ayo, ed. *Ideologies of Liberation in Black Africa: 1856-1970.* London: Rex Collings, 1979.

Lewis, C. S. *English Literature in the Sixteenth Century.* In *Oxford History of English Literature.* London and New York: Oxford University Press, 1954.

Lewis, Ewart. *Medieval Political Ideas.* 2 vols. New York: Cooper Square Publishers, 1974. Volume 1.

McIlwain, Charles H. "Mediæval Institutions in the Modern World." In Karl H. Dannenfeldt, ed. *The Renaissance: Medieval or Modern?* Problems in European Civilization Series. Boston: D. C. Heath, 1959.

Merkl, Peter H., and Ninian Smart, eds. *Religion and Politics in the Modern World.* New York: New York University Press, 1985.

Mulk, Nizám al-. *The Book of Government for Kings (Siyását Náma).* London: Routledge & Kegan Paul, 1960.

New York Times. 14 April 1990.

Niebuhr, H. Richard. *Radical Monotheism and Western Culture.* New York: Harper and Brothers, 1960.

O'Brien, Conor Cruise. *God Land: Reflections on Religion and Politics.* Cambridge: Harvard University Press, 1987.

_____. "The Wrath of Ages: Nationalism's Primordial Roots," *Foreign Affairs* (November-December 1993), pp. 142-49.

Pro Mundi Vita Dossiers. "The Church and Christians in Madagascar Today," Africa Dossier 6 (July-August 1978).

Rippin, A., and J. Knappert, eds. *Textual Sources on Islam.* Manchester: Manchester University Press; Chicago: Chicago University Press, 1986.

Rosenthal, E. I. J. *Islam and the Modern National State.* Cambridge: Cambridge University Press, 1965.

_____. *Political Thought in Medieval Islam.* Cambridge: Cambridge University Press, 1958.

Sekyi, Kobina. *The Parting of the Ways.* In J. Ayodele Langley, *Ideologies of Liberation in Black Africa, 1856-1970.* London: Rex Collins, 1979.

Stackhouse, Max. "Politics and Religion," *Encyclopedia of Religion,* vol. 11, Mircea Eliade, ed. New York: Macmillan, 1987.

Waldman, M. W. "The Church of Scotland Mission at Blantyre, Nyasaland: Its Political Implications," *Bulletin of the Society of African Church History,* 2/4 (1968).

6

"The Crown and the Turban"

Public Policy Issues in Christian-Muslim Relations

Whatever one's attitude toward so-called fundamentalist Islam, there is no question that it is from that quarter that the major intellectual initiative has been taken to call for an uncompromising assessment of the comprehensive claims of secular political primacy over religion. The liberal mainstream abandoned that role when it staked its reputation on faith in human progress, with the secular state as necessary machinery. Human well-being in the liberal scheme requires the state instrument and, to a degree, that we be shackled to the state. Right-wing conservatism for its part seeks capture of the state to mobilize market-driven individualism and the sanctity of personal property. Thus liberals and conservatives together reinforce state power from ostensibly opposite standpoints.

This doubly reinforced secular ideology has provoked Muslim fundamentalism into attacking head-on modern confidence in political ultimacy, in the state as our finality. The controlling idea of this chapter is the search through comparative analysis for the religious underpinning of democratic liberalism and the connection between the political enterprise and the life of faith. I assess in this light Islamic objections to the notion of religion only as personal faith based on private persuasion and choice, however much such a notion might be fruitful of tolerance, pluralism, and the autonomy of the secular state. If religion is right in what it claims about the meaning and purpose of human life, then it cannot be banished from the public sphere, which is the Islamic contention; nor can it, at the same time, be coopted as public commodity, which is the liberal democratic tendency.

To place Muslim objections to secular primacy in comparative historical context, we need to examine the roots of Western political secularism, whose origins lie in the sixteenth-century crisis that overtook Christendom. The teaching of Jesus about maintaining an appropriate separation between God and Caesar (Mk 12:17; Mt 22:21) provided the doctrinal remedy for those wishing to stop the damaging religious wars that wracked late medieval and early modern Europe. This teaching later came to be formulated as separation of church and state and given institutional expression. It has continued to inspire secular Europe by making freedom of religion an indispensable principle of political freedom. In the main, political authority was distinguished from confessional rules, with church membership no longer normative for national identity or political affiliation. Christianity then broke up into numerous groups and sects in a context that removed public sanction from religious differences and disagreements, resulting in Christianity abandoning any public role, except when being subsumed under the national state gave it that role. We should thus stress the crucial importance of the religious factor in giving rise to secularism, defined here as recognizing the separate and equally valid spheres of God and Caesar or church and state. That separation is necessary for secularism as well as pluralism to thrive. Conversely, the fusion of the two retards secularism and pluralism.

This is the context in which we have seen the rise of modern Christianity and the missionary movement that effectively spread it. Cut loose from the Old World colonization movements of Spain and Portugal, the modern missionary movement made faith as a personal decision the basis of a new form of community and identity, and that did not require converts to become members of a divine political system. However they may have regarded non-Christians, modern missions conceded all citizens to be equal in law. In that sense the modern missionary movement fostered pluralist religious practice within autonomous national communities. The denominations and confessions thrived within and across national and political boundaries rather than being reduced to a single territorial designation, such as one church, one land, one faith, one race, or one truth, one tribe. In that sense, modern missions were an important secularizing force.

This situation, or something closely resembling it, is what characterizes Christianity in much of the West and in modern Africa, where in time the Western experience exerted itself. We may say that the contemporary Muslim encounter with Christianity is essentially an encounter with the religion as anti-theocratic and pluralist in tendency. Consequently, in the wake of the Christian retreat from theocratic politics we have a rising tide of Muslim demand for religion as a state idea. Canonical Islam has always conceived a political role for religion, whatever the ambivalence of modernist Muslim liberals.[1] However, what is new and different now is that Muslim temporal pressure is being brought to bear in numerous African states still struggling to hold their own against a significantly unamenable citizenry. In places in the West itself this temporal religious pressure is being increasingly felt as well, so that the issue is not simply a matter confined to distant and exotic societies. On this matter, as on so much else, Africans and Westerners face a common challenge and may benefit from common responsibility.

For example, current Muslim political activism in the West means immigrant Muslims are demanding rights that are not simply religious, narrowly defined, but also educational, legal, political, economic, social, and medical, including

---

[1] Isma'īl al-Farūqī (1921-1986) has written: "The Muslim is perpetually mobilised to bring about the actualisation of the absolute on earth" (cited in Kenneth Cragg, *Troubled by Truth* [Cleveland: Pilgrim Press, 1994], p. 127). See also note 30 below.

public-health matters concerning abattoirs, matters that the Western rank-and-file have left in the hands of state and secular institutions.[2] Consequently, Westerners are caught in a bind in the face of Muslim demands: the logic of religious toleration, not to say of hospitality, requires making concessions to Muslims, while the logic of privatizing Christianity, of taking religion out of the public arena, disqualifies Westerners from dealing in any effective sense with Muslim theocratic demands.

We need caution here. For many people pluralism or multiculturalism has become a shibboleth of peculiar force, tending to displace any serious thinking about particular and rival claims to truth and to encourage complacency among reasonable people. Complacent pluralism in this sense can blind us to the real opportunities of interfaith encounter, with platitudes replacing commitment and accountability. Espousal of pluralism can be a disguise for religious retreat, a feeling that since there are so many religions, no one religion really matters in the end. If the current global religious revival, including world Christianity, has any future, then the West in its current mood is likely to miss it. Yet few can escape the consequences of a religiously active world, including the West. In the global Islamic resurgence, for example, the West is necessarily implicated, even though the West's response has been to minimize the religious importance. The West is still surprised that Muslims show little inclination to follow the secular path that it has confidently laid out. But the West may be forgiven for assuming that other cultures will follow where it leads, because for over two centuries it has been the decisive culture of reference. Yet in matters of faith, human affairs are more subtle and complex. Thus militant Muslims have risen against an ideological secularism, for the idea seems riddled with religious compromise, as the West has proved.

Our Western brand of piety, with religion as a private, individual matter, has blunted our grasp of genuine religious pluralism and left us with a strictly sociological and political view of it. The impact of technology and the information revolution, with their web of global interconnections at our fingertips, has also pushed—or allowed us to push—religion to the margins. Religion scarcely figures in the West's design of the new world order. Yet religion and technology in one sense correspond with a spiritual ideal: diverse expressions of faith and practice sustained in a cumulative global solidarity with God at the center. Muslims are equally included in this new global horizon where technology has shaped the landscape. There is something in common with the field of religious encounter as defined by a nonprivatized transcendence and the unpatrolled frontiers of cyberspace. However, religious claims have their source in timeless truths.

The question is how religions, especially proselytizing ones, impinge on the imperatives of a common humanity, and how we can harmonize the claims a tradition makes about itself with the demands of interfaith tolerance so that a community's ownership of its tradition does not become inbred and anti-foreign. A major obstacle is the disincentive which religious privatization breeds. As it is,

---

[2] John Locke says that the secular magistrate may intervene in the slaughter of beasts only if "an extraordinary murrain" has threatened the stock of cattle (*A Letter concerning Toleration* [Buffalo, NY: Prometheus Books, 1990], p. 48).

there are resources enough in most religious traditions to combine commitment with criticism, to make personal persuasion compatible with public scrutiny. If we are to hope for any progress in interfaith relations, we must resist the view that our particular tradition is superior, or else, because of a progressive view of convergence among religions, is destined to be used up from within. Meanwhile, the pervasive language of religious privatization leaves us with the bland consensus of diplomatic politeness, a consensus that may save our manners but scarcely anything else. Thus religious privatization fosters a code of silence which is ultimately ineffective against indifference from the left or fanaticism from the right. We should explore here the limits of privatization against the challenge of political Islam and how we might meet the challenge.

Part of the difficulty is that religious privatization appeals to people grown weary from the bitter legacy of religious territoriality, even though with regard to Muslim demands they may be religiously tone deaf on account of it. However, even if privatization is unsatisfactory, the drive for freedom that leads to it is central to religious pluralism and democratic liberalism. Thus, in the conclusion I argue that democratic liberalism and religious pluralism have their basis in the notion of religious freedom that set so much store by persuasion and personal conviction, and that the converging of democratic liberalism with religious freedom invests religion with a public rationale, and on that basis we may promote interfaith relations in our time. Let us deal with the issue in three stages.

STAGE I: CHRISTIANITY AND THE DEMISE
OF TERRITORIAL CHRISTENDOM

The church was never more involved in politics than during the era of the Holy Roman Empire, when faith and territory were joined as a principle of membership in church and state. Constantine secured the freedom of Christianity, not its establishment as an exclusive state religion. He saw himself as Pontifex Maximus, the visible earthly vessel of an all too misty divinity whose intuitive, malleable purpose he could attach to the robust will of the state. He claimed to be the colleague of the bishops of Nicea, but only as a "bishop of external affairs" and of those things in Christianity deemed useful and convenient.

The real shift came with Charlemagne, who took Christianity out of the sacristy and established it as *Christendom*, weaving it into the fabric of the state. The political ruler was seen as God's appointed agent, the herald and instrument of God's mission. Thus political affairs and religious matters were two strands of one and the same reality. It follows from this that church and state were united in purpose even though as institutions they represented different functions. While the church reserved to itself custody of the absolute moral law, the state was concerned with enforcing the rules of allegiance and conformity that gave practical expression to the higher spiritual law. Conformity rather than personal persuasion was the chief end of religious activity under this corporate arrangement.

Christendom identified itself with territoriality in the sense of making religion a matter of territorial allegiance. Church membership was coterminous and interchangeable with territorial location, and territorial rule was established on and made legitimate by the ruler's professed religion.[3] Christian mission under these circumstances was inconceivable except as colonialism, the forcible swallowing up of the tribes as vassal subjects of, say, Ferdinand and Isabella, the earthly representatives of Christ. Thus the Indians were dispossessed in the *encomienda*, the distribution system in which by royal decree the tribes and their property were "given away" as the only way to evangelize them.[4] In Christendom, to evangelize was to colonize, and to colonize was to evangelize, though nothing broke down the walls of Christendom as effectively as the wider and later repercussions of European colonialism and Western missions. By the same token, Christians living in a territory ruled by a nonbeliever were considered resident aliens, even though prevailing conditions of peace and tolerance might reduce the necessity for embarking on acts of conscientious withdrawal, what Muslim sources refer to as *hijrah*.[5] Christendom prevented such situations from arising or proliferating, since religious integrity and territorial cohesion meshed or were supposed to mesh.

As an arrangement Christendom would work only if there continued to be a more or less homogenous, cohesive society apportioned into more or less stable social classes. Such homogeneity and cohesion became increasingly difficult to maintain in the face of growing pluralism and social mobility. Finally, with the rise of national ethnic consciousness and fueled by the drive for religious freedom, the formal structures of the Empire collapsed, lost irretrievably in the rubble of Napoleonic Europe, and Christendom as a territorial reality broke up into its constituent parts.[6]

For leading Christian thinkers of the time, the demise of Christendom was a consummation the godly had devoutly wished for, because it allowed religion to become a matter of personal experience rather than of membership in a divinely designated race or church. Religious faith prospered as the church was transformed from territoriality to voluntarism. Alexis de Tocqueville observed this in religious practice in America, saying it was a fact "that by diminishing the apparent [territorial] power of religion one increased its real [spiritual] strength."[7] John Locke turned to the principle in his *A Letter concerning Toleration*, in which he states that Christians as members of a "voluntary society" came together for "the public worship-

---

[3] For a succinct, lucid summary see Sir Ernest Barker, *Principles of Social and Political Theory* (Oxford: Clarendon Press, 1951).

[4] Gustavo Gutiérrez, *Las Casas: In Search of the Poor of Jesus Christ* (Maryknoll, NY: Orbis Books, 1993), pp. 280ff.

[5] The Muslim *jihádist* ʿUthmán dan Fodio (d. 1817) wrote an exhaustive treatise on the legal and doctrinal foundations of *hijrah*. See his *Bayán Wujúb al-Hijrah ʿAla-l-ʿIbád*, ed. and tr. F. H. El-Masri (Khartoum: Khartoum University Press and Oxford University Press, 1978).

[6] A. J. P. Taylor examines some of the deeper social and political ramifications of the dissolution of the Holy Roman Empire in his *The Habsburg Monarchy: 1808-1918* (1948; reprinted London: Penguin Books, 1990).

[7] Alexis de Tocqueville, *Democracy in America*, tr. George Lawrence, ed. J. P. Mayer (New York: Harper Perennial, 1988; originally published by Harper & Row, 1966), p. 296.

ping of God in such a manner as they judge acceptable to Him, and effectual to the salvation of their souls" (Locke 1990, 22). The overriding concerns of such a society, he felt, ought to be spiritual and moral, "and nothing ought nor can be transacted in this society relating to the possession of civil and worldly goods." Such a religious arrangement allowed for the triumph of personal faith.

However, between that conception of religion and of the state Locke drew a neat if overly formal distinction. He gave to civil government the responsibility for ordering our material well-being, which includes "life, liberty, health, and indolence of body," as well as "possession of outward things, such as money, lands, houses, furniture, and the like" (ibid., 18). Just as the church should not concern itself with amassing wealth and material possessions, so the government should not concern itself with the salvation of souls.

This distinction between the nature of religion and the nature of the state is not satisfactory either in detail or in principle, as Locke recognized, for he went on to observe that government should not be given authority over religion because "it appears not that God has ever given any such authority to one man over another as to compel anyone to his religion" (ibid., 19). For Locke, as for many Puritan divines, religion was incompatible with state coercion, not simply because the state is a blunt and oppressive instrument to use in delicate matters of faith, but because "though the rigor of laws and the force of penalties were capable to convince and change men's minds, yet would not that help at all to the salvation of their souls" (ibid., 21). That is true even if it is a democratic will.

Locke reasoned as he did because theological issues were paramount for him in the following sense: a soul that was compelled was a soul that had lost its religious worth; it would not be a legitimate subject for spiritual regeneration. He asserted: "true and saving religion consists in the inward persuasion of the mind, without which nothing can be acceptable to God. And such is the nature of the understanding, that it cannot be compelled to the belief of any thing by outward force" (ibid., 20). Similarly, the political commonwealth would be a tyranny if nothing beyond compulsion held it together. Such a religious conception of the moral integrity of the human person was necessary to Locke's conception of the tool-making character of civil government. Religion and civil government, Locke continued, have an overlapping legitimate interest in "moral actions" that belong "to the jurisdiction both of the outward and the inward court; both of the civil and domestic governor; I mean both of the magistrate and the conscience" (ibid., 56). In other words, religion as a voluntary society made possible the birth of the theory of limited state authority. In this complementarity of church and state we find the "good life" wherein "lies the safety both of men's souls and of the commonwealth" (ibid.).

The Muslim challenge was not far from Locke's mind, and he considered how Muslims and others might be integrated into a society where religion was not enforced or enforceable. That form of Islam, he said, that represented a rupture with the tradition of voluntarism would be difficult if not impossible to assimilate, but only by force of circumstance, not on principle. The crucial test for Muslims, according to Locke, is whether they, too, would abjure the judicial and political weapon in religious life and accept that "nobody ought to be compelled in matters of religion either by law or force."

Atheism would present a no less troubling challenge. "Those that by their atheism undermine and destroy all religion, can have no pretense of religion whereupon to challenge the privilege of toleration" (ibid., 64). This statement shows that Locke is aware that the argument for religious toleration itself rests on a religious idea, and that it is a contradiction in terms for people to repudiate religion while supporting tolerance and inclusiveness. That is why Locke insisted that neither atheist nor Muslim nor any other "ought to be excluded from the civil rights of the commonwealth, because of his religion" (ibid., 70). We may summarize Locke's reasoning to the effect that, on the one hand, moral integrity requires us to reject the use of political instruments of Christendom in securing religious ends, while, on the other, we cannot surrender the religious ground concerning the liberty of conscience without making civil government in the narrow sense and religious toleration broadly conceived ultimate casualties. This is the sense in which we should understand the New England Pilgrims of 1620, whose brand of piety freed religion from political and territorial establishment and placed religiously inspired curbs on state supremacy. Thus, for example, Roger Williams of Rhode Island argued that God had placed the Ten Commandments on two tablets; on one God wrote the laws regulating the divine-human relationship, and on the other the laws dealing with the relationship of men and women among themselves. In that way, Williams concluded, we have a basis for the fundamental distinction between the divine jurisdiction and human tribunals. It would be improper to mix these two tablets or confuse them, because to do so would imperil our soul and our political welfare. So the separate branches of church and state have a single theological root, and, by extension, a common moral source.

Innumerable other Western religious thinkers have given similar attention to the character of a free society and the proper relation within it of religion and politics. They separated the two by repudiating a theocratic state without jettisoning the religious ground as such. One seventeenth-century theologian insisted that religious persons of conscience cannot allow "a secular sword [to] cut in sunder those knots in religion which [it] cannot untie by a theological resolution."[8] The reason for this is that "to employ the [civil] magistrate in this kind of compulsion is a prejudice to the Lord Jesus, and the provision he has made for the propagation of the Church and truth" (Woodhouse 1974, 256).[9] Another writer who paid close attention to such matters (even though his fame rests in the impact

---

[8] A. S. P. Woodhouse, ed., *Puritanism and Liberty: The Army Debates (1647-9) from the Clarke Manuscripts* (London: J. M. Dent & Sons Ltd., 1974), p. 256. Richard Overton, another seventeenth-century Puritan thinker, expressed similar sentiments about the use of "human compulsive power or force" in religion (ibid., 332ff.).

[9] Pope John Paul II, addressing a gathering of Muslim youth in Casablanca in August 1985, spoke in a similar vein about the importance of religious freedom. "We desire," he said, "that all may reach the fullness of the divine truth, but no one can do that except through free adherence of conscience, protected from exterior compulsions which would be unworthy of the free homage of reason and a heart which is characteristic of human dignity. There is the true meaning of religious liberty, which at the same time respects God and man" ("The Speech of the Holy Father John Paul II . . . at Casablanca," *Islamochristiana*, II [Rome, 1985], p. 203).

of his scientific ideas) was Robert Boyle, with whom Locke was for a time closely associated. For Boyle political authority could never be absolute and indeterminate lest it conflict with the higher authority of God. The political ruler should, therefore, be reminded that civil disobedience is an intrinsic right with which our Creator has endowed us. "For God being, as our only Creator, so the supreme governor of man, his laws are those of the truest supreme authority: and princes themselves being his subjects, and but his lieutenants upon earth; to decline their commands, whenever they prove repugnant unto his, is not so much an act of disobedience to the subordinate power, as of loyalty to the supreme and universal sovereign."[10] Milton declared himself to the same effect, namely, that if they turn to tyranny, kings and magistrates "may be as lawfully deposed and punished, as they were at first elected." Such political rights have their source in theological doctrine,[11] to wit, that men and women "were born free, being the image and resemblance of God himself," with government instituted among themselves "by common league to bind each other from mutual injury." Government is the servant of people, not their master, Milton asserted.[12]

In his trenchant observations on religion in American life, de Tocqueville argued for separation, saying that when a religion allies itself with government, "it must adopt maxims which apply only to certain nations. Therefore, by allying itself with any political power, religion increases its strength over some but forfeits the hope of reigning over all" (de Tocqueville 1988, 297). The compromise involved in bringing religion into alliance with partisan politics is fatal to the fundamental claims of religion, because "when it is mingled with the bitter passions of this world, it is sometimes constrained to defend allies who are such from interest rather than from love; and it has to repulse as adversaries men who still love religion, although they are fighting against religion's allies. . . . Alone, [religion] may hope for immortality; linked to ephemeral powers, it follows their fortunes and often falls together with the passions of the day sustaining them" (ibid., 297-98).

Such teachings are the flaming sword by which this age has defended liberal democratic pluralism and religious freedom and under which we have conceived all human history as tending toward what R. G. Collingwood has called "the general development of God's purpose for human life."[13] The democratic liberal state

---

[10] Cited in Eugene M. Klaaren, *The Religious Origins of Modern Science* (Lanham, Md.: University Press of America, 1985), p. 144.

[11] Augustine had written that there is an emperor in human affairs and a "King for otherworldly matters. There are a king for temporal life and a King for life eternal" (cited in Hugo Rahner, S.J., *Church and State in Early Christianity* [San Francisco: Ignatius Press, 1992], p. 136. Translated by Leo Donald Davis, S.J., from the German, *Kirche und Staat im Frühen Christentum* [Munich: Kösel Verlag, 1961]).

[12] John Milton, *The Tenure of Kings and Magistrates*, in *Political Writings*, ed. Martin Dzelzainis, tr. Claire Gruzelier (Cambridge and New York: Cambridge University Press, 1991).

[13] R. G. Collingwood, *The Idea of History* (London and New York: Oxford University Press, 1946), p. 49.

is sovereign not because its laws are unquestioned or unquestionable but because of the rights of personhood established in natural and divine law. Democratic liberalism is a derived value, not itself the moral source. De Tocqueville affirmed a similar sentiment when he said that in a free, democratic society obedience and obligation are incumbent even on persons who do not believe, and that persons who are free are to the same degree constrained to believe (de Tocqueville 1988, 444).

Unfortunately, the development of Locke's ideas in one respect would not be fruitful for preserving the delicate balance between religion and government, for elsewhere he gave grounds for abandoning the primacy he gave to religion vis-à-vis government. In his *Second Treatise on Civil Government* he inserted private property rights under the rubric of the sacred, saying divine truth harmonizes here with "the voice of reason." Thus is justified the ultimate sanction of killing lawfully in defense of one's property. In the hands of his disciples, Locke's doctrine of property was given the explicit metaphysical status he implied for it. American philosopher Richard Weaver wrote an impassioned defense of property rights, including the rights of capital, against the presumptions of social justice and of the rights of the laboring classes

> When we survey the scene to find something which the rancorous leveling wind of utilitarianism has not brought down, we discover one institution, shaken somewhat but still strong and perfectly clear in its implication. This is the right of private property, which is, in fact, the last metaphysical right remaining to us. The ordinances of religion, the prerogatives of sex and of vocation, all have been swept away by materialism, but the relationship of a man to his own has until the present largely escaped attack.[14]

These words make clear how in a unitary secular order the moral law would be usurped for the ends of property and profit, and how banishing religion from the public realm would result in political territoriality as a sacred covenant for private wealth. Thus on secular grounds alone, separation, without the religious precaution, would enshrine interests and the instruments for defending them. Therefore Locke's ideas on property, what he defines as "lives, liberties and estates," would make human beings, by reason of their labor, belong first and last to themselves and not to God. That would blow a hole in the safety net of separation,[15] removing the distinction between property and religion.

These were decisive reasons why religion as territorial principle or state authority was opposed by many Christian thinkers, as well as by many non-Muslims today, including Christian Africans, though many such people feel encouraged by Islam's witness to divine justice in temporal affairs. It is, however, a

---

[14] Richard Weaver, *Ideas Have Consequences* (Chicago: University of Chicago Press, 1948). Cited in C. L. R. James, *American Civilization* (Cambridge, Mass., and Oxford: Blackwell, 1993), p. 243.

[15] John Locke, *Two Treatises of Government*, ed. Peter Laslett (Cambridge: Cambridge University Press, 1963; New York: Mentor Books of the New American Library, 1965).

question whether religion as personal faith only is adequate to the contemporary global situation with its rising Islamic challenge.

STAGE II: ISLAMIC TERRITORIALITY
AND THE COUNTER-TRADITION

The late Ayátulláh Khumayní of Iran once complained that Muslims have been robbed of their heritage through the connivance of the West. Western agents, he charged, "have completely separated [Islam] from politics. They have cut off its head and [given] the rest to us."[16] The reference is to the creation in Muslim countries of the secular national state as the successor to the transnational Islamic caliphate. As we saw in the previous chapter, a similar complaint was made by Sádiq al-Mahdí, the Sudanese political leader who pilloried the secular national state for being the means by which antireligious forces have entered non-Western societies and been fomented. He assured his bewildered co-religionists that Islam was the God-ordained answer for their undeserved ills.[17] Such sentiments have resonated with rank-and-file Muslims, in part because they invoke powerful religious symbols and in part because they exploit widespread popular disenchantment with Western-inspired economic programs. The religious objections to Western-style reforms have undercut the credibility of the state as an imported Western institution. Thus the appeal of religion reflects the disaffection with the West almost as much as it draws upon Islam's canonical tradition, or what is claimed for it.[18]

In terms of that tradition, modern Muslim views on political authority have their roots in the Prophet's own personal legacy in Medina and Mecca, where he established territoriality, *dár al-Islám*, as the handmaid of religious faith.[19] It was not long before the early Muslims were rallying round the political standard *lá hukm illá bi-illáhi* ["no government except under God"].[20] The words have echoed down to our day, refined and mediated by the medieval theologian Ibn Taymiyya (d. 1328), as a stringent theocratic credo. A contemporary Muslim writer

---

[16] Cited in A. Rippin and J. Knappert, eds., *Textual Sources on Islam* (Manchester: Manchester University Press; Chicago: Chicago University Press, 1986), pp. 191-92.

[17] Cited in G. H. Jansen, *Militant Islam* (London: Pan Books, 1979), pp. 126-27.

[18] Nazih Ayubi argues for Islam as "a religion of collective morals" rather than as "a particularly political religion" (*Political Islam: Religion and Politics in the Arab World* [London: Routledge & Kegan Paul, 1994], p. 120).

[19] See W. Montgomery Watt, *Muhammad at Medina* (Oxford: Clarendon Press, 1962), still regarded as the definitive study of the subject.

[20] An authoritative Muslim political tract put it as follows: "The [religious] law of the sultan is the [political] law of the country" (*Usúl al-Siyásah* [*On the Fundamentals of Government*], reproduced in B. G. Martin, "A Muslim Political Tract from Northern Nigeria: Muhammad Bello's *Usúl al-Siyása*," in Daniel F. McCall and Norman R. Bennett, eds., *Aspects of West African Islam*, vol.5 [Boston: Boston University Press, 1971], pp. 82-83).

cites an identical opinion from the second of the Four Righteous Caliphs, 'Umar ibn Khattáb (d. 644) to the effect that "there is not Islam without a group, no group without power (authority), no authority without obedience. If someone is made master on the basis of jurisprudence, this will be for their and his good, and if he is made master otherwise [say, by a secular constitution], this will be destruction for all of them."[21] However, it is from Ibn Taymiyya, among others, that modernist Muslim reformers in the last two hundred years have received their marching orders, from Jalál al-Dín Afghání to Sayyid Qutb and Ayátulláh Khumayní.

In view of Ibn Taymiyya's influence on modern critical Muslim assessments of the West, a few words are in order on his ideas. He spoke about the indispensability of God and the Prophet in political affairs, what he calls *siyásah iláhíya wa inába nubúwíya* ("divine government and prophetic vicegerency"). He contended:

> To govern the affairs of men is one of the most important requirements of religion, nay, without it religion cannot endure. . . . The duty of commanding the good and forbidding the evil cannot be completely discharged without power and authority. The same applies to all religious duties (holy war, pilgrimage, prayer, fast, almsgiving), to helping those who are wronged, and to meting out punishment in accordance with the legal penalties. . . . The purpose of public office is to further the religion and the worldly affairs of men (*isláh . . . dínahu wa-dunyahu*) . . . when the pastor exerts himself in proportion to his ability to further both, he is one of the most excellent fighters on the path of God. The exercise of authority is a religious function and a good work which brings near to God, and drawing near to God means obeying God and his Prophet.[22]

Thus authority is the possession of moral truth.

These are uncompromising words that impute territoriality to religious orthodoxy, words that would make Muslims discontented with a merely liberal pragmatic political ethic. Yet they are words that also make it difficult to coexist in a pluralist society. One way out of Ibn Taymiyya's rigid scheme is to make "the duty of commanding the good and forbidding the evil" (*amal bi-ma 'rúf wa nahy 'an al-munkar*) (Qur'án III:104)[23] the basis for a theocentric view of the world rather than the justification for a theocracy. A theocracy would ironically still be the rule of mere earthen vessels, a limitation echoed in the Qur'ánic verse about intrinsic human weakness (Qur'án 30:54). Thus government *faqihs* seduced by power would dismay even dyed-in-the-wool stalwarts by the ease with which they add new and not so subtle inflections to the injustice of conjugation of the ill-

---

[21] Cited in Yasir al-Mallah, "The Relationship of Religion to the State in Islam," *Al-Liqa' Journal*, vol. 3 (May 1994): 39. *Al-Liqa'* is a Palestinian review published in Jerusalem by the Center for Religious and Heritage Studies in the Holy Land.

[22] Cited in E. I. J. Rosenthal, *Political Thought in Medieval Islam* (Cambridge: Cambridge University Press, 1958), pp. 51ff.

[23] See Abú Hamíd al-Ghazálí, *Kitáb Ihyá'Ulúm al-Dín*, trans. Al-Haj Maulana Fazul-ul-Karim (New Delhi: Kitáb Bharan, 1982), vol. ii, chap. 10, pp. 225-28.

omened verb *to corrupt*. The twists of the turban may be politically more fraught than the religious sum of its folds.

It is a similar consideration that has led many other Muslims to question whether even under Islamic territoriality it is wise to employ force and coercion to propagate religion. One early caliph, for example, agonized over the safety of religious truth when upheld by the instruments of the state. This was the Caliph al-Ma'mún, who declared in a public meeting in 830 A.D. that although under his rule many had converted to Islam for purely religious reasons, many others had done so from less honorable motives. "They belong to a class who embrace Islam, not from any love for this our religion, but thinking thereby to gain access to my Court, and share in the honor, wealth, and power of the Realm; they have no inward persuasion of that which they outwardly profess."[24] This anticipates Locke's notion of the jurisdiction of the "outward and inward," and why territoriality offends conscience as much as it undercuts democratic pluralism, for if religion looks to political power for its ultimate defense, then it will find in that its sole vindication and reward, and, in time, its demise. We would, like the agonized caliph, be unable to determine the true from the spurious, sincerity from self-interest, or commitment from opportunism. Consequently, revealed law may not be domesticated into human schemes without direct risk to truth and the political scheme itself.

In an instructive piece of debate between two Muslim scholars on the need for a theocratic state we find identical issues being raised. One of the scholars in question, Muhammad al-Kánemí (d. 1838), the ruler of Kanem-Bornu in West Africa, challenged the *jihád* leader, 'Uthmán dan Fodio (d. 1817), with regard to the use of the sword for religious ends. Al-Kánemí said the sword is too rough and ready a weapon to use in settling religious questions, especially questions between Muslims themselves, since they would then attempt to resolve by *force majeure* what might be substantial matters of theology or even only differences of opinion. He insisted that Muslims must either settle for tolerance and mutual acceptance or else unleash a smoldering permanent war that would exempt, in his words, not even "Egypt, Syria and all the cities of Islam . . . in which acts of immorality and disobedience without number have long been committed." "No age and country," al-Kánemí cautioned, "is free from its share of heresy and sin,"[25] and any immutable division of the world between *dár al-Islám* and *dár al-harb* would fly in the face of this reality and reduce to ashes all sincere but inadequate attempts at truth and obedience. We could not find revealed truth in the blinding flames of fanaticism fed by short-fused *fatwas*.

It might be appropriate here to recall the words of Locke about religious triumphalism, for the point he makes is pertinent to the issues raised by al-Kánemí.

---

[24] 'Abd al-Masíh ibn Isháq al-Kindí, *The Apology*, ed. and tr. Sir William Muir (London: S.P.C.K., 1887), pp. 29-30. Al-Kindí, himself a supreme controversialist, added that people turned to Islam in these circumstances "some by fear of the sword, some tempted by power and wealth, others drawn by the lusts and pleasures of this life."

[25] Text reproduced in Thomas Hodgkin, ed., *Nigerian Perspectives: An Historical Anthology* (London: Oxford University Press, 1960), pp. 198ff.

Let us imagine, Locke argues, Christian missionaries, destitute of everything, arriving in a so-called Pagan country and inserting themselves into the society by taking advantage of the kindness and hospitality of their so-called Pagan hosts. The new religion then takes root in the country and spreads gradually. As long as Christians remain a minority they publicly espouse peace, friendship, faith, and justice for all. But at length they grow powerful and achieve a substantial victory with the magistrate of the country converting and becoming a Christian. This fact emboldens the Christians to break all previous accords with the Pagans on whom they turn, requiring them to repudiate their ancient religion and customs on pain of being dispossessed and reduced to servitude. Such a Christian religion, Locke concludes, would be merely "the pretense of religion, and of the care of souls" and would be "a cloak to covetousness, rapine, and ambition" (Locke 1990, 50).

That constructed tableau has an uncanny similarity to the condition of count-less communities in Muslim Africa. To take one well-known instance of two hun-dred years ago, the Sarki, or king, of one West African Pagan state, Gobir, woke up one day to find his Muslim guests had grown in number and confidence, turned implacably militant, and were threatening his kingdom. They were in no mood for conciliation and concession. He had been too sanguine and rued the day, he said, when he gave friendly sanctuary to Muslims. He later complained to his fellow kings "that he had neglected a small fire in his country until it had spread beyond his power to control. Having failed to extinguish it it had now burnt him. Let each beware," he lamented, "lest a like calamity befall his town also."[26] By then the flames were raging, and Locke is small comfort; the Sarki's warning had come too late.

In contrast to that way of religious proselytization, we have an example where a whole religious vocation has developed among certain groups of Muslim West Africans on rejecting political and military means for spreading and maintaining religious faith and institutions. One such group are the Jakhanké clerics, whose professional roots go back to medieval Africa through a cleric called al-Hájj Sálim Suwaré (hence the appellation "Suwarians" in some sources). I have described elsewhere their professional religious life. In received traditions al-Hájj Sálim is described as handing down teachings that represent a scrupulous disavowal of political and military coercion in religious matters and the repudiation of secular political office for the professional cleric, an astonishing position given the un-ambiguous rulings of the Qur'án and the jurists. Yet equally astonishing is the durability of this pacific strain in Muslim West Africa, whose antiquity and dis-persed, mobile character have led scholars to offer a Semitic hypothesis as its origin. Indeed Jakhanké chronicles identify them as *Baní Isrá'ila* ("children of Israel"), which appears to lend at least conjectural credence to the Semitic theory.[27]

---

[26] Muhammad Bello's correspondence with al-Kánemí, in Bello, *Infáq al-Maysúr*, ed. C. E. J. Whitting (London: Luzac & Co., 1957), p. 131; also cited in J. Spencer Trimingham, *A History of Islam in West Africa* (London: Oxford University Press, 1962), p. 199.

[27] For a detailed study of the subject, see Lamin Sanneh, *The Jakhanké Muslim Clerics: A Religious and Historical Study of Islam in Senegambia* (Lanham, Md.: University Press of America, 1989). This is the first and only book-length study in any language.

At any rate, as professional clerics the Jakhanké people established educational centers as cells of influence among diverse ethnic groups, a clerical *cordon sanitaire* of mobility and dispersal whence they wafted the felicitous breath of pacific counsel. So distinctive was this tradition that local religious militants who defied it found themselves exposed to the virus of religious mutiny from within. Local populations that had come under the influence of clerical pacifism were so deeply affected that a theocratic dispensation was more disconcerting to them than the prospects of continuing pluralism.

This is not to say that pacific Muslim clerics did not clash with unamenable secular strongmen, for they did. But that clerical pacifism undermined the extreme program of a corporate theocratic state. The attempt was made many times in the nineteenth and twentieth centuries to create theocratic governments in Muslim West Africa, and each time it failed from the prevailing unfavorable quietist climate of opinion. Even the effort by European administrations to coopt such pacific clerics into the colonial brand of political committedness by giving them chieftaincies foundered on the same pacific rock, with the clerics offering their sympathy or even cooperation but stopping short of becoming collaborators and active allies. In an era of the total political mobilization that some colonial regimes preferred, such clerical independence was deemed an affront. It brought on the collision it was designed to avert and forced the clerics to reassess the heritage in the light of new realities. For example, in 1911 a clerical leader who was arrested along with his followers at the point of a gun and sent into humiliating exile and imprisonment spoke eloquently of clerical pacifism not simply in terms of personal survival but in terms of a long, self-consistent vocation. The French administrator and scholar Paul Marty, who saw the relevant document, found it difficult not to be impressed by the argument. Marty said the leading cleric in question "formulated conclusions, stamped with the indelible mark of loyalty, and remarked that his fidelity, had it not been born of natural sympathy, would have been for him a necessity of the logic of history" (Sanneh 1989, 132-33). Marty described the attack on the pacific clerics as a St. Bartholomew's Massacre. Such conflicts were clearly painful personal setbacks but scarcely a fatal loss for pacific credibility, or mobility, since the clerics conducted themselves with dignified restraint under violent provocation and then subsequently emigrated as haven-seekers.

The Máliki *muftí* of the Republic of Senegal, a seasoned child of the clerical peripatetic tradition, told the present writer of being invited from his country retreat in Casamance by the Senegalese president to travel to the capital to meet the king of Saudi Arabia. He declined on the grounds that it would be tantamount to political sponsorship, which he would wish to reject. When he finally yielded, it was as a courtesy to the royal visitor rather than as a concession to collaborating with political office. He and clerics like him are happy to make their peace with political territoriality but are less willing to collapse religion into such territoriality. Admittedly religious withdrawal, even with the clerical pacific principle at its heart, may not deal well enough with the problem of the doctrinaire ideological secular state, but it does sustain the moderate pacific counsels by which Muslim Africans have extended and deepened the tradition of genuine pluralism.

There is thus a large body of material in both Christian and Muslim traditions to support a public role for religion without requiring theocratic rule. Sufyán Thaurí, a classical Muslim writer, has a witty aphorism apt on this point: "The best of the rulers is he who keeps company with men of [religious] learning, and the worst of the learned men is he who keeps the society of the king."[28] That is to say, religion and worldly affairs prosper together when political rules are qualified by moral principles, and they suffer when moral principles are qualified by political expedience. Ibn Khaldún defends this position, though in his case he was stepping forward with the same distrusted secular foot twice. He wrote:

The state whose law is based upon violence and superior force and giving full play to the irascible nature is tyranny and injustice and in the eyes of the law blameworthy, a judgment in which also political wisdom concurs. Further, the state whose law is based upon rational government and its principles, without the authority of the *Sharia*, is likewise blameworthy, since it is the product of speculation without the light of God . . . and the principles of rational government aim solely at worldly interests (Gibb 1962, 173).

In that statement Ibn Khaldún describes and criticizes the Hobbesian state where political sovereignty is the basis of moral jurisdiction, with people's rights being what is secured to them by the national political sovereign.[29] Yet his alternative of a religious state creates the situation in which religion as a fundamental personal matter is placed under state prerogative. Ibn Khaldún thus excoriates the power state only to reward it with jurisdiction over religion. In the Lockean view, by contrast, liberty is a principle of the people's God-given rights rather than an indulgence granted by the sovereign national state. In that scheme, political rules may be effective without being sacred, and moral injunctions may produce practical fruit without being expedient. In neither case would people have to dance to the Vicar of Bray's tune, in which the morality of taking the king's shilling is fixed at the king's bidding.

STAGE III: THE ROOTS OF CONTROVERSY: CAESAR CROWNED AND TURBANED?

The Muslim challenge and tradition examined in this brief account bring up the issue of how national secular state jurisdiction may find acceptance in the religious community. Muslims consider the *ummah* as a supra-national commu-

---

[28] Cited in Nizám al-Mulk, *The Book of Government for Kings (Siyásat Náma)* (London: Routledge & Kegan Paul, 1960), p. 63. This work was written in the eleventh century.

[29] At the United Nations Human Rights Conference in Vienna in June 1993, the delegation of the People's Republic of China took the Hobbesian position that "no rights inhere in persons other than those accorded them by the state" (as reported in Thomas Michel, S.J., "Differing Perceptions of Human Rights: Asian-African Interventions at the Human Rights Conference," in Tarek Mitri, ed., *Religion, Law and Society* [Geneva: World Council of Churches, 1995], pp. 131-37, 132).

nity, one that transcends national identity. The reality, however, is that Muslims are not all assembled under one Islamic roof but are instead spread over many countries and subject to diverse and conflicting political jurisdictions. In virtually all cases, state authority has jurisdiction, however contested, over membership of the *ummah*, so that loyalty to the religious community would override or else conflict with the claims of territorial sovereignty. Yet modernist Muslims, modifying the fundamentalists, would compromise with the national secular state by holding it to standards of justice and respect for human rights or would otherwise settle for a benign liberal democracy with room for religious freedom. In its turn, the secular state, committed to toleration, would abjure the right to interfere with religion.

That liberal compromise commands wide support, bringing, as it does, religion into qualified association with the affairs of state and making it possible for church and state to be *united* instead of existing in a mutually damaging adversarial relationship. Since religion stakes its reputation on moral commitment, the state cannot ignore it without risk of popular disaffection. In its turn, if religion is politically domesticated, political differences escalate into major theological schisms. If the state intervenes to suppress or enjoin appropriate forms of religion, that would infringe its own liberalism. It follows, then, that liberalism and religious freedom share one foundation, though church and state function as a split-level structure. Thus a way must be found for them to cooperate in society while restricting the state in its invasive power to encroach on conscience and keeping religion from turning expedient and partisan, as expressed in some of the Muslim fundamentalist debate.

In many significant cases, however, the secular state considers itself a competitor with religion for the moral ground, a competition which proves that the state is not neutral. The Leviathan national state, whose inauguration the Abbé Sieyès trumpeted with such confidence, is in its nature girded for combat against all irrational forces, especially organized religion. The Muslim instinct to distrust it is, therefore, understandable, though with regard to Africa such distrust should be mitigated by Africa's recent encounter with the Western secular Leviathan. Given that fact, Muslim (and, one should add, Christian) leaders in many parts of Africa sense all is not lost, so that, confronted with an ideological secularism and its iconoclastic view, they feel they can respond with a religious alternative. In Nigeria and the Sudan, for example, we have two cases where the ferment has created extreme public debate on the conflicting claims of religion and the state. More than academic, the debate in the two countries has produced political movements.

Thus at Kaduna, Nigeria, the Supreme Council for Islamic Affairs was founded in 1973, and thus too did Hassan al-Turabi's National Islamic Front, a radical Islamic movement, mastermind the 1989 coup d'état that installed Gen. Omar Hassan al-Bashir as head of state in the Sudan.[30] The Islamic revolution in the

---

[30] See the report in *The New York Times*, "A Fundamentalist Finds a Fulcrum in Sudan," 29 January 1992. See also William Langewiesche, "Turabi's Law," *The Atlantic* (August 1994): 26-33.

Sudan thus attempts to replace national state allegiance with religious obligation. As Turabi puts it, "Islam is becoming temporal"[31]; that is, Islam is acquiring temporal power as an inevitable and necessary holy duty. In both countries Muslims have demanded the introduction of the *Sharí'ah* in public life, and in the Sudan the process has gone further with implementation of parts of the *Sharí'ah* code. In Nigeria, by contrast, the plan has hit a major political snag. A proposal along the lines of the Sudan was voted down in Nigeria in April 1978 by the Constituent Assembly that met to draft a new constitution for the nation. The choice, as Muslims see it, is straightforward and unambiguous enough: either a state buttressed by the religious code, such as the *Sharí'ah* provides, or a secular state that is "godless." Muslims do not feel sanguine about a national state that has unrestricted access to unrivaled resources and power which it would use to uphold secular, "godless" aims and programs. On the pretext of religious neutrality, the secular state could cut off public funds for religious schools and institutions but allocate them to secular and atheist programs. Such a posture exposes the antireligious bias of the national secular state and shows too that political authority is setting itself above religion. Even when it professes neutrality toward religion, the secular state is in fact engaged in a contest with religion and is thus deeply entangled with it. Such views were reported in the national paper, *New Nigerian*, from March to September 1977.

However, the *ummah* is unlikely to be the panacea doctrine claims for it; ethnic, linguistic, and historical differences are too endemic to conform to its uniform rule. Besides, the present world security and economic system is too firmly invested in the secular state structure to survive the disarray involved in a shift based on a religious code. The secular state is attractive because of its capacity (and despite its limits) to absorb the great diversity and plurality of social and religious groups existing within its borders. The *ummah* as a religious community could not concede the secular principle of egalitarian individualism without self-contradiction. In this situation religion as temporal power would incur—and in turn incite—instability, injustice, and disaffection. Thus have Sudan's unassimilated southern tribes long constituted an obstacle both to Khartoum's policies of arabization (and islamization) and to the effectiveness of the unitary secular state. Such minorities, already persecuted, would also be stigmatized under the dispensation of the *ummah*. Nigeria has been faced with no less fundamental a choice.

In this sense, matters in Nigeria received a boost in 1986 when the Christian Association of Nigeria (CAN), an ecumenical grouping of Protestants, Catholics, and African Independent Churches founded explicitly to respond to Muslims in general, and in particular to the military government's unpublicized decision to enroll Nigeria as a member of the OIC (on which more presently), issued a statement protesting federal government backing for *Sharí'ah* courts in north Nigeria and asking for an identical public status for Christianity. But CAN's strategy of demanding privileges for Christians comparable to those being offered to Muslims sets it on the Muslim side of the fault line, with Christians wheeling and

---

[31] Cited in Judith Miller, "The Islamic Wave," *The New York Times Magazine* (31 May 1992).

dealing on a stage Muslims have constructed for their own purpose. For example, the Kaduna Branch of CAN published a statement asking the government to offset any concessions to the *Sharí'ah* with similar concessions to Christians by establishing a Christian constitution based on ecclesiastical courts (*Nigerian Tribune*, 21 October 1988). No wonder Muslims welcomed CAN's platform, forcing a catch-22 upon Christians by challenging them to say which they prefer, English Common Law, ecclesiastical canon law, or secular law. The divisions among Christians, Muslims point out, are responsible for Christian confusion, contradiction, and indecisiveness toward the agenda of the secular state. And until Christians can make up their minds and decide either for transcendent truth or for secular humanism, Muslims, they believe, must carry the burden of the challenge.

However, Muslim confidence should be tempered by the realities of the world, because even in places where *qádí* courts have operated, the Islamic code has not been free of its share of corruption and exploitation, and Muslims who have had cause to resort to them have not always found relief or justice. With the *Sharí'ah* becoming part of the political debate, Islam risks being reduced to a political enterprise in which the ultimate is turned into the expedient and vice versa. Many Muslim modernists say such a course risks irreparable damage to the claims for revealed truth. Such modernists see a tolerant secular state as less threatening than a theocratic state. After all, there is plenty of scope in a tolerant secular state for exercising the duties called for by Islam's ethical system with regard to *zakát*, economic probity; education; domestic tranquillity; marriage; care for widows, orphans, the poor, and the sick; rearing of children; good neighborliness; honesty; forbearance; and so on. Modernists feel grievances in such matters are as much the consequence of internal failures and inadequacies as they may be of external infidel malice, and no amount of flaming *fatwas*, or infidel quarantine, can immunize against so endemic an infection.

All religious systems are equally vulnerable to the relentless incursions of temporal compromise and to the vagaries of human instrumentality even, or especially, where human stewardship is claimed in the service of revealed truth. The preface to the First Book of Common Prayer (1549), taking somber stock of what had overtaken a religion trapped in human systems, expresses the sentiment well when it says, "There was never any thing by the wit of man so well devised, or so sure established, which in continuance of time hath not been corrupted." Herein is echoed 'Uthmán dan Fodio's own painful musing in his poem *"Wallahi, Wallahi,"* where he bemoaned the corruption that had riddled the theocratic reform program he had initiated with the highest public ideals.[32] Religious truth cannot survive this corruption, for believers would become either cynics or Eliot's "hollow men," a presence without consequence. The only reasonable answer is to separate church and state, to desacralize the political instrument while safeguarding religion's independence.

These considerations prompt the following thought: Such separation need not deny the connection of ethics and politics, of church and society, of principle and

---

[32] See Mervyn Hiskett, "'The Song of the Shehu's Miracles': A Hausa Hagiography from Sokoto," *African Language Studies*, vol. 12 (1971).

precedent, or of faith and public order, a connection well described by Stackhouse as a "buffer zone" between church and state, between piety and power.[33] For example, religious ethics may provide for the maintenance and security of the public order in such matters as family life, the socialization of children, interpersonal trust, philanthropy, compassion, and humility without the public order being excluded from shared responsibility, though in that partnership public agents might be tempted to sequester religion as expedient leverage only, taking short-term advantage of revealed injunctions which are the source and spring of ethical life. All this indicates that liberal arguments for distinguishing between public and private spheres would be hard to sustain on purely free-speech grounds, as Locke has cogently shown, for, however we define them, the private and public spheres are affected by identical rules of order, freedom, and responsibility. State institutions would be expected to observe standards of freedom, justice, honesty, truth, and decency no less than persons in community. In other words, the state in its nature distinguishes between right and wrong, punishes wrongful acts, and offers incentives for right conduct. It is not morally neutral. Even in the intimate domain of family life, for instance, the rule of safeguarding and promoting the welfare of children is no less valid when transferred to the public realm than when it is viewed in its natural sphere of parental responsibility. Thus while separation defines the public and private domains, it does not abrogate the large area of partnership and overlap that turns out to be extremely fruitful of a humane and just society. There would be room in that partnership and overlap for absorbing Muslim ethical teachings and other values within an open, free, and pluralist community.

In spite of such considerations, the debate as it has been conducted in Nigeria has been a one-sided affair in which Muslims have taken the offensive and Christians have reacted with high-decibel slogans about pluralism and multiculturalism—and with strategies of ecumenical unity striking for their ephemeral, tactical skittishness. If, by contrast, the example of Christendom and its disastrous consequences for genuine pluralism and multiculturalism were available to Muslims, it might calm passions and provide instructive lessons about the liabilities of religious territoriality in Africa or anywhere else. In that case, the secular state, shorn of its antireligious bias and conceived as a pluralist apparatus, might be less objectionable and might thus remove any conspiratorial odor from Christian support for such a state. It turns out, however, that events have preempted the issue, with the regime of General Ibrahim Babangida, which ruled Nigeria from 1985 to 1993, acting in 1989 to allow *Sharí'ah* court jurisdiction in the north, thus setting aside the position taken by Christians and endorsed in the decisions of the Constitutive Assembly.

International Muslim solidarity has aided and abetted national efforts and has distracted local Christian attempts to respond to Muslim initiatives. After several years as an observer, in 1986 Nigeria joined the Organization of Islamic Countries (OIC) (*Munazzamah al-Mu'tamar al-Islámí*), which was set up following

---

[33] Max Stackhouse, *Public Theology and Political Economy* (Grand Rapids: Eerdman's, 1987), p. 109.

the meeting of the Third Conference of Islamic Foreign Ministers in March 1972. Its first secretary general was Tunku Abdur Rahman, who resigned as prime minister of Malaysia to assume that position. The OIC was registered with the United Nations in February 1974. A number of Islamic agencies was established within the OIC, whose religious character was spelled out in an official statement. This religious objective was described as the commitment "to propagate Islam and acquaint the rest of the world with Islam, its issues and aspirations" (*The Guardian*, 27 January 1986). The statement then went on to cite from the Declaration of the Third Islamic Summit of 1981, as follows:

Strict adherence to Islam and Islamic principles and values, as a way of life, constitutes the highest protection for Muslims against the dangers which confront them. Islam is the only path which can lead them to strength, dignity and prosperity and a better future.[34]

The statement in that form and in its fuller version proposes a frankly utilitarian political view of religion, with the unsettling theological implication that Islam seeks for its adherents political and judicial instruments for their protection, and that only a temporary sacrifice need be involved in the process. Those who share in Islam's struggle, its *jihád*, will also share in its fruit, no more and no less. The problem with this reasoning is that it does not seem to work in reverse: many affluent and thriving communities, who are otherwise "lodged in this world in a goodly lodging" (16:43), claim no scriptural credit for such advantage. By promising similar fruits to its adherents, religion, any religion, would be trafficking in double standards by placing the moral diacritic on political and economic goods but impugning those goods when their source is perceived to be the secular national state. If in the nature of the case the secular state or religion exists only to secure our material interest, that would make ends and means identical and make religion nothing more than mere everyday usefulness. If both state and religion have as their common end the single goal of being "lodged in this world in a goodly lodging," then the one would only be a duplicate of the other, and distinguishing between the two would defy even the most discerning. Religious pursuit and political interest would merge. We can avoid this situation only by drawing the distinction between church and state which moral principle and worldly expedience alike require. African states are embroiled in this struggle.

The OIC statement ended by quoting the Qur'án at 3:106 to the effect that Muslims "are the best nation ever brought forth to men, bidding to honour, and forbidding dishonour, and believing in God" (Arberry). The phrase "bidding to honour" is not sufficiently exact to reproduce the sense in the Arabic original of "commanding the good and fitting" (Qur'án iii:106), a sense involving power and authority. "The duty of commanding the good and forbidding the evil," Ibn Taymiyya insists, "cannot be completely discharged without power and author-

---

[34] 'Abdulláh al-Ahsan, *OIC: The Organization of the Islamic Conference: An Introduction to an Islamic Political Institution* (Herndon, VA: The International Institute of Islamic Thought, 1988), p. 19.

ity." Member states of the OIC accept the binding authority of its charter, though the power and authority implied in the Qur'ánic verse it invokes might conflict with the sovereignty of national constitutions. At present the view has been expressed that the OIC lacks the power to hold member states accountable, even when it comes to the payment of dues. As it happens, this inadequacy in the structure of the OIC reduces its ability to challenge sovereign national states whose own internal domestic pluralism would, as in Nigeria, make doctrinal conformity difficult to enforce.

In terms of its historical origin, the OIC began as an organized Muslim response to the arson in August 1969 at the *Aqsá* mosque in Jerusalem under Israeli occupation, and in its original charter Jerusalem was designated as its de jure headquarters, with Jeddah being adopted *faute de mieux*. Before long, the activities of the OIC extended to numerous fields covering social, political, economic, media, publishing, educational, and intellectual activities. Membership in the organization was limited to sovereign nation-states, which are Muslim by definition, although several states with minority Muslim populations have joined, including Benin, Sierra Leone, and Uganda. However, somewhat inconsistently, India and Lebanon, which have significant Muslim populations, have not been allowed to join. They have been disqualified by the territorial rule, for their heads of government by practice are non-Muslim. In *territoriality* the religion of the ruler is the religion of the country, as we have remarked earlier. In other respects the OIC has applied stringent confessional criteria, from deciding on the venue of its meetings to granting economic assistance from its $2 billion development fund and awarding scholarships.

Although the OIC has agreed to work within the framework of the international security system in terms of explicit recognition of national state jurisdiction, it strives, in spite of that, to redirect the attention of member states to issues of international Muslim solidarity in terms of the primacy of the *Sharí'ah* and the unity of the *ummah*, that is, code and community. Indeed, the religious counsels it has invoked as its reason for existing commit it to appeal to Muslims without regard to state protocol. For example, in its founding charter the OIC declared that "jihád [is] the duty of every Muslim, man or woman, ordained by the *sharí'ah* and glorious traditions of Islam," and called "upon all Muslims, living inside or outside Islamic countries, to discharge this duty by contributing each according to his capacity, in the cause of Allah Almighty, Islamic brotherhood, and righteousness" (al-Ahsan 1988, 60). Such appeals reveal the OIC's distrust of secular national states even though publicly it says it respects and recognizes them. The ambivalence is also no doubt to be explained by the need to respond to Israel's dominance in the Middle East, as OIC's founding documents reveal.

Be that as it may, the OIC distinguishes itself from other international organizations such as the United Nations, the European Community, the Organization of African Unity (OAU), and even the Arab League by stressing its Qur'ánic identity as *ummah*. Yet the OIC as such has no independent sovereign power and relies on member states to carry out its decisions. It has, nevertheless, identified the secular character of modern states as the consequence of Western intellectual hegemony and therefore as something that is in the nature of the case in tension, if not in conflict, with Qur'ánic norms and with the authentic Muslim aspirations they enshrine. By implication, Christian support or sponsorship of the secular national state is open to an identical objection.

The OIC issue has released a potent ferment of the fundamentalist debate and has thus caught Nigerians unawares. Yet even here we have possibility for inter-faith understanding, because it can be said that the secular national state which is the butt of criticism among Muslims is an issue also for Christian Africans, and for them, as for their Muslim compatriots, the great stumbling block continues to be the idea of secularism. It does not change very much to tinker with the notion and break it up into, say, "secularity," "secularism," and "the secular." For Christian Africans the secular laic state is the least of all possible evils, and for Muslims it is the worst of available alternatives. Watched by Muslims, Christians are disinclined to side with the secular state as a "godless" institution,[35] but neither are they ready to buckle under Muslim pressure and endorse religion as state ideology because of what that would imply for minority groups in the community. For their part, Muslims are not reassured by the doctrinal minimalism of Christians and others who are willing to accept humanly constructed national constitutions for a secular state but refuse the role of revealed law in public affairs. Or, equally inconsistently, Christians plead for ethnic or cultural priority over any claim for religious primacy, and yet insist that they speak also as religious people. Yet, how can religion count for anything when thus reduced to an ethnic decoy or a cultural filler? Here we see Ockham's razor dissected by the Muslim *sayf al-haqq*, the sword of God.

At this point historians of religion ought to notice the special circumstances of an African Christianity that received from the mainline Western churches the tradition of an enlightened worldliness first preached by their eighteenth-century forebears. This worldliness furnished the basis for a "bland piety, a self-satisfied and prosperous reasonableness, the honest conviction that churches must, after all, move with the times. This—the concessions to modernity, to criticism, science, and philosophy, and to good tone—this was the treason of the clerics,"[36] that is, the absolute liberal compromise. It is the principle of "finders, keepers, losers, weepers," whereby the church pleads its right to keep whatever it finds congenial in secular traditions, though such stolen property might taint its reputation. Christian reasonableness in this sense was a code for religion as the cultural helix which cuts and shapes religion as a social ornament. When the church entered confi-

---

[35] In a forthright statement supporting the establishment of a secular state in South Africa, Archbishop Tutu said that did not mean a "godless state." He declared: "A secular state is not a godless or immoral one. It is one in which the state does not owe allegiance to any particular religion and thus no religion has an unfair advantage, or has privileges denied to others. In some Muslim countries Muslim Sharia law is enforced on all and sundry. We do not want to impose Christian laws on those who are not Christian, even if we are the majority" (*Constitutional Talk*, Official Newsletter of the [South African] Constitutional Assembly, Supplement to *The Cape Times*, 12 July 1995).

[36] Peter Gay, *The Enlightenment: An Interpretation*, vol. I: *The Rise of Modern Paganism* (New York: W. W. Norton, 1977), p. 343.

dently and uncritically upon the heritage of its secular captors, it gave up its autonomy as the price for being included in the affairs of state. This created a peculiar situation: the church appropriated the national cultural enterprise as a devout vocation, fitting into Locke's idea of "the reasonableness of Christianity," though the idea of vocation with intrinsic religious merit was abandoned. Religion as cultural helix was corkscrewed into official submission, with the cultural coil guiding the religious axis. It would be difficult, as society became more materialist and pluralist, to maintain such a vital nexus of religion and culture. As Herbert Muller says of an earlier age, "As the commonplace was made holier, the holy became commonplace."[37] That development was unchallenged by the attendant scholasticism, which constructed its system of human cognition with a built-in slight toward non-Western cultures.[38] The brilliance of its rational disputation exhausted itself in deductive reasoning that permitted no new discovery and quenched even the slightest flicker of any interest in non-Western cultures. For the schoolmen of scholasticism, absorbed in dispute over the choice of horns in dilemmas, God disappeared in a blaze of verbal fireworks, and as divinity floated away into the mists, it lost all connection with lived social practice except in a gross, alien, popular piety that had the universe infested with spirits, demons, sprites and goblins.

As a consequence, from the intellectual captivity of the gospel cultural respectability resulted, with moral fervor and cultural devotion becoming synonymous. Thus was religion sequestered to become the national cult. Compromise does not have to be imposed to be fatal, and the church, relaxed and mellow, was trimmed with undue fuss and domesticated into the cultural matrix of its captivity, its solemn religious trunk pared down to remove all offense to good taste. "There was much comfort and little anxiety in sermons purporting to prove that the course of a Christian life was easy, that reward for good conduct [i.e., conformity to the status quo] was sure and glorious, that God had commanded men nothing 'either unsuitable to our reason or prejudicial to our interest; nay, nothing that is severe and against the grain of our nature,' and that, on the contrary, 'the laws of God are reasonable, that is suited to our nature and advantageous to our

---

[37] Herbert J. Muller, *The Uses of the Past: Profiles of Former Societies* (London: Oxford University Press, 1952; repr. New York: Mentor Books, 1963), p. 277.

[38] Richard Gray writes: "Most missionaries trained in the scholasticism of the first half of the twentieth century found it difficult to accept the legitimacy or even the feasibility of an African theology. This was true even of some of the most intelligent and sympathetic of missionaries. One of my most vivid recollections of the seminar on Christianity in Tropical Africa, organized by the International African Institute and held at Legon in 1965, was of René Bureau, fresh from presenting his brilliant, if Eurocentric, analysis of the impact of Christianity on the Duala, vehemently disputing with the Zaïrean, Vincent Mulago, the possibility of an African theology. 'Theology,' Bureau maintained, 'was a universal science, and one could not contrast African with Western theology.' We were all increasingly part of a universal, technological civilization founded on Jewish thought and Greek ideas, and another Western missionary maintained 'it was as unreal to talk of an African theology as of a lay theology'" (*Black Christians and White Missionaries* [New Haven: Yale University Press, 1990], p. 72).

interest."'[39] Such justification, remarkable for its supreme, airy confidence, pulled religion by its roots from its social connectedness.

Historians struck by the survival in Christian Africa of vestiges of European influence will do well to remember that it was a scholasticized faith that came to Africa, and that in its European form the church demanded little engagement with local priorities and attitudes. Jesus of Nazareth was swallowed up in abstract dogma, his earthly life refined as fuel for enlightened minds. Encountering such a religion, Africans soon discovered its inadequacies for the flesh-and-blood issues of their very different societies. The bracing religious commitment needed for creative cultural innovation and for a radical understanding of local social systems was at odds with Christianity as a system of human cognition, and the churches as transplants in Africa were too out of step with the African experience to enable people to decide what religious foundations to put in place for constructing a new society in new times. Thus, Muslims may be justified in thinking that Christians have abdicated from the religious center, confining themselves to the sidelines on the great issues of state and society. However, if it is the case that Christians are mere rookies at the game of politics and state building, then it is hard to see how they could be charged with public responsibility for the policies of colonial regimes in Africa and for the enduring effects of those policies in postcolonial Africa. Such theological minimalism is uncontroversial, content as it is with religion occupying a residual role in public life where it subsists on political dole. It results in apathy in the face of maximal political participation, such as that involved in setting up and running a state.

Furthermore, it is important to recognize the noncontroversial context of Muslims in modern African states not as the subjugated people of a colonial overlord but as masters of their own affairs, even where they are only a tiny fraction of the population. A similar context obtained even under colonial rule, where Muslim life endured and thrived, in part because the muscle of secular colonial administrations could be harmonized with the momentum of a dynamic Islamic order to produce the Constantinian state, and in part because, flowing from this logic, colonialism became guarantor of the Pax Islamica which discouraged Christian missionary activity or anything else that might offend Muslims. Colonialism became the Muslim shield, and the riposte to the church's theological minimalism. In one example in British-administered Adamawa in Nigeria, the resident colonial officer presided over a meeting called by Muslims who headed the Native Authorities set up by the British. The meeting would receive charges from the Muslims against the Danish missionaries of the province for allowing classes for religious instruction to be taken by village catechists in mission schools. The meeting, held at Yola, the provincial headquarters, considered how these classes were in fact political platforms producing "young rebels," that is, a class of young people not under the direct influence of the Muslim native authorities. The colonial administration backed the Muslim demands to abolish the religious instruc-

---

[39] Gay, 1977, 345, citing Archbishop John Tillotson in Norman Sykes, *Church and State in England in the XVIIIth Century* (London, 1934), pp. 258-59.

tion classes.[40] Thus colonialism became the Muslim shield and the guarantor of Islam as the public alternative to Christianity for Africans.

Examples are numerous. In 1910, when a traditional ruler of Bauchi Province converted to Christianity in what appeared a sincere act, the resident in charge objected and had him deposed because the ruler's authority depended on observing local rituals which as a convert he had now forsaken. In another example, the colonial district officer upheld the decision by the Muslim chief to have Christian places of worship torn down—though he intervened after protest by the missionaries and prevented the chief from carrying out the demolition.[41] In yet another incident, the district officer felt that anti-mission feeling was getting out of hand after some Mission boys were ordered flogged by the district head and his elders because some of the people associated with the mission had refused to be married under native custom and were thus flouting native authority (Barnes 1995, 417). One colonial officer, Fitzpatrick, expressed the widespread view that colonialism was the alternative to Christianity when he wrote, "The Christianised African in Kabba is presently a difficulty and is rapidly becoming a problem. To-day his attitude and his actions make it hard for the Native Administration to govern: tomorrow they may make it impossible" (ibid., 417). This view led Fitzpatrick to launch an attack on mission Christianity, especially the Protestant form of it, as a subversive, dangerous influence on Africans. Christianity, he wrote in a fit of uncompromising candor, was "synonymous with idleness, impudence, inefficiency, with all that is meanest and worst in a native or any other polity" (ibid., 421). Fitzpatrick's views were backed by his superiors, including the governor, Sir Hugh Clifford, who wrote that native administrations should receive the backing of political officers against Christian insubordination (ibid., 422). Barnes is more forthright, saying that administrators saw Christianity as giving African converts the temerity to presume that they could transcend "their status as members of a lesser race" (ibid., 423). Thus the policy of *indirect rule* promoted the territorial interests of Islam as an effective block to Christianization with its tendencies, so inimical to religious territoriality and constituted authority, toward the separation of the religious and the secular and the emancipation of the individual. Missionaries there or elsewhere would plead forlornly and in vain for a role for educated youth in modern society, rather than their being stigmatized and subject to harassment and reprisal. Thus colonialism, while strengthening Muslim territoriality, reinforced the privatization of Christianity.

However, such historical cooperation has not removed all Muslim grievances, so that their need for transnational solidarity has pitted Muslims against the West as the source and guardian of the secular national state, a state that divides Muslims and sets at nought the just claims of the *ummah*.

---

[40] Niels Kastfelt, *Religion and Politics in Nigeria: A Study in Middle Belt Christianity* (London: British Academic Press, 1994), pp. 41-42.

[41] Andrew E. Barnes, "'Evangelization Where It is Not Wanted': Colonial Administrators and Missionaries in Northern Nigeria during the First Third of the Twentieth Century," *Journal of Religion in Africa*, vol. XXV, no. 4 (1995): 412-41, 416.

In spite of differences of culture and language and in spite of a common desire to succeed economically, such religious groups are, even in the West where they have chosen to immigrate, in the words of the legal manuals,

bound together by the common tie of Islam that as between themselves there is no difference of country, and they may therefore be said to compose but one *dár* [that is, *dár al-Islám*, "the abode of fraternal Islam"]. And, in like manner, all who are not [Muslims], being accounted as of one faith, when opposed to them [Muslims], however much they may differ from each other in religious belief, they also may be said to be one *dár* [that is, *dár al-harb*, "the sphere of war and enmity"]. The whole world, therefore, or so much of it as is inhabited and subject to regular government, may thus be divided.[42]

De Tocqueville called attention to this strand in the Muslim tradition, noting how the refusal of Muslims to grant the principle of a separate jurisdiction in church and state makes the religion a liability in an enlightened, pluralist democracy (de Tocqueville 1988, 445), since faith and the public interest must under those circumstances coincide. Consequently, the pursuit by radical religious activists of Islam's comprehensive doctrine perpetuates the difficulty.[43]

Our comprehension of this new reality, however, must keep abreast of moderate Muslim counsels concerning the anachronism of territoriality, and ecumenical groups need to come to a common mind about religious freedom, whether in Maiduguri, Manchester, or Medina. Religious toleration cannot survive by conceding the extreme case for religious territoriality, because a house constructed on that foundation would have no room in it for the very pluralist principle that would make the national secular state hospitable to religious voluntarism. The fact that such religious activity has grown and thrived under national state jurisdictions at a time when religious minorities established in religious territorial states have, if press reports are to be believed, continued to suffer civil disabilities shows how uneven the situation has become. As a prominent national political figure and TV commentator put it, playing somewhat to the gallery with a bait of his own, "While Moslem minorities proliferate and prosper in Western societies that preach and practice freedom and tolerance, in nations where Moslems are the majority, Christians find the profession of the faith difficult, the preaching of the Gospel impossible."[44]

---

[42] *Digest of Moohummadan Law: Containing the Doctrines of the Hanifeea Code of Jurisprudence*, ed. and tr. Neil B. E. Baillie (1869-75; repr. Lahore: Premier Book House, 1974), pp. 169-70.

[43] In a rambling polemic against the West, a U.S.-based Muslim fundamentalist group claims that for Muslims politics is a sacred duty, and Islamic fundamentalism must assume responsibility for it ("A Political Progress for Muslim America," produced by Muslim America, Inc., Olympia, WA 98503).

[44] Pat Buchanan, "The Global Ascent of Islam," *Colorado Springs Gazette*, 20 August 1989. Pat Buchanan was a Republican presidential candidate in 1992 and again in 1996.

The substance of that view, shorn of its crowd baiting, is that a split-level structure in interfaith relations becomes untenable, and poses a risk to democratic public institutions whose preservation demands that human rights be enshrined in the actions of the national secular state. Three points should be made here: (a) religious toleration is an essential part of human rights and, thus, of democratic pluralism; (b) it is necessary to separate church and state in order to protect human rights and to foster pluralism, and c) the matter cannot rest there, because religious toleration requires arguments that go beyond those of public usefulness. Normative toleration as a safeguard of individual conscience is theological in the sense of being founded on the divine right of personhood, with obvious political implications. Now, while conscience or the sanction for it is not the concern of state jurisdiction, nevertheless, in its assumptions of moral agency, it touches inexhaustibly on the public order. Thus might religion produce fruits in projects of social welfare and their effects on public social ethics without religion turning into a mere expedient ethic, and thus, too, might state interest converge with religion without the state becoming a divine organ. They complement each other when church and state are separated, but each corrupts—and is in turn corrupted—when the other coopts it.

This consideration leads to the following conclusion: voluntary religious practice promotes ends that are constitutive of the values of a liberal democratic political community, though religion would be corrupted if it were coopted merely as a tool of authority, and politics turn tyrannical if it ceases to be morally accountable. In this regard the temporal Islam of conservative Muslims—the claim for a public sphere for religion—may be reconciled with the ethical Islam of liberal Muslims without yielding to theocratic extremism on the right or to prescriptive atheism on the left. Thus we may concede the point of Ibn Taymiyya that "the exercise of authority is a religious function" in the sense of accountability and subordination to the higher moral law, without granting that this requires establishing a theocratic order for the purpose. The political community is also the moral community, though the political and the moral, while necessarily connected, are not identical. Truth is no less so even if it is not politically expedient, while political expediency may serve the higher end without turning into the end itself. The political community, stretched to its extensive overlap with the moral law, cannot return to the exclusive dimensions of prescriptive atheism, so that, for example, when Ibn Khaldún separates dogma and politics, truth and pragmatism, he expands the religious view while qualifying the political. Similarly, from the left we may agree with Locke when he argues for the "outward" and "inward" jurisdiction, with religion at the center, without going so far as to say that separation removes religion from any role in the political economy. A theocratic state in Ibn Taymiyya's terms would be no better than an ideological secular state in John Locke's terms, for in both views God and obedience to God would be reduced to tools of authority, with truth-seeking becoming a strategy for self-interest or group advantage and vice versa. Separation of church and state, when taken to its logical extreme, would produce a doctrinaire secularism aided and abetted by religious collusion; without separation the situation may be reversed, yet identical consequences will follow, for then Caesar's political commissars will anoint themselves with the moral norms they confiscate from the church. Separation does not mean exclusion, nor does it imply as alternative Hobson's choice of the state's absorption of the church. It only means that religion is so important that the state should take it seriously and yet is too important for the state to expropriate it, and that although religion and politics are comprehended within the human scheme, religion exceeds the human measure by pointing beyond to the divine.

CONCLUSIONS

In view of growing signs of pressure for temporal Islam, often expressed in terms of *Sharí'ah* and political power, and in view of the utter inadequacy of the sterile utilitarian ethic of the secular national state in meeting this challenge, Christian Africans and their Western predecessors are faced with a question about supporting the pragmatist case for the secular state with moral principles. The state as the vehicle for tolerance, human rights, equality, and justice must now be conceived in terms that are hospitable to claims for truth. Too much is at stake in the survival of the state as a noncorporate, nondoctrinaire institution to allow it to fall victim to our Enlightenment scruples about not mixing religion and politics. The pragmatist liberal scruple that proceeds upon religion in the fashion of individual entitlement and free speech is in one sense the spoiled fruit of the original insight about keeping Caesar and God separate, about ensuring religious freedom against state power and jurisdiction. That insight became twisted into religion as individual entitlement and free speech, as a rights issue under state jurisdiction, in fact as a matter of private, individual choice without public merit. So Muslim critics are correct that rights without God are meaningless, but mistaken to suggest that a religious state would do better, because under such a state rights would as a last resort spring from duress and intimidation, and that would just be another name for jungle power. To work, rights must presume an authority above and beyond individual or collective will, by general consent a transcendent tribunal that can support and adjudicate conflicting claims and interests. If we only have human authority as final arbiter of human rights, then there simply is no basis for saying one individual has rights of person and property against the multitude; against the individual, the multitude's will is irresistible and final by reason merely of numerical preponderance. Human rights as such are meaningless in that environment precisely because the individual has been assured no God-given rights. That is why human rights must presume a public tribunal insulated from the tyranny of numbers by being grounded in faith in the divine right of personhood, a faith that fosters the twin culture of rights and obligations, of freedom and community. In this context, state capture of religion is bound to dismantle the machinery of civil society, so that in one move the brakes are removed from political excess and in turn applied to freedom and commitment, in effect pressing political expediency into the service of a false absolute. All of that diminishes freedom and tolerance, two priceless and indispensable pieces of the apparatus of democratic liberalism.

In the nature of the case, democratic liberalism seeks political sovereignty from the people rather than taking it to them, and so, to be successful, it rules and governs through consent. It is, therefore, a profound condition of its strength that religion flourish in it in the obvious sense of democratic liberalism using legitimate methods in the pursuit of ethical ends. "Despotism," de Tocqueville insisted, "may be able to do without faith, but freedom cannot. Religion is much more needed in [an egalitarian democratic society] than [in a privileged, aristocratic society]" (de Tocqueville 1988, 294). It is when the ties of political control are relaxed that those of religion are tightened, when freedom expands that personal responsibility increases with it, and that as men and women take control of their own affairs that they should be subject to the law of God. That much is clear on the political side of the equation. On the religious front, we may say that the ethical life requires our ability to think and act voluntarily. As Pope Nicholas I (d. 867) put it, there is no good that is not ultimately voluntary. Thus religion may relinquish territoriality to the state without giving up the public sphere altogether, so that people can enter into ultimate religious commitment freely. That free commitment signifies the limitless possibility of human worth and allows people to conceive a separate, limited domain of political action. It is on that basis that we can distinguish between the norms of moral truth and the calculations of political action. Political sovereignty and state jurisdiction have their common foundation in the higher wisdom of the people's God-given rights, with religion the expression of that political axiom. Freedom is an act of faith.

Jefferson (1743-1826) appeals to this principle, invoking it as the last resort of democratic liberalism. "I have no fear," he affirms, "but that the result of our experiment will be that men may be trusted to govern themselves without a master. Could the contrary of this be proved, I should conclude either there is no God or that he is a malevolent being." Jefferson fervently supported separation of church and state, not because he opposed religion, or his notion of it, but because he felt deeply that government would use religion to bolster its despotic powers. Religion was at its best, he argued, when it did not feel the necessity to compel compliance, and, he might have added in the same breath, democratic liberalism was at its soundest when it allied itself to religion's spirit of freedom. John Dewey (1859-1952), for his part, comes to the issue with the instinct of a pragmatist, saying that those who are committed to democratic liberalism must "face the issue of the moral ground of political institutions and the moral principles by which men acting together may attain freedom of individuals which will amount to fraternal associations with one another."[45]

Religion thus constitutes the pillar upholding democratic liberalism, secured as it is on the consent of persons constrained by right rather than cowed by might. The state that can reach its people only through force will turn society into a battlefield, and religion allied with such a state becomes moral coercion, making salvation a political prerogative. We would be ill advised to abandon our faith in divinity on the basis of state fiat or base it on the will of the collective, Rousseau's

---

[45] John Dewey, *Freedom and Culture* (Buffalo: Prometheus Books, 1989), p. 125.

general will with its unrealistic assumption about innate human goodness and reasonableness. Instead, we should see that the notion of peoplehood on which democratic liberalism depends itself hinges on the doctrine of persons "born free, being the image and resemblance of God himself," as Milton expressed it, a view echoing the religious basis of peoplehood of classical Muslim thought, too.

At this stage we may redirect the Miltonian or Lockean view of religion and politics toward its modern-day natural convergence with democratic liberalism in the following way. A liberal democratic state, however laisser faire, must still impose laws and rules impartially on all citizens, and it is necessary to its success that such a state depend on a broad consensus concerning the fundamental constitutional axioms upon which laws and rules are based without a controversy about "beliefs" in each round of rule-making. Thus disagreements may arise in society as to the material effects and consequences of rules, but not about the fundamental axioms and their source in religion and tradition. For example, the axiom "Thou shalt not kill" as a scriptural injunction would permit laws against murder to be promulgated and stipulated without the operative validity of those laws depending on prior assent to the authority of Scripture. Life is sacred because of divine affirmation, though the murderer or society need not affirm that to be subject to the law. In the law against suicide, for example, the point is poignantly made. Similarly, as a penal concept truth-discovery and punishment are valid even if the criminal rejects confession and repentance as a religious duty. It is the fact that these laws and rules may be detached from their source in religion and made impartially operative that gives them their force. Thus liberal democratic regimes are concerned with those procedural tasks deriving from a Miltonian or Lockean doctrine, even if in substance those tasks do not require avowal of the religious source. You do not have to bring up the roots to know the tree is sound.

Political realism and religious integrity thus have a common purpose in distinguishing between a Caesar crowned and a Caesar turbaned, and that purpose is to prevent constituted government from meddling with religion. Politics as a self-sufficient comprehensive system of values concerned primarily with public-order matters is already too well equipped to tempt it further with jurisdiction over religion. In the power state religion is addictive, for transcendence is fodder to triumphalist politics. Hence the caution that, although political liberalism can scarcely flourish without its foundational attachment in religious freedom, yet it will spoil from assuming political primacy over the religious domain. If it knows anything about religion, the impulse of secular liberalism is to "commodify" religion for short-term exchange, or, to amend de Tocqueville, government by habit prefers the useful to the moral and will, therefore, require the moral to be useful. By thus shortening the odds on the long-range, timeless truths of religion, the secular realm ends up removing the safety barrier against political absolutization and coming into conflict with George Herbert's religious rule that what "God doth touch and own cannot for less be told." Much of the church-state tension stems from the proximity of the two spheres, so that religion is too enmeshed in life not to profit or suffer from the state instrument, and vice versa, though marrying the two introduces an even greater risk of malignancy between them. Government with unlimited power will metastasize, leading to the adoption of injurious, despotic measures in the name of a prescriptive political code. At the same time, religion as a public-order strategy will become just a power game. Ultimately, whether the state repudiates or coopts religion, it ends up feeding off religion; private piety as a liberal political concession is little different in restriction from the belligerent antireligious stance preferred by the atheist state. We need the prophylaxis of separation to tame the state and to create a public space for religion without religious differences becoming a public liability. In the contemporary global situation, such qualified separation also provides a crucial shield for pluralism and minority rights, enabling nonconformist groups and minority communities to play an assured role in the public sphere without fear of stigma.

Concerning the ultimate OIC case for the *ummah*, it may well be that, in principle, advocates of temporal Islam are right in their criticism of the national state as biased toward the secular metaphysics of the state as a moral idea, indicating that the secular state is not neutral toward the religious source of the moral idea but is actively at work to supplant it for self-serving reasons. The suspicion is that the state wishes to establish the public sphere as a religion-free zone so as to designate it as a religious "no-go" area. Yet this stringent criticism is reserved also for the doctrinaire state, now dressed in purple velvet, whose religious metaphysics gives no immunity from despotism, since the religious state is still the captivity of dogma in the service of expediency. The actions of the religious state ultimately can be guaranteed to spare not even its religious sponsors, either as agents implementing harmful laws or as the targets of such laws. That is why religion and government should be united in requiring the safety net of separation, a separation in terms of coequal spheres of responsibility. Once we have secured that, then tolerance and pluralism can thrive, and with them religion, and especially politics, as a fundamental issue of personal choice within a culture of persuasion. All of which would ensure that minority status and religious or political preferences could possess public merit without necessarily carrying any stigma or reprisals or the threat of any. Open and fair contest would determine for the most part, or for the part that matters, what survives or does not survive of the ideas and values best deemed to advance our freedom and welfare. The culture of persuasion developed under religious freedom is essential and indispensable to that open public choice.

CHAPTER BIBLIOGRAPHY

Abdin, Tayyid Z. Al-. "The Implications of *Sharí'ah, Fiqh and Qánún* in an Islamic State." In Tarek Mitri 1995.
_____. "The Role of Religious Institutions and *'ulamá'* in a Contemporary Muslim Society." In Tarek Mitri 1995.
Abul-Fadl, Mona. *Where East Meets West: The West on the Agenda of the Islamic Revival.* Herndon, VA: The International Institute of Islamic Thought, 1992.

Ahsan, 'Abdullah al-. *OIC: The Organization of the Islamic Conference.* Series no. 7. Herndon, VA: The International Institute of Islamic Thought, 1988.

Alharazim, M. Saif'ud Deen. "The Origin and Progress of Islam in Sierra Leone," *Sierra Leone Studies*, old series, no. 21 (1939): 12-26.

Ayubi, Nazih. *Political Islam: Religion and Politics in the Arab World.* London: Routledge & Kegan Paul, 1994.

Baillie, Neil B. E., ed. and tr. *Digest of Moohummadan Law: Containing the Doctrines of the Hanifeea Code of Jurisprudence.* 1869-75; reprinted Lahore: Premier Book House, 1974.

Barker, Sir Ernest. *Principles of Social and Political Theory.* Oxford: Clarendon Press, 1951.

Barnes, Andrew E. "'Evangelization Where It is Not Wanted': Colonial Administrators and Missionaries in Northern Nigeria during the First Third of the Twentieth Century," *Journal of Religion in Africa*, vol. XXV, no. 4 (1995).

Breiner, Bert F. "Secularism and Religion: Alternative Bases for the Quest for a Genuine Pluralism." In Tarek Mitri 1995.

————. "*Sharí'ah* and Religious Pluralism." In Tarek Mitri 1995.

Buchanan, Pat. "The Global Ascent of Islam," *Colorado Springs Gazette* (August 20, 1989).

Burckhardt, Jacob. *Force and Freedom: An Interpretation of History.* New York: Meridian Books, 1955.

Collingwood, R. G. *The Idea of History.* London & New York: Oxford University Press, 1946.

Cragg, Kenneth. *The Call of the Minaret.* Revised ed. Maryknoll, NY: Orbis Books, 1985.

Dewey, John. *Freedom and Culture.* Buffalo: Prometheus Books, 1989.

Economist, The. "Islam and the West." 6 August 1994.

Esposito, John. *The Islamic Threat to the West: Myth or Reality?* New York: Oxford University Press, 1990.

Fasholé-Luke, Edward W. "Christianity and Islam in Sierra Leone," *Sierra Leone Bulletin of Religion*, vol. 9, no. 1 (June 1967).

Fodio, Uthmán dan. *Bayán Wujúb al-Hijrah 'Alá-l-Ibád.* Edited and translated by F. H. El-Masrí. Khartoum: Khartoum University Press and Oxford University Press, 1978.

Gabid, Hamid al-. "The Organization of Islamic Conference (OIC) and the Development of Africa." In *Islam in Africa: Proceedings of the Islam in Africa Conference.* Edited by Nura Alkali, Adamu Adamu, Awwal Yadudu, Rashid Motem, and Haruna Salihi. Ibadan: Spectrum Books Limited, 1993.

Gay, Peter. *The Enlightenment: An Interpretation.* Vol. I: *The Rise of Modern Paganism.* New York: W. W. Norton, 1977.

Ghazálí, Abú Hamíd Al-. *Kitáb Ihyá 'Ulúm al-Dín.* Vol. 2. Translated by Al-Haj Maulana Fazul-ul-Karim. New Delhi: Kitáb Bharan, 1982.

Gray, Richard. *Black Christians and White Missionaries.* New Haven: Yale University Press, 1990.

Guardian, The, 27 January 1986.

Gutiérrez, Gustavo. *Las Casas: In Search of the Poor of Jesus Christ.* Maryknoll, NY: Orbis Books, 1993.

Hansen, Holger Bernt. *Mission, Church and State in a Colonial Setting: Uganda: 1890-1925.* London: Heinemann, 1984.

Hodgkin, Thomas. "The Fact of Islamic History (II): Islam in West Africa," *Africa South*, vol. 2, no. 3 (1958): 88-99.

_____. "Islam and National Movements in West Africa," *Journal of African History*, vol. 3, no. 2 (1962).

_____. "Islam, History and Politics," *Journal of Modern African Studies*, vol. 1, no. 1 (1963).

_____, ed. *Nigerian Perspectives: An Historical Anthology.* London: Oxford University Press, 1960.

Huntingdon, Samuel P. "The Clash of Civilizations?," *Foreign Affairs* (Summer 1993).

James, C. L. R. *American Civilization.* Cambridge, Mass., and Oxford: Blackwell, 1993.

Jansen, G. H. *Militant Islam.* London: Pan Books, 1979.

Kastfelt, Niels. "African resistance to Colonialism in Adamawa," *Journal of Religion in Africa*, vol. viii, no. 1 (1976).

_____. *Religion and Politics in Nigeria: A Study in Middle Belt Christianity.* London: British Academic Press, 1994.

_____. "Rumours of Maitatsine: A Note on Political Culture in Northern Nigeria," *African Affairs*, LXXXVIII (1989): 83-90.

Kerr, Malcolm. *The Arab Cold War: Gamal 'Abd al-Nasir and His Rivals: 1958-1970.* 3d edition. London: Oxford University Press for the Royal Institute of International Affairs, 1971.

Klaaren, Eugene M. *The Religious Origins of Modern Science.* Lanham, Md.: University Press of America, 1985.

Kokole, Omari H. "Religion in Afro-Arab Relations: Islam and Cultural Changes in Modern Africa." In *Islam in Africa: Proceedings of the Islam in Africa Conference.* Edited by Nura Alkali, Adamu Adamu, Awwal Yadudu, Rashid Motem, and Haruna Salihi. Ibadan: Spectrum Books Limited, 1993.

Kumo, Suleimanu, "Shar'ia [sic] under Colonialism-Northern Nigeria." In *Islam in Africa: Proceedings of the Islam in Africa Conference.* Edited by Nura Alkali, Adamu Adamu, Awwal Yadudu, Rashid Motem, and Haruna Salihi. Ibadan: Spectrum Books Limited, 1993.

Langewiesche, William. "Turabi's Law," *Atlantic* (August 1994): 26-33.

Locke, John. *A Letter concerning Toleration.* Buffalo, NY: Prometheus Books, 1990.

_____. *Two Treatises of Government.* Edited by Peter Laslett. Cambridge: Cambridge University Press, 1963; New York: Mentor Books of the New American Library, 1965.

Martin, B. G. "A Muslim Political Tract from Northern Nigeria: Muhammad Bello's *Usúl al-Siyása.*" In Daniel F. McCall and Norman R. Bennett, eds. *Aspects of West African Islam*, vol. 5. Boston: Boston University Press, 1971.

Miskin, Tijani, El-. "Da'wa and the Challenge of Secularism: A Conceptial Agenda for Islamic Ideologues." In *Islam in Africa: Proceedings of the Islam in Africa Conference*. Edited by Nura Alkali, Adamu Adamu, Awwal Yadudu, Rashid Motem, and Haruna Salihi. Ibadan: Spectrum Books Limited, 1993.

Mitri, Tarek, ed. *Religion, Law and Socety: A Christian-Muslim Discussion*. Geneva: World Council of Churches, 1995.

Moore, Kathleen M. *Al-Mughtaribun: American Law and the Transformation of Muslim Life in the United States*. Albany: State University of New York Press, 1994.

Mulk, Nizám al-. *The Book of Government for Kings (Siyását Náma)*. London: Routledge & Kegan Paul, 1960.

New York Times. "A Fundamentalist Finds a Fulcrum in Sudan," 29 January 1992.

Poston, Larry. *Islamic Da'wah in the West: Muslim Missionary Activity and the Dynamics of Conversion to Islam*. New York: Oxford University Press, 1992.

Rahner, Hugo. *Church and State in Early Christianity*. San Francisco: Ignatius Press, 1992. Translated from the German by Leo Donald Davis, *Kirche und Staat im Frühen Christentum: Dokumente aus acht Jahrhunderten und ihre Deutung*. Munich: Kösel Verlag, 1961.

Rippin, A., and J. Knappert, eds. *Textual Sources on Islam*. Manchester: Manchester University Press; Chicago: University of Chicago Press, 1986.

Rosenthal, E. I. J. *Political Thought in Medieval Islam*. Cambridge: Cambridge University Press, 1958.

Sanneh, Lamin. *The Jakhanké Muslim Clerics: A Religious and Historical Study of Islam in Senegambia*. Lanham, Md.: University Press of America, 1989.

Sayeed, Khalid Bin. *Western Dominance and Political Islam*. Albany: State University of New York Press, 1994.

Sivan, E. *Radical Islam*. New Haven: Yale University Press, 1985.

Smith, Jane Idleman, and Yvonne Yazbeck Haddad, eds. *Muslim Communities in North America*. Albany: State University of New York Press, 1994.

Taylor, A. J. P. *The Habsburg Monarchy: 1808-1918*. 1948; reprinted London: Penguin Books, 1990.

Tocqueville, Alexis de. *Democracy in America*. Translated by George Lawrence, edited by J. P. Mayer. New York: Harper Perennial, 1988. Published by Harper & Row, 1966.

Watt, W. Montgomery. *Muhammad at Medina*. Oxford: Clarendon Press, 1962.

Weaver, Richard. *Ideas Have Consequences*. Chicago: University of Chicago Press, 1948.

Woodhouse, A. S. P., ed. *Puritanism and Liberty: The Army Debates (1647-9) from the Clarke Manuscripts*. London: J. M. Dent & Sons Ltd., 1974.

Yadudu, Auwalu Hamisu. "The Prospects for Shar'ia [sic] in Nigeria." In *Islam in Africa: Proceedings of the Islam in Africa Conference*. Edited by Nura Alkali, Adamu Adamu, Awwal Yadudu, Rashid Motem, and Haruna Salihi, Ibadan: Spectrum Books Limited, 1993.

Yahya, Dahiru. "Colonialism in Africa and the Impact of European Concepts and Values: Nationalism and Muslims in Nigeria." In *Islam in Africa: Proceedings of the Islam in Africa Conference*. Edited by Nura Alkali, Adamu Adamu, Awwal Yadudu, Rashid Motem, and Haruna Salihi. Ibadan: Spectrum Books Limited, 1993.

Yúsúf, Bilikisu. "Da'wa and Contemporary Challenges Facing Muslim Women in Secular States—A Nigerian Case Study." In *Islam in Africa: Proceedings of the Islam in Africa Conference*. Edited by Nura Alkali, Adamu Adamu, Awwal Yadudu, Rashid Motem, and Haruna Salihi. Ibadan: Spectrum Books Limited, 1993.

Afterword

A Childhood Muslim Education

Barakah, Identity, and the Roots of Change

PREFACE

The material contained in this section is a portrait of the world of the Qur'án school as seen from within, focusing on the teacher and the community, and on a child's view of that world. The Qur'án school exists to give unrivalled preeminence to the word of God; it demonstrates the authority of the word, its scope in the education process, its role in the lives of individuals and society, and its future under Western secular pressure. Such a central place for the Qur'án school sets it squarely on the front line of the encounter with the West. Can the Qur'án school perform two different functions: keeping society in touch with its religious roots, and being open to change? Can received identity survive in modernity? Is education for religious virtue, what is described here as *barakah*, compatible with education for skills? Is competition reconcilable with community? Can a child at Qur'án school learn about moral truth and combine that at a Western school with education as objective science that is morally neutral and ethically agnostic?

Education has defined the terms of Muslim self-understanding, and making provision for it has been a priority of the first order. Education is not just a professional activity, something reserved for qualified professionals trained in dispensing factual information. On the contrary, education is a religious duty, demanded of Muslims for the purpose of fulfilling their religious obligations. Thus religion and learning are joined together in the Muslim tradition. It is worth citing here the famous dictum of al-Ghazálí (1056-1111): "I sought knowledge without God, but God forbade it that knowledge should be without Him" (*'utlibu-l- 'ilm min dúni -lláh fa abá Alláhu 'an yakúnu li-khayrihi*).

Ibn Khaldun concurs. Writing in 1377 in his *Muqaddimah*,[1] he cites accepted custom as giving "preference to the teaching of the Qur'án. The reason is the

---

[1] Ibn Khaldún, *Al-Muqaddimah: An Introduction to History*, 3 vols., tran. Franz Rosenthal (Princeton: Princeton University Press, 1968), III:304ff.

146

desire for the blessing and reward (in the other world resulting from knowledge of the Qur'án) and a fear of the things that might affect children in 'the folly of youth' and harm them and keep them from acquiring knowledge." Ibn Khaldún recognizes that a few authorities differ from this approach to education, one of them, for instance, urging that education begin with poetry as "the archive of the Arabs," but says that is a minority view. He continues, saying that children put on that kind of syllabus "might miss the chance to learn the Qur'án. As long as they remain at home, they are amenable to authority. When they have grown up and shaken off the yoke of authority, the tempests of young manhood often cast them upon the shores of wrongdoing. Therefore, while the children are still at home and under the yoke of authority, one seizes the opportunity to teach them the Qur'án, so that they will not remain without a knowledge of it."

The modern West rejects such fusing of religion and learning. The West does not view knowledge as accountability to the past but rather as individual entitlement. Milton's formula is the opposite of al-Ghazálí's, to the effect that the goal of learning is to repair the ruins wrought by our forebears and to create for ourselves the right conditions for our improvement and progress, in effect "to be like God" (*Of Education*). Modern attitudes to education as individual entitlement are in continuity with that sentiment whose force continues with the idea of education as the unfettered search for truth and the rolling back of the frontiers of ignorance. The quest for truth is regarded as the greatest safeguard against bigotry, intolerance, repression, and conformity. As Milton puts it in a famous passage, "Though all the winds of doctrine were let loose to play upon the earth, so Truth be in the field, we do injuriously by licensing and prohibiting to misdoubt her strength. Let her and Falsehood grapple; whoever knew Truth put to the worse, in a free and open encounter?" Thomas Jefferson (1743-1826), a great educator himself, echoed Milton when he said that truth "is great and will prevail if left to herself, that she is the proper and sufficient antagonist to error, and has nothing to fear from the conflict, unless by human interposition disarmed of her natural weapons, free argument and debate, errors ceasing to be dangerous when it is permitted freely to contradict them."[2] Committed to this understanding of education, the West in its historical encounter with Muslim society was determined to cut asunder the venerable cord of religion and learning that Allah has knit. Muslims would resist.

To shift to another level, the pedagogic style of the Qur'án school sets it apart from the Western school. The Qur'án school promotes knowledge as rote memorization and the correct pronunciation and articulation of the word; the Western school, by contrast, requires comprehension and understanding. Also, the Qur'án school prescribes the word of God to preserve the soul for divine happiness, while the Western school offers skills for future employment; material success is its goal, not eternal life. While the Western school makes the development of the child its focus, with classes graded according to age, the Qur'án school seeks to impose an established canon and to discourage innovation and originality, lest

---

[2] Adrienne Koch and William Peden, eds., *The Life and Selected Writings of Thomas Jefferson* (New York: The Modern Library, Random House, 1993), p. 290.

heresy slip in. In pursuit of that goal, the Qur'án school repudiates the child's mother tongue as a suitable vehicle for instruction, and instead lays emphasis on learning the sound, tones, and accents of the sacred Arabic of the Qur'án. Merit and virtue are its proffered fruit, not the award of diplomas as license for employment.

We may expect that, faced with the economic power of Western schools, which are backed with the authority and prestige of the state, the Qur'án school would weaken and in time disappear, yet this has not happened. In its age-old functions, the Qur'án school, far from becoming a historical relic, has survived many centuries of practice. More recently it has also survived a relentless onslaught from a hostile, uncomprehending West, able to continue its tradition of uniting religion and learning and placing God at the center of it.

As described here, the Qur'án school is not a forum for interfaith encounter, for it belongs structurally with the shaping and directing of Muslim life, too much so to fall naturally into a stage in interfaith relations. That is why it is tucked into the far corner of this book in an Afterword as a safeguard against ecumenical pretensions. It is thus offered to the reader with that *caveat emptor*, to be skipped should the reader so choose. Yet, because the Qur'án school is central to the faith and social formation of Muslims, and because it conditions their religious psychology, it seems justified to include it here as an opportunity at least for intercultural eavesdropping. It is material, therefore, of a special kind, not demanding agreement or approval from the reader but a willingness to listen, and perhaps to learn. At a minimum, this material may offer insight into the Muslim understanding of the Qur'án as the word of God and so may avert potential misunderstanding with Westerners for whom the phrase "word of God" has little of the Muslim sense. And wherever we can reduce the risk of mutual misunderstanding we can to the same extent advance the greater cause of interfaith understanding. So let that stand as the excuse. The piece asserts no claim on ecumenical priorities.

HISTORICAL BACKGROUND

The Gambia, where the following story took place, was a British colony until February 1965, when it gained independence. As a political entity its roots go back to the medieval empire of Mali, of which it formed the extreme western point. Records attesting to its history reach much further back, in fact as far back as 500 B.C. when Hanno the Carthaginian sailed down the west coast and left observations on the country and its culture. There is a tradition, for example, that the Greeks first saw in Senegambia the instrument, totally new to them, to which they gave the name *xylophone*. The name simply means "wooden instrument," which is what the *balafon*, the indigenous name, is in that part of West Africa. It is constructed without any metal parts. The French scholar Raymond Mauny, in his work *Tableau Geographique*, proposes a bold, novel hypothesis of sailors from the Senegambian/Mauritanian coast crossing the Atlantic centuries before Columbus and his crew. In any case, all of that is by way of making the point that the Senegambia region is full of history, which is preserved in documentary, archaeological, and oral forms. A good deal of it is enacted in local musical traditions in which the *balafon* features prominently.

The country was named after the river, which was the most navigable waterway in premodern Africa. A ship drawing fifteen feet of water could sail over one hundred and fifty miles inland. At the headwaters of the river are soils rich in gold, which made its way down the river to European trading ships. Coffee, ebony, hides, wax, ivory, and spices were also brought down the river, which thus became an essential artery of the regional economic trade. The major point from which trade might be controlled was James Fort, built on an island in the estuary, twenty miles from the sea, and described in one source as "a slab of friable rock which scarcely projects above the river at high tide."

James Fort was originally built by Baltic Germans who were servants of the Duke of Courland in Latvia. The fort was constructed on an island purchased from the local chief and changed hands several times before the English acquired it in 1661, renaming it after James II. The English abandoned the fort in 1709, then returned through the Royal African Company in 1713. In 1715 a Welsh pirate captured the fort only for the Company to reoccupy it in 1721. In 1725 the powder kegs in the storeroom accidentally exploded, killing eleven of the nineteen Europeans and doing considerable damage to the buildings. Repairs restored the fort to some semblance of life, until its final destruction in 1778 by the French. Though the English succeeded in retaking it and expelling the French, the fort was allowed to languish in its dilapidated state, and henceforth it sank into the country's marine psyche as a biodegradable relic.

The river once teemed with marine life, and it is still one of the world's best bird sanctuaries, with over 450 different species. The country is famous for its beef and cattle, and there is also abundant seafood, including shellfish. The cash crop is groundnuts, farmed by the men; rice, which is produced by the women, is the staple food. The Gambia has sixteen languages, two main seasons, wet and dry, with a cool spell between October and March, called the Harmattan, after the northwest trade winds that sweep from the Himalayas and across the Sahara, blowing fine desert dust right up to the western rim of the Atlantic, and thus feeding into the ocean currents which arch off the African continental shelf.

With a population of just over a million and few natural resources, the country has been bypassed by modern communication routes and consigned to the cosmopolitan backwaters. But historically the Gambia had been at the crossroads of attempts to open up Africa, an indispensable coordinate in geographical knowledge and exploration of the continent. The river brought the traveler virtually to the doorstep of the great trans-Saharan routes that dissected and linked the grain and gold-producing regions of the area. Today, however, the country languishes in relative obscurity, protected from the glare of exploitative world attention, and mostly free from internal upheaval. However, in July 1994 a group of junior army officers in their twenties seized power in a bloodless coup d'état, with first reports speaking of no general disturbance, only a minor, brief traffic jam a few miles from the capital. The president and his family fled to a visiting U.S. frigate berthed in the harbor, to take sanctuary first in neighboring Senegal and eventually in London. The president had ruled for over thirty years with few accomplishments to his name. After the coup there was an abortive counter-coup. Discussions aimed at returning the country to democratic civilian rule have so far stalled, and all local political activity has remained suppressed. Lacking the reflex of political excitement, the country seems to have returned to its customary sluggishness.

In that soporific state the Gambia has resisted attempts to yank it into the mainstream of world events, either into the primeval eddy of militant *jihád* or into the path of aggressive missionary endeavor. Its predominantly Muslim population follows the orders of the Prophet with mild disposition and gentle means, which fosters amicable relations with its Pagan and minority Christian neighbors. The Christian population is formed from a nucleus of freed slaves or recaptive Africans with some conversion occurring among the autochthones, those leaderless populations that Islamic orthodoxy has for the most part ignored or annexed as tributaries. Right from the heyday of colonial rule, Christians have settled into the easygoing ways of the population, offered education to the largely Muslim population without expecting or wanting converts among their pupils, as if instinctively surrendering the policy of active evangelization in return for the Muslim rejection of *jihád*. The two traditions of a pacifist Islam and an accommodating Christianity have created an ethos of religious and political moderation which has fitted in well with the country's pluralist makeup. The Gambia is probably the first and only Muslim country in the world that has observed as national holidays Christian feasts such as Good Friday and the Feast of the Assumption of the Blessed Virgin.

Georgetown, the district headquarters of the local colonial administration, is the birthplace of the present writer's mother. It is an island about 170 miles from the mouth of the river. It had been a Portuguese slave fort until centuries later when the district commissioner made his home there, as did the chief. The government established a secondary boarding school in the town in 1927 for the sons of chiefs and instituted a stiff Islamic religious regime to persuade otherwise reluctant Muslim parents to send their children there. The Methodist mission opened a primary school, but it was maintained by the local district council. A Creole schoolmaster and his wife were in charge. The school was effectively shunned by local Muslim parents until a colonial education officer, a maverick Irishman, went on a campaign to persuade town elders to support the school with assurances of government backing and exaggerated promises of riches. He would follow the women to their farms and tell them in his sanitized Mandinka that if they sent their children to school they would be able to retire from their drudgery with the income of their educated offspring. My mother, for one, heard the message and allowed me to enroll later in the school after several years of attending the Qur'án school. Briefly, then, that is the background to the present account and makes me recall the famous words of Samuel Johnson (1709-1784):

> The rod produces an effect which terminates in itself. A child is afraid of being whipped, and gets his task, and there's an end on't; whereas, by exciting emulation and comparisons of superiority, you lay the foundation of lasting mischief; you make brothers and sisters hate each other.

Muslim children from about the age of four are enrolled in Qur'án school where they learn by rote verses from the Holy Book. The school is important as a social experience for children. They study the word and learn to interact among themselves and with others, watching each other progress through the school, forming friendships, resolving disagreements, and learning to test and trust each other. But most important in the lives of the children at this stage is the figure of the teacher, a figure of authority, knowledge, and assurance. In his hands rest the security of the children in this life and their welfare in the next. The teacher will not let them forget that.

In the case of my own experience in Qur'án school, it was important as a primary rule of survival for us children to establish rapport with the teacher, so we would observe him closely. We saw an adult who looked very different from those who told favorite children's stories. This teacher was a lanky, middle-aged man with a dark mark in the middle of his forehead, a sign that he had said his prayers regularly. He wore a thin white gown called an *abayah* and a white skull cap. He constantly worked at his teeth with a piece of chewing stick, which gave him a slightly impatient and clumsy appearance. When the chewing stick was at the back of his mouth at the molars, for example, and he was about to say something, he twitched his eyes wildly, his cheek puffing impatiently. Then he moved his hand forward, sucked the saliva from the chewing stick, spat it out, cleared his throat, and said what he had to say. As soon as someone started to reply, he went back to his teeth, repeating the process while he listened. He seldom looked anyone in the eye. When his hands were observed, the firmness of the muscles seemed to indicate a firmness with children. The signs did not look good. The hands flicked about a lot, with the haste and energy that implied he would not suffer fools, or, for that matter, children gladly. We concluded that we did not like him very much but we were afraid of him and did not try to cross him. We sometimes gave him a nickname, such as Mount because of his sinewy limbs, or Giraffe on account of his elevated head. But perish the thought of his ever discovering that we had done so! We wondered if he knew how closely observed he was.

THE TEACHER

The parents imposed on their children a duty which tied them to the teacher in an authoritative way. To earn *barakah*, they said the children should call him "Teacher." *Barakah* was virtue that could be attached to a person or removed; it assured blessing and success in life. The Qur'án school was a source for *barakah*, with Teacher its sole agent. The short distance children traveled from home to the school gave no indication of the great symbolic distance they were traveling to be for the first time under the control and direction of the *barakah* of Teacher, whom they held in respect bordering on fear. Teacher's habit of theatrically clearing his throat became in time an overhanging threat, a sign that he was about to descend on the children without mercy. No doubt the children's disposition to distrust him exaggerated his intentions, but experience would teach that we took the man for granted at our peril. For his part Teacher came to regard deference to him as confirmation of his view that his students were now beholden only to his personal *barakah*, which was his to give or withhold. Indeed this was conceded to him many times when nervous parents asked him, indeed begged him, to mend their wayward children, often with the cane and sometimes with physical labor, so that they would earn his *barakah*. It was widely assumed, or widely feared, that one such as the Qur'án school teacher, who had such an intimate knowledge of the Qur'án and of the divine language, Arabic, had a particularly powerful *barakah* at his disposal, and it was this which led many parents to entrust their children to him. In the past we had watched children being formally handed over to Teacher. Now it was our turn.

The ceremonies over the induction into the Qur'án school were quickly done, partly because Teacher was a highly practical man who had little time for preambles and partly because parents did not like public displays of any kind. Then followed the serious business which was to engage Teacher for all our childhood life, that of instructing children in the Arabic Qur'án.

In our particular example, our teacher (we could not get away from the possessive pronoun) did not pretend to us that this was an easy matter. The lessons started with the alphabet, which began with the *alif,* a sort of upright dagger, and with that we pierced the sacred veil of the mysteries of the divine language. The bilabials and the hard consonants presented little difficulty. Letters with similar pronunciations, however, became mixed up. For example, the *ha,* with a softer sound, was not differentiated from *ha,* with a more assertive thrust behind it. Only in writing did we distinguish between the two. Similarly, and even more unpardonably, the 'ayn and the *ghain* suffered from a tendency to bring everything down to one level. *Ghain* was difficult. In sound it was like another letter, the *qáf.* But since there was yet another consonant, the *káf,* we went further with simplification by watering down the *ghain* until it became an indefinite and indistinct *gkain.* With elisions we committed offenses so abominable it would be kinder not to say a word.

As soon as we were able to press ahead to the twenty-eighth and last letter, the *ya,* we were ready to begin spelling single words. Knowledge of the alphabet was a great asset. With it we plunged into the mysteries of divine revelation. The *fátihah,* the opening chapter of the Qur'án, was the first we memorized. We memorized the recurrent formula: "In the name of God . . . " which comes, with one exception, at the beginning of every *súrah* or chapter of the Qur'án. Then the *fátihah* proper, which opens with the words "Praise be to God, the Lord of the worlds" and ends with "Guide us on the straight path . . . the path of those who go not astray." Finally we said "Amen." Thanks to the bliss of rote learning, we thought the "Amen" was simply part of the whole piece rather than being what it patently is, a response coming at the end of a prayer. Thus we rushed to the end of the *fátihah* with a resounding "Amen" as a sort of great personal triumph. With it we slammed the door on ignorant humanity and felt jubilant.

But the *fátihah* means what it says; it is simply an opening, a significant step forward, yes, but still only a beginning. By the standards of the school it was a very small beginning at that. We had to press ahead. New boys had a period of grace in which no bad marks were recorded against them until they had learned to settle into the school. So at the beginning they were inviolate. But, thanks to

Teacher's proclivity for quick and practical answers, that period was very short indeed. Consequently, slamming the door on ignorant humanity with the *fátihah* was a hasty reaction.

A few weeks later, Teacher (the possessive became understood, and in its place "Teacher" stood alone, the symbol of a monopoly title to *barakah*) pulled us one by one by the ear. His voice, charged with *barakah*, trembled as he cleared his throat. He reprimanded a number of big boys and then proceeded to impose an atmosphere of defeat over the entire school. He pulled out a scruffy little piece of paper and began to call roll. A few boys were absent, and Teacher jotted down their names in his black book. When he called a boy's name and there was no answer, he would hum to himself as if evoking a lost tune, and with an expression of impatience on his pale face he would wet the point of his reed pen with his tongue and scrawl a few characters into his black book. Then he would clear his throat and emit a long stream of saliva, which he always managed to direct whichever way he wanted with masterly precision. After the roll call, the chief end of which had been to find out not who was present but who was absent, Teacher started to assign new tasks and redefine old ones. He operated a kind of merit system, and rewarded the faithful with appropriate favors, from being in charge of the overall running of the school, with powers to punish and correct, to being relieved from carrying out some of the more strenuous school duties. Conversely, he meted out punishment on a sliding scale depending on the seriousness of the offense. To his special favorites there were unexpected bonuses such as entrusting new recruits to them. On this particular day it turned out that some senior boys had won his special favor and were therefore rewarded with the privilege of supervising those of us who were new to the school. Children would soon learn this was more theory than fact, for Teacher still continued to exercise supreme control. Perhaps his assigning us to some of the senior boys was his way of sealing the stamp of defeat he had already riveted on the entire school.

For Teacher, power and *barakah* belonged together, and that was why discipline and vigilance were necessary. His task was to lead and educate, and that was what power was about. In fact, his bamboo cane was the symbol of the school. Without the cane the gathered children would be a mere herd, good for the wild but scarcely for the garden of learning. Spare the rod and spoil the child was his rule. Teacher valued the cane for that reason, and carried it, often across his shoulder, as a professional emblem. With it he would point to a word on the slate and tap it several times next to the child's right index finger, indicating that it was not being correctly pronounced. And then as punishment, he would smack the finger still stuck on the offending word. The child was not allowed to pull away his hand when the cane was beside it, or on it, as Teacher preferred. In that position, Teacher was free to spike it.

PUPILS

The senior boys assumed their functions as watchdogs of *barakah*. When they allotted new work they expected their subordinates to be prompt in discharging their duty and the result to be impeccable, and they therefore squeezed us hard. After all, Teacher had set them up as noncommissioned vigilantes of virtue, not from any accomplishment but from a pecking order.

Among the rest of the boys certain rules on bravery and cowardice were in force. To be weak or timid was considered a bad thing, whereas to be known to be brave or strong was a noble thing. There was one incident I vividly remember where this crucial distinction was made. In the early afternoon we children usually went to the nearby bush to gather a few twigs and sticks, which we brought back to the school to use as fuel in the evenings when we had lessons. This was a very important aspect of school life; good and brave boys fetched extra loads of firewood of good burning quality. To guard against lazy boys benefiting from a lucky find—such as stumbling on a neat pile a farmer might have gathered on the boundary with another farm (farms otherwise had no fences)—Teacher looked for a consistent track record. This maintained a high level of performance while keeping pressure on the laggards among us.

Going to the bush to fetch the evening supply of fuel involved the risk that one or another of the boys would attempt to settle old scores or make humiliating demands. In the bush old loyalties were reawakened and alternative alliances formed across official Qur'án school lines. Boys broke up the old formations and formed new ones according to their age groups, their common affiliation to an initiation rite like the circumcision ritual, their common tribe or ethnic unit, the closeness of their family connection, blood-ties (brothers of the same mother hardly ever found themselves on opposite sides, although half-brothers of the same father sometimes did), or even according to their common interests in games and other forms of play. Thus in addition to public rules of compliance there was another set of complex rules sustained by jealousies and vigilant sensibilities. That made going to the bush a hazardous business.

Late one afternoon, after we had collected the evening supply of fuel, we brought the bundles to a central place where we all usually gathered before making our way back to the school. While we were sitting near our bundles a sudden silence fell. The boy who broke it turned out to be the chief protagonist in a quarrel with another boy. His opponent also made a challenging stir, and before long they were asking each other aggressive questions which neither of them stopped to answer. Their language grew more belligerent, and as the stakes rose they used fierce and uncompromising words. The verbal violence escalated to such an extent that when their bodies touched it sparked the final confrontation. They flung each other about, stamped, kicked, and wrapped their long wiry legs around each other in the style of traditional wrestlers. In the dust which they raised it was hard to say who was gaining the upper hand. Some of the other boys were cheering, not so much one side against another, but the fight itself. One of the big boys was circling the fighters, clapping his hands and encouraging them. He would have been disappointed had the two contestants stopped suddenly, for he was committed with the intensity of a participant, with as much of his own honor at stake as that of the two pugilists. Flaunting the matador's banner seemed much more appropriate to his character than playing the role of peacemaker. From spurring on the fighters he turned to organizing us. He asked us all to sit around in a circle. After the contest was over, he had us all swear an oath of secrecy.

The fight was a draw. Neither of the contestants gave in, and the inciter was satisfied that he had been amply rewarded for his exertions. Some of the younger boys felt very intimidated and frightened, but they would feel better as time went on. There were a few bloodstains on the collars of the fighters, and these were quickly attended to by the inciter, who washed them off at a nearby pond, so there were no telltale signs. The fight reinforced the high value put on bravery and strength, and it delineated more sharply the division between the strong and the weak. A new alliance was forged between the two fighters, who had until then represented rival factions. Teacher might have been a very knowledgeable man, but here was a whole world about which he knew little. What he did know was siphoned off from boys under direct pressure from him but who were under even heavier pressure from the other boys not to spill or by some chance remark alert him. Sometimes he reacted by ignoring such an incident; at other times he followed the clues with scientific thoroughness. If he failed to get to the bottom of the affair, he inflicted heavy punishment on us all, as if we were a subspecies that could be extinguished at his hands.

This bush fight turned out to be one of those incidents that Teacher followed up with relentless energy. He had caught wind of it, and the parents of the boys concerned had taken up the matter with the chief. Teacher's reputation was at stake. This, plus the fact that he was in danger of appearing ignorant of a whole way of life right under his own nose, strengthened his resolve. One Friday morning, before we adjourned school to prepare for the Friday congregation prayer, he summoned us into his presence and demanded an explanation. He first revealed that he knew the entire story, but that he would give us a chance to tell it ourselves, such being the implicit honor code he instituted in the school. If not, we would be admitting guilt in a collective way and then it was up to him to decide what should be done. A unanimous silence fell. This did not please him. He picked up one small boy, who, crushed between Teacher's direct pressure and the hidden but no less powerful counter-pressure of the other boys, staggered to his feet and made as if to run away. He fell down near the entrance. Teacher perhaps thought this was an act of unsolicited surrender, but any illusions he might have had on that score were dispelled by the lad blubbering and bursting into tears. Teacher had him dragged away.

It was a rule with Teacher that when he was going to cane a child he halted abruptly and then rocked slightly from side to side before steadying himself. He looked the consummate professional, born to his craft. Beating children was for him something of a sacramental duty: he formulated the pious intention and had it silently declared, his hands gathered as if in supplication to God and his teeth clenched to signify unflinching resolve in undertaking and completing the Lord's business. The tyranny of the cane must stand between the unregenerate anarchy of misbehaved children and their imperiled destiny before the Creator. Indeed, everywhere tyranny is better than anarchy, as the masters tell us. There was one doctrine to which he consistently adhered: children were what he called God's sun-baked mud bricks, made of unregenerate mud, extremely fragile, and needing recasting and remodeling. He caned them at the same time as he cleared his throat, giving a loud yell as if prodding a donkey, and ended the ritual by reminding them that as God's mud bricks they needed all the thrashings they could get. As long as this need was there, he was happy to oblige.

That Friday morning Teacher confirmed the notion children were, without exception, God's mud bricks. These bricks were clearly uneven in quality; some were made of sterner stuff than others. If there was any credit to be claimed for these, it was because he, Teacher, had worked hard to get them transferred from his black book to his roll of honor. Essential to that slow process was the cane, judiciously wielded and selectively applied. In the case of students of unequal talent, the cane was again unquestionably valuable. It raised morale and brought about a leveling process in which the slow were made to catch up with the not-so-slow. Teacher struck several blows before anyone screamed. Presently, however, some of the little ones started screaming and yelling. Then the general confusion died down to a long and monotonous sob, with an odd voice or two rising above the rest. It was difficult to say which was more gibberish, little boys crying after being flogged or shouting their chants in an incomprehensible foreign language like Arabic. No doubt Teacher would have said that the divine language, no matter how badly chanted, had superior merits. The sobs of the children were just the sound of inferior bricks snapping.

The floggings did not make canaries out of the children, and, if anything, it stoked the flame of resistance. This was a delicate matter. Teacher went apoplectic with any hint among the children of anarchy, the riotous condition, for in his view such a condition was akin to bad manners. Resistance, however, he considered more rationally; it was evidence of native fiber and could, when reclaimed and directed, be the opportunity for personal improvement.

The matter of the bush fight and its consequences at school went beyond all previous bounds. The parents of the children heard about it. Our fathers did not react immediately. It was the mothers who started to get worried. They began to imagine the worst possible things that could happen among their children in the bush and gave them advice about choosing friends. The mothers let off steam with occasional and scattered vents of anxiety. They were like a thatched roof over a kitchen out of which smoke filtered in short, small puffs rather than the entire roof going up from suppressed force. By the time they had got round to another one of their bursts of warnings the children had gone off. Toward evening they all drifted toward the school in preparation for the evening recitations.

BONFIRE

Reciting the Qur'án by the light of the bonfires was the highlight of everyday life at the school, a time when everybody, including the smaller boys, came together to recite the portions of the Qur'án they had copied to their slates earlier in the day. Abler students who had memorized their scripts often went through the evening exercise with flying colors. Slower students had a more difficult time of it, struggling with old scripts of a day or two previous. Teacher hovered menac- ingly over the slow students, ignoring completely their successful colleagues. Those who had little, he felt, should have even that little taken away, such being the logic of the higher wisdom. The bonfires, however, were a collective indul- gence. Teacher would have us believe that our fire was different from heathen fires. The heathens, he said, treat fire as an object of worship, their egos absorbed in its rage as they fret distractedly after salvation and immortality rather than being tamed with the word from high. It is hard to tell how much Teacher was subliminally influenced by fire rituals prevalent in much of non-Muslim Africa, and if in his reaction he was deflecting attention from his own pre-Islamic roots in the culture. For example, his own non-Muslim Fulbé cousins practiced fire-eat- ing—putting a bundle of loose, smoking straw into their mouths, then blowing and puffing to fan the flames and removing the bundle as it blazed, with the audi- ence bursting out with loud applause. We as children attended many of these fire rituals, which were staged in defiant proximity to the Qur'án school.

At any rate, Teacher spoke derogatorily of heathen fires that blazed and babbled as short-lived spectacles, the tongues of flame leaping in vain to reach the sky above only for their brief upward darts to be quenched in the trackless void. Hea- then fires presume to bring God down to our level, while the Qur'án school fire pointed us to the exalted truth above. The school's fire thus retained an abiding luminous merit at its heart even after the sparks had subsided, as was appropriate to its role in assisting human beings take custody of the word of God. We were not allowed to stare into the fire or to be silent before it lest, being at the center, the fire should incite us to mute heathen introspection, consuming us in its brief glare and then abandoning us to the darkness beyond.

Yet the school made a concession to the fire's obvious centrality in the children's education, and Teacher did this by infusing into the nightly practice elements of ethical teaching and orthodox assurance. He said that at the Last Day, when all the souls were assembled before the judgment throne of God, the flames of the Qur'án school would rise before God as witness to plead for mercy and forgiveness. He said that on the strength of that plea God would wipe out the sins of children, increase their merit, and count to their benefit all the good works they had done on earth. The flames would also bear witness to the number of times the children had attended the evening recitations, and God would multiply all their good works by that number. He said even friends and relatives who were in mortal danger of hellfire would find that the approaching flames of punishment would be turned away by the merciful flames of the Qur'án school. Teacher said—and the children found all this very impressive teaching—that God would never let any of God's faithful creatures suffer punishment by fire when these same creatures had stud- ied the divine revelation by the bonfires of the Qur'án school, nor would God let them toil in the heat of ultimate loss after they had toiled in the heat of the noon- day sun, gathering firewood for the Qur'án school. He said that just as some of the boys were unstinting in the way they went in search of fuel for the school, so God would be unstinting in collecting good marks for them and would raise their rank in Paradise. The entire school gave Teacher its complete and total attention whenever he waxed strong on this theme. Any discussion about the ultimate judgment and God's providence always received the undivided attention of the school, partly because it was widely believed, and feared, that Teacher was the only man qualified to say anything authoritative about it, and partly because many children had dreams about death and the judgment which puzzled them. They were pleased that someone could explain some of their secret questions.

It was therefore important who Teacher chose as head boy for the evening recitations, often a favorite who was well versed in his scripts and generally ahead of the rest of the school. The children referred to him as the fireman, though Teacher would have given him a less mundane title, such as night angel or companion of the commander of the word. His job was to make sure that there was enough fuel to keep up a constant blaze in order to enable the children to recite their scripts reasonably well. Sometimes the fireman would forget to bring more firewood. Having mastered his own script, he forgot that the rest of the children still needed illumination. Teacher might be somewhere in his house or have his back turned to the children, but he would notice immediately if they were not reciting their scripts properly. He would give one of his characteristic signals, like clearing his throat or flapping his baggy trousers with the cane, and that was enough to send the children scurrying to their slates. The fireman would hasten to place a handful of sticks on the fire. As these burned he would grab a few heavier pieces of wood and toss them in as well. He was overreacting, attempting to dispel any suggestion of tardiness, though he would be equally unwise to spend all the fuel in one blind moment of enthusiasm. It would be quite a time before the fire needed restoking.

SCHOOL

The Qur'án school was something like a moveable feast, taking up residence wherever there was need and demand. Of course certain rules of collective decision making were followed to establish it. The particular school described here was "called" by a leading head of family whose many wives and other women relatives of the the extended family household had produced and were producing large numbers of children. Such a school could be supported from the labor the children would provide on the farms. The men would produce the millet and sorghum, and the women rice and vegetables, with well-wishers contributing cash and other gifts. To have many children was considered a blessing, but to have them learn the Qur'án was even more blessed, for the special *barakah* of it would rub off on the entire community. Children made Qur'án schools, but it is far truer that Qur'án schools made children, and made them into the image of God's word. You might know a Muslim community by its many mosques, but you could not make a Muslim community except by Qur'án schools. The brighter the bonfires of learning, the sturdier the rod that marshals the children, we could hear Teacher say, the greater the community's aggregate *barakah*, as if the Prophet had said, "by the fire and the rod you shall receive *barakah*."

A word is necessary about the stages of learning through which Teacher himself went. As a Fula, Teacher had had the education Muslim Fulbé gave their children. There are four main stages in that system: *jangugol*, reading; *windugol*, writing; *firugol*, vernacular exegesis; *fennu* (Arabic *funún*), higher studies. Reading is a laborious process consisting of singling out and chanting the separate words of the *fátihah*, then picking through the first rubric division of the Qur'án (*hizb*, pl. *azháb*) (súrahs 94 to 104 in reverse order), then the student returns to the *fátihah* for pronunciation and covers the same rubric division. Then follows a third going over when the *fátihah* is studied for proper reading and enunciation, what the Fulbé call *rindingol* or *fineditugol*. By this stage *windugol*, writing, has commenced and is pursued concurrently.

Special in this system was the use of the Fula language in oral exposition and rhetorical training. This allowed the language in time to be fixed with the transcribed conventions and conceits of literary Arabic as the masters employed it in theological argumentation, rhetorical demonstration, oral ornamentation, and didactic guidance. In effect, Fula was transformed into a tool of scholastic practice, a halfway house between the penalty of primitive stigma and the merits of revealed truth. The religious use of the language excited Fulbé ethnic consciousness, with religion often providing the channels that guided political expression and shaped social identity. Even non-Muslim Fulbé found they needed the linguistic materials developed in religious work, leaving these ethnic Fulbé only one step short of conversion to Islam. In one historical example, it needed only the presence of a Christian medical mission among non-Muslim Fulbé to bring about indirectly the conversion of the whole community. Muslim Fula and Mandinka clerics came periodically to the clinic for medical attention, and while undergoing treatment they stayed for weeks at a time with their non-Muslim Fulbé compatriots, propagating Islam. By the time they finished treatment, they had converted the entire village to Islam, thanks to the Christian missionaries who opened a path for them![3] However, two centuries of active Islamic preparation had sowed the seeds for this otherwise sudden flowering, and Teacher was the seasoned fruit of that long and deep preparation.

To return to the Qur'án school now placed under his absolute authority, there were certain occasions when it and the general town community joined together in the religious performances. One such occasion was the all-night chanting on Islamic feast days. As far as we could remember, Teacher did not attend these occasions, but he let his students go. It was the other Muslim community leaders who took charge, usually by volunteering to give their time and services. The Qur'án school had its own sessions of all-night religious vigils, but they were not very popular, largely because they were no change from the normal routine of Qur'án school life; vigils in the community, however, took place outside the school and without the presence of Teacher. Later some local Tijání[4] leaders became closely identified with organizing all-night vigils, and this virtually completed

---

[3] John Spencer Trimingham, *Islam in West Africa* (Oxford: Clarendon Press, 1959), 38.

[4] Members of the Tijániyya, a *Súfí* order founded in the eighteenth century by Ahmad al-Tijání. The order is widespread and popular throughout the Muslim areas of West Africa.

Teacher's exclusion, because he was a staunch Qádirí[5] and would not be seen consorting openly with his Tijání arch-rivals. In Teacher's view the Tijání clerics were the Cherubim who looked to their hearts for loving God, and the Qádirí clerics were the Seraphim who attended to their heads for knowing God's ways. As a consequence, the Tijání people flirted with demagoguery while the Qádirí people sought after virtue in knowledge and understanding. These fine doctrinal points were sharpened by the unstated though no less real subject of ethnic sensibilities. Teacher was a Fula, originally from Futa Jallon in Guinea, while the men who led the Tijání vigils were Wolof from neighboring Senegal. The two peoples rarely socialized together. The Wolof Tijánís were too populist for Teacher, who as an affiliate of the stringent Qádiriyáh confraternity had too high-minded a view of the word of God to trust the crowds with it. Crowds want regulation not speculation, confinement not exposure. For that reason the Tijánís were a public hazard and a religious nuisance, though to answer them would play into their hands.

His scruples notwithstanding, the vigils continued, organized by compound heads. A large open courtyard at the town center was the setting. A canvas tent was erected on bamboo poles and rhun palms. The community leaders sat in an inner ring, and around them sat other community elders, counselors, advanced Qur'án students, and so on to the periphery, where the women sat. A small wooden table was placed in the middle, and on it were offerings of kola nuts, candles, and other things. A small kerosene lamp glowed. The Muslim leaders who organized the vigil sat around the table, dressed in thin white robes and wearing white skull caps. In front of them were copies of the Qur'án and a few religious texts, such as eulogies on the Prophet (*Madíh*), accounts of his life and the lives of his Companions (*Síra*). The chanting was interrupted by brief homilies and selected recitations from well-known religious works. Sometimes prose passages, after being read out in the original Arabic, were translated into the vernacular, but verse was not translated, presumably for fear of losing the poetic effect.

The chanting was also interrupted to serve refreshments. Just like the other aspects of the vigil, these interruptions were informal. We did not serve any refreshments if people were chanting or listening to a recitation. Many of the chants were not written down but recited from memory. A man would begin with a short familiar chorus, and after this been well-received he would follow it up with a long impressive solo performance. Then the company would recite in unison. After this would come refreshments. It was here that some of us lads became useful. The candles and the kola nuts were beyond reach, but we were given charge of distributing biscuits, bringing in buckets of tea, and passing round the tin mugs. We distributed the tea from tall metal jugs. After people had refreshments, they resumed the religious exercises while we collected the mugs to wash them up. Refreshing the saints required the performance of less elevated chores!

---

[5] Member of the Qádiriyya, a *Súfí* order founded in the twelfth century by ʿAbd al-Qádir al Jílání. This sect, too, is widespread throughout West Africa. Some rivalry exists between its adherents and those of the Tijániyya, which finds expression in West African politics as well as in religious attitudes.

History came alive during the vigils. Scenes representing Muslim armies engaged in battle were recalled. Many chants celebrated the bravery of Muslim generals and the miraculous victories of hard-pressed Muslim armies. Moving scenes involving the conversion of hitherto implacable enemies of the faith, such as certain Quraysh leaders, were evoked, and the growing strength of Islam in its early days was vividly brought out. The vigils ended with the Prophet ascending and appearing before God (the *mi'ráj*), confessing his unworthiness but pleading on behalf of his followers. God granted his intercession, and so Muslims throughout the world were bound together in a community of mutual intercession. That was the extent of the freedom even Tijání adepts would allow to religious credulity. Although in the vigil a *muríd* devotee might appeal to a personal saint, the crowd was never publicly invited to seek saintly intercession or even to invoke the permanent patronage of the founder, Shaykh Ahmad al-Tijání himself, notions alien to the form of rigorist Máliki Islam the community had received. A vivid example was the rigorist teaching that following the fortieth day after death, the soul of the deceased lapsed permanently, having no further contact with the living. The Tijání masters would have liked to ameliorate such teachings and to introduce ideas that were in provocative contrast to Teacher's attitude of stringent adherence to the unembellished facts of law and injunction.

At the dawn prayer, the vigil broke up and the Cherubim took flight. The dawn prayer, a ritual obligation, took precedence over the intercessory exercises of the vigil. We had offered to God the free and voluntary submission of our hearts; now we were to perform obligatory prayer as commanded from on high, with the Seraphim at hand to watch over us. The mystic disposition to seek "God's face" must yield to the appropriate humility of prostrating before the exalted law.

Teacher, nosy proxy of the archangel himself, but coming down to earth through the effective spy network he had planted among us, was up to date on all the happenings at the vigil. No saints would be allowed to stand between him and his spoils. He knew, for example, which of the students performed well and which of them fell asleep during the night. He regarded falling asleep during religious exercise as proof of idleness and felt duty-bound to rectify this. Offenses during vigils did not immediately lead to corporal punishment but merely to being tagged with the stigma of an offender released on the promise of good behavior. The next offense, however slight, brought the cane.

DISCIPLINE

Not long after the vigil a lad called Karamo had occasion to fall into Teacher's grip. He had been reported to him as one of those who had fallen asleep on a mat near the tea buckets. Teacher knew that Karamo had been current on his lessons and that he seldom had cause to rebuke him on that score. In spite of that he took a serious view of the matter. A little later Karamo fell foul of him again. He called Karamo one morning and asked whether he had finished reciting the portion of the Qur'án he had copied to his slate the previous day. Karamo said he had memorized it, and when he asked him to recite in front of him he did so, whereupon he directed him to wash off the old material so that the slate was clean and ready for the new material. During midday recitations he asked if Karamo had washed his slate. When Karamo answered yes, he asked him to bring it to him. Karamo brought the wooden slate to him, but the Arabic characters were still faintly visible on it. That was not really Karamo fault because the ink used for writing was crudely made by the children under Teacher's own supervision, and they did so by rubbing the surface of metal cooking pots. Sometimes not enough soot had collected on the pots and no amount of scraping would coax any more of the precious substance. The scraping added rust to the soot, and rust stained the wood. It was difficult to remove with one washing of the slate. The scraping, in fact, was bad for the ink, causing it to dry and to stain the wood. This was what happened in Karamo's case. He had scrubbed the stubborn surface with all his strength, but after it dried the characters were still clearly visible. Teacher was furious. As he turned the slate over and over, Karamo noticed his thin, bony hands flicking and a growing impatience rising in his voice. It was only a matter of time before he reached for his cane and tap-tapped the slate, a sign that Karamo was to keep his right index finger where the offense was, Teacher's way of rubbing it in. However, Karamo's hand recoiled by reflex. When he steadied it enough to point to the slate, he made circles in a futile bid not to be smacked. Teacher, fed up with the lad's dodges, abandoned the chase and settled on capture.

Teacher's face tightened and furrowed, and then his throat vibrated menacingly as he cleared it. He raised his cane, placing it first behind his neck across his shoulder and then bringing it down to rest where he was seated on the prayer rug. He then picked it up, and, as his fingers closed round the cane, his face loosened and his wrist relaxed. He was muttering to himself, his tone one part declaratory and the other doxology. He loved his craft, and now he would thank God for it.

Teacher pulled both Karamo's ears, as Karamo crawled on the ground toward him. Karamo stooped as low as he could without touching the ground, and then he felt Teacher's hand fly past his head as he tried to hit it. I think he cursed him secretly. There was a legend at school that Teacher's left hand delivered the most deadly slaps across the face. So when any of the children went to him expecting to be punished, they moved as close to the left hand as possible, trying thus to reduce the effectiveness of his left-hand swipes and leaving him with the weaker right hand. Karamo remembered this, and when Teacher pulled him by the ears he dragged himself to Teacher's left side as close as possible. But the poor fellow was at a disadvantage. With his two ears firmly in Teacher's hand he could balance him on either side of him as he pleased. He swayed him to the right at arm's length, and when Karamo tried to recover his balance, Teacher closed in with a powerful left-hand swipe. Then he grabbed him by the ears again, pinched his ear lobes tightly, piercing the cartilage, and shook him hard, as if to test his grasp on the substance of power.

This side of Teacher was not easily understood by parents and guardians, but it was one which children had no difficulty in appreciating. For his part, Teacher approached this aspect of his job with as much care and thought as he did the religious and educational aspects. By constantly referring to the children as God's mud bricks he took the divine law into his own hands. One could not say he actually enjoyed beating his students. But he always stood for strict discipline and saw even the ritual prayers as God's way of containing us, of reducing us to postures of submissive obedience, as close as we could be on this side of the grave to the dust of our origin. The mud bricks idea attained the same purpose. His cane rested beside him as by divine order. His hands were as much adapted to wielding the cane as his prominent forehead was to touching the floor during the prayer prostrations. A devout servant of God, Teacher regarded himself as responsible, before God, for the minds and bodies of his pupils, and he expected to receive his reward from God in accordance with the diligence with which he performed his duty.

RITE OF PASSAGE

A common practice at the school was to collect the water with which the children had washed their slates if the relevant portions were from highly auspicious parts of the Qur'án. We collected this water in small bottles and took it home for use as medicine. We had to obtain Teacher's permission for that, but he was never known to object. In fact, it was he who told us which sections of the Qur'án were useful in that way. He never publicly or formally taught that the holy water could help us acquire quick minds, for fear, in all probability, of contravening Málikí doctrinal strictures. Yet it was precisely such hope that sent many parents in search of the right Qur'án medicine, at great expense and trouble, which they made their children drink, alas, often in vain.

Although the number of parents who resorted to this mind-quickening device was large, that did not mean that there were not bright boys at the school. Teacher could in fact boast of a fair number, and occasionally he had a chance to receive public honors for the many bright boys he had helped to set on the right course. On one such occasion a number of his pupils had finished reciting up to súrah 36 of the Qur'án, *Yá Sín*. This was considered to be an advanced stage of proficiency and was traditionally celebrated by the community on the school premises and occasionally at the mosque on a Friday. Given the peculiar numbering of the súrahs of the Qur'án, so that it reads back front, with the higher súrahs occurring earlier, *Yá Sín* in fact was the second stage in Qur'án recitation. The first was the sixty-seventh súrah, *al-Mulk*, "the kingdom." That particular chapter opens with a general prayer: "Blessed be He in whose hand is the kingdom, He is powerful over everything, who created death and life. . . . Thou seest not in the creation of the All-merciful any imperfection. . . . And we adorned the lower heaven with lamps." It was considered a meritorious act to make some kind of voluntary offering after reaching that súrah, but in importance it ranked below *Yá Sín*, which starts by venerating the Qur'án.

EXAMINATION

On the occasion above, when Teacher was to present his successful students before the community, a few preliminaries started the proceedings. It was a Friday, and people were returning from the congregation prayer. A number of distinguished visitors had also come to town. The mothers of the boys had cooked big meals to feed the crowd. The local imám and his followers were among the visitors. However, the Qur'án school was out of bounds for certain visitors, such as the chief and colonial officials. Even the imám did not come there as a rule. The wife of Teacher was not expected to do any cooking, but she supervised the seating arrangements in the forecourt. The candidates themselves were specially prepared for the exercise. Their heads were shaved, and they wore clean gowns. They were expected to perform ablution—ritual cleansing—before attending the ceremonies. A small offering of kola nuts was brought by the parents, and this was formally introduced to the gathering and then laid aside to be distributed after the introductory prayers. Important dignitaries and visitors were specially welcomed, and other proceedings of protocol duly completed before coming to the highlight of the occasion. Prayers were an important part of the proceedings and were led by the imám, who usually began by having everyone join in reciting the *fátihah* and ended by thanking Teacher for his leadership of the school. Then Teacher would introduce the pupils and announce the portions of the Qur'án each would recite.

By the time they reached that stage the students had had sufficient time to pull themselves together and to get used to the rather august atmosphere of the meeting. Teacher, the imám, and distinguished guests and visitors sat near Teacher's house, directly opposite the gate of the compound. Facing them were the students, who were in turn surrounded by former students and other Muslim dignitaries, friends, and relatives. The women waited in a nearby house and appeared when it was their turn to distribute the food and the other refreshments.

Then came the climax of the ceremony. The students began with the formal opening, announced the súrah and verses from which their selections were taken, and then commenced the long, arduous task of recitation. Teacher was supposed to prompt them if their confidence wobbled, but he preferred instead professional detachment, like a giraffe with elevated head overseeing a fish market. Teacher had never seen his task as that of helper of the disadvantaged, as a one-man affirmative action brigade, for that would put him on the same side as the students. After all, as priest of the word he was selectman of heaven rather than an equal opportunity agent. He would not compromise his standing by being seen on the side of half-baked children floundering through God's word. Fortunately, in this case there was no need to suffer for his principles. One by one the students recited their pieces with confidence, to the great satisfaction of the people present. That was Teacher's supreme moment of triumph, which had enabled him gracefully to endure the long and complicated preamble. The verdict of the examiners was still to come, but there was no doubt the students had fully justified Teacher's faith and high hopes. The main part of the business thus completed, the assembly started to disperse. People shook hands, offered short extempore prayers, and departed. There was no public congratulation of the students, or rather, such congratulation took other forms. People came to them and prayed for them but beyond that ignored the children completely. I have often wondered if, because the adults wanted on such occasions to have the Qur'án hold center stage, they made a point of ignoring the children beyond mere form lest children come to see themselves as central. So the children, their egos enticed and then ignored by public clamor, were left to seek remedy in boasting, posturing, and other forms of macho behavior, behavior by which they looked to themselves to remedy the slight they suffered at the hands of the all-powerful adults.

While the dignitaries were dispersing, most of the children stayed behind; it was time for refreshments and food. That was also an important part of the day. The elders had shared the kola nuts among themselves, and now it was the children's turn for a share of the good things. Among them on this occasion was Karamo, who was just getting up from where he was squatting when an elderly man walked up to him and stroked his shaved head with his rough hands. "My son," he said, "I shall look forward to the day when you also will be inducted into the holy order of Qur'án scholars. I pray for the hastening of that day." His thick hands brushed down the side of Karamo's head, touching the right ear Teacher had pinched so severely. Karamo ducked quickly and uttered a faint "Amen," perhaps more to celebrate his escape than in answer to the prayer of the elderly visitor. Then he turned his mind quickly to the meals which were being served in a neighboring compound.

That evening at the Qur'án school Teacher announced that the examiners had returned a unanimous verdict in favor of the students, and that having attained such high standards it was now up to the boys to decide whether they wanted to continue at the school as full- or part-timers or go elsewhere for further education. Some of the children indicated that they were opting for a Western-type education and this did not please Teacher at all. He advised them to continue at the school on a part-time basis while at the same time attending the other type of school, which he could not bring himself to name directly. They would earn *barakah*, which they could not forego, only as his pupils.

The competition he faced from Western-style schools hardened Teacher. The Western school, he contended, created a drop-out culture. Although it boasted of its principled abjuring of the cane, by inciting in children attitudes of superiority and inferiority and, withal, a festering insecurity, it resorted to a weapon far more callous.

The Western school was, therefore, a moral breach, Teacher charged; an extension of infidel and alien penetration into African soil. He predicted that children would be torn from their roots, and young men and women detached from the stem of tribal solidarity, all of them transplanted into a culture of competitive individualism which had not a shred of compassion and offered the illusory promise of economic advancement. A few such people, he warned, would make it, but the great majority, drop-outs all, would reap only personal disenchantment and loss of identity. Brothers and sisters would be turned against each other and driven apart by competition. Whether they passed or failed in their exams, the children would have lost all sense of family and community solidarity. Consequently, the society needed all the ammunition it could muster to avert such a calamity, and so Teacher's own example of wielding the cane should find collective resolve in community resistance. But Teacher was dreaming, for, even if he had moral right on his side, he knew an irresistible force had entered the land heralding a permanent, aggressive new world order. It would be the hegemony of the infidel West, which would seek to make public example of the very tradition Teacher was raised to foster. As it was, some of the children (God forbid!) would bend and be lost to it.

Teacher's dramatic personality, to which orthodox stringency gave a sharp edge, was bolstered by the spectre of the infidel West. Religion polarized his thought, causing him to divide the world neatly between truth and error, between lawful and forbidden, purity and pollution. For him, education not founded on religion was in principle unsound, and a state education which made religion suit all tastes rendered religion worthless. The end of education should be, he stressed, *sapiens atque eloquens pietas* ("piety endowed with the power of thought and expression"), as the Puritans would put it. This theocentric view of education, Teacher felt, would not be spared by a Western humanism, in which human experience is given primacy over revealed truth, and where the connection between education and religion is severed for good, driven by the specious argument of education as a neutral channel for ideas. This neutral humanism would make our ultimate end the dissolution and dissipation of all life into the universe, whereas religion sees death not as the end but as the harbinger of a fuller, more complete existence. Secular humanism promises freedom in education but in fact sets up a structure of opposition to God. Education for freedom is the banner cry of the West, yet freedom without purpose is human delusion. So the West masks the delusion by emphasizing the building of national character and civic virtue as the goal of education. The delusion thus remains, because nations, especially proud ones, are a nuisance among themselves and to their people unless they too live under God's law. (Teacher had escaped the draft in World War II but had come close enough to sense how nations boasted vainly in the sword.) Society must not be satisfied with the view that giving its children the tools of literacy and professional skills will ensure prosperity and virtue, for without ethical character, without integrity and spirit, in fact without *barakah*, no system of education, however efficient, can inculcate habits of virtue and love for truth. On the contrary, efficiency may produce ruthlessness. The child is not just a hollow vessel which the school packs with information and facts; rather, the child bears the divine imprint, a living spiritual entity whose security and welfare should come before any neutrality ideology. The child must be formed, not just tutored; directed, not just informed; inspired, not just instructed; motivated, not just rewarded; affirmed, not just evaluated; and commissioned, not just congratulated. The child is not an animal. It must know God, the master of the world, and is, thereby, fit for knowledge. That, in a nutshell, was the whole case for education and the cause that fitted (and fired) Teacher's Puritan temper.

Since all children were created equal before God, God also made their egalitarian formative education a high and holy calling. Education is moral growth, and though its effects are practical and national, its enduring fruits are spiritual and symbolic. The Western school system, by contrast, is based on class, rank, status, race, money, and power, which necessarily divide us. It makes secular education an individualistic enterprise and repudiates the values of cooperation, community, and commitment, the "three C's" of moral education. It is a denial of

God's sovereign justice. By taking over the education of African children, Teacher would intone remorsefully, Western colonial powers—the English, the French and the Portuguese, to be precise—had imposed captivity without visible chains. In the sparsely clad children of Africa, the Western colonial powers saw defects which well-tailored school uniforms would hide. The whites think thus: Bring his children to a sense of sexual embarrassment, and the pygmy father will throw away his ancient tribal heirloom and welcome his modern Western savior. After all, what is straw beside the torch of knowledge?

Western education sets its face against community and conformity, but it is dishonest, for such education standardizes children by the very banner of individualism and suppresses their individuality by the rule of battery run individual tests which are objective only in a subversive sense. Separated from kith and kin, children become conventional, their tribal kit and caboodle replaced by the school uniform, and their leisure organized by gym rules. In response, Muslim Africans must resist by passive defiance first, and then with the curse in their daily devotions. If the West opposes God, Teacher would say with his cane-bearing hand trembling in pained defiance, then the people of God should make the West an anathema, a ransom to divine displeasure. Compromise, which had no honor with him, had on this subject abandoned him entirely, and he would retire, still ill at ease, from battle with the invisible and imperturbable enemy. However, assured of the adulation of his students, whom he would rouse to strong chanting of the Qur'án, his hackles began discernibly to subside.

CONFORMITY

Teacher had indicated with his own attitude that times had changed and that children would now live their lives in a world completely different from the one in which he grew up. They would have to adapt to succeed. Precisely how or when, nobody knew, except that the children could see their elders juggling their options and biding their time. Even in the confined world of children old patterns were beginning to shift in the final years of the Qur'án school. Numerous bush fights had produced a rapid turnover in friendships and alliances, and tension increased among the boys. That hardened the mood and drove them to seek relief from duties the elders had imposed on them. Teacher's authority was accepted implicitly, but they wondered whether its source in divine injunction was entirely to their benefit. So they asked why the ritual prayers could not be skipped, why it was necessary to observe the obligatory fast of Ramadan in all its tiny details, why in Islamic law duties were classified as required, recommended, indifferent, reprehensible, or forbidden? Why not just recommended and indifferent? That would take the coercive and the punitive out of religion. The boys who pressed such questions came to be looked upon as rebels, causing the rest of the children to side with Teacher as champions of orthodoxy.

In many ways that particular Qur'án school was a mild regime compared to other schools. In school the children might talk lightly of conformity, but other schools had a far harsher regime, indeed something of a bootcamp culture of confinement and draconian measures of labor and submission. This is a widespread practice in all Muslim Africa.

In time many of the children began to develop definite feelings about the Qur'án school, although they never questioned openly some of the fundamental principles on which it was based. Teacher, as the driving force of the school, made that kind of opposition impossible to contemplate. They accepted the rule of *bila kayf*, meaning "without asking how." Teacher might give it a more instrumental interpretation, such as that the more grounded children are in Scripture the more stored they would be for the future. Thus everyone accepted the teaching that God gave children minds to train and develop in divine service so that at the end of our appointed earthly course they could render an intelligible account of their stewardship to the Creator. That was one of Teacher's basic teachings. He said God had no use for illiterate minds. The Qur'án school was the obvious place where children could learn to be literate in Arabic. The entire school also venerated the teaching that the flames of the bonfires of the Qur'án school would rise to defend the children on Judgment Day, bearing witness to their diligence and perseverance *fí sabíl illáh* ("in the way of Allah"). God's mud bricks, as Teacher was accustomed to regarding the children, needed expert handling if they were to occupy their rightful place in the ranks of heaven. Off-limits to political officials like the chief and the district commissioner, the Qur'án school was their province of virtue. Pious people, visiting religious notables, and important community dignitaries came there on visits. The children had the benefit of seeing some of these men at close quarters and learning about the wider Muslim world. The accounts of travelers to the school filled everyone with great curiosity and longing. Moreover, for those of the students who were destined to play important roles in the larger Muslim community outside, to have had the school in their academic pedigree was an advantage. That, plus the attractiveness of travel to other Muslim lands, made the school an essential and necessary part of early childhood education and training. The mood of questioning, however intense, did not change the basic attitudes toward Teacher and the school.

One day at meal time my brother asked our father if he thought it would have been more pleasant and less risky if God had allowed people never to have left heaven rather than plunging them willy nilly into the world and all its hazards. Why put people to a test few could pass? He asked this question after a night of heavy rains accompanied by thunder and lightning. Because he was frightened he thought it not equitable for God to be sheltered in heaven, leaving us to face life's trials here. Our father coughed advisedly and asked my brother to put his mind to other things. But the bait, once cast, could not so easily be withdrawn, and the questions kept tumbling out: Why was it that, although merciful and kind, God still would like to roast people in hellfire? Why did God create all of us and then place some with the good and some with the bad instead of making us all bad or good, or not making us at all? And why must people like Teacher automatically be destined for Paradise when the rest of us had a fifty-fifty chance? And why . . . ? We were not quite finished, but we did not have time to put in another question.

Father fixed his cold and deliberate eyes on us and we froze. "God," he said, "is not a subject for idle speculation." It did not help, though, to be told we were too young to question the Creator's ways when we were held old enough to bear the burden of learning God's word, but that unsatisfactory situation would take several years to produce an effect. In the meantime, Father resorted to the evasiveness so natural to parental authority by explaining that when he was a child and going to Qur'án school he was taught that all children were born as believing Muslims, although many children grew up without the chance to develop that God-given side of them because of wrong parentage and environment. Nevertheless, when a child died it automatically went to Paradise as an angel. This reassurance, however motivated by generosity, did nothing to absolve us from present responsibility, but father was in no mood to be challenged. So we tried unsuccessfully to imagine Paradise as a place for children who died a premature death. The problem was that our language had no word for heaven or Paradise, so the myth of infant immortality had little hold on our imagination.

But our father, roused to duty, would not be deterred. He explained that as children he and his friends fulfilled their duties at their school because it ensured their security in the unseen world. He said they obeyed their teacher to attract *barakah* to themselves, for such *barakah* would be an undiminishing asset which they could pass on to their families. He said it was such *barakah* that helped otherwise vulnerable little children to fend off the unsolicited attention of the evil one and to be destined for noble ends. Then he referred to the example of the Prophet. He said when the Prophet was a baby and his mother wanted another family to rear him, everybody refused to take care of him. Eventually it was a kind but poor peasant woman who took him into her home. The woman had lived a life of prayer and that was why, aware of the great *barakah* prayer achieved, she took in a tiny baby in the belief that she would be blessed by the God who created it, little aware that she would be suckling the Prince of Creation and the Apostle of God. That short preliminary about the Prophet was by way of introduction. Then he went on to tell us that once upon a time a poor family, desirous of receiving the divine *barakah*, made a modest food offering to which they invited children from the neighborhood. The children who came were from many different backgrounds: Fulbé, Bambara, Wolof, Mandinka, Serakhulle, Diola, Berber, Pagan, and Muslim, neighbors and strangers, high and low. After the children consumed all the food—a meal and milk offering—they washed their hands in the big calabash bowl from which they had just eaten and made the customary call for *barakah* on the household. The woman of the house then collected the water in the calabash, and making her secret wishes over the water, she poured it over the entrance of the compound. The water was supposed to run in trickles across the gate as a symbol of protection, the idea being that the *barakah*-charged prayers of the children would seal the home against malevolent forces.

After the woman had carried out that part of the ritual she turned to go inside her house. At that point she discovered that two of the boys had remained behind. Puzzled why they had not gone with the rest, she asked them what they wanted. The lads said they thought there might be some household chores she wanted done and that they would be glad to help. They even offered to fetch her supply of domestic fuel from the surrounding bush. When the woman asked them why, they replied that they had missed Qur'án school and wanted to substitute deeds of merit to earn *barakah*. The woman later discovered that these boys were the sons of an important local chief. Our father then looked straight at us but did not say a word. There was no need to. We took the point well. He had spoken in this round-about way about the Qur'án school as the repository of *barakah*, and this was why he wished his children to obey Teacher unquestioningly and call him "Teacher." In the name of *barakah*—what our father's Pagan Manding forebears knew as *yirwa*—children came to be God's mud bricks, to be chiseled and laid down four-square, vessels for the streams of *barakah* set to pour from Teacher's favorable disposition.

It is difficult to exaggerate the role *barakah*, the indigenous *yirwa*, played in children's upbringing and early education, an idea with deep roots in pre-Muslim Africa. Both individuals and communities could receive *barakah* or lose it; they could regain it and retain it. Whatever the case, *barakah* demands trust in its efficacy rather than emotional attachment. It is more like a living trust and doing than it is a psychological mood or feeling. *Barakah* bespeaks a world of social interaction, of the goings and comings of people, of their relationships and human interests. Those who receive enough of it will obtain immunity against misfortune. Those who have *barakah* should expend it, and the more they expend it, the more it increases. Those who attempt to hoard *barakah* will lose it, because it spoils from inactivity or miserliness. *Barakah* loves a generous spirit, and it will conspire with one to create another. It is not possessive or boastful. It does not seek its own but prefers others. It does not reproach except to correct. It will relent if offended. It is just but not vengeful. It does not hurt or think ill of others. It is not loose or wild but is gentle and mild-mannered. It is not evasive, impulsive, intrusive, or indulgent. It loves the truth but is not sectarian or self-righteous. It is positive and compassionate but not sentimental or soft. It does not wag its tongue at others, but craves the best for all. It is loyal without being exclusive. It shelters under patience and forbearance, and it flourishes from public acclaim but is not ostentatious. It does not compromise, though it shuns rancor and spite. It cannot be purchased, though it loves a cheerful and generous giver. It does not covet and is not envious. Everyone who seeks it will find it; all it requires is a sincere spirit. It does not wilt or cloy from familiarity. It encourages but does not flatter. Like *yirwa, barakah* promotes company though it transcends it; it rejects no one; and it forgives and embraces all. The hope of *barakah* springs eternal, and its rewards are a joy forever.

Children seek *barakah* from their parents and teachers, and a mother's *barakah* is as important as a father's. *Barakah*, when dispensed as virtue, follows strict rules of observance: husbands give *barakah* to their wives, teachers to pupils, saints to supplicants, paupers to the well-off, pilgrims to others, the old to the young, the blind to the sighted, but the best and choicest *barakah* is that of the Prophet who also bears the honorific *al-Mubárak*, "the blessed one." In virtually all these cases *barakah* does not work in reverse: children do not give *barakah* to their parents, pupils to their teachers, supplicants to saints, wives to their hus-bands, the well-off to paupers, non-pilgrims to pilgrims, the young to the old, the sighted to the blind, or, what would be the ultimate scandal, believers to the Prophet, unless, that is, *barakah* as offering thanks. Also, *barakah* as virtue can be tempo-rarily nullified by a breach of the rules of respect, deference, and honor. Though a person may earn *barakah*, he or she cannot give it to themselves. Such belief in *barakah* emphasizes the social reality of persons and their relationships with one another. Muslim doctrine reinforces this by confronting the believer with a moral *barakah* vested in ethical duty, of becoming an authentic person from our actions rather than from anyone else's, whether relatives or friends. People are thus brought into active relationship with each other as believers, that is to say, as persons beholden to a common code of conduct. The Qur'án as code and oracle expresses it thus, "Neither your blood-kindred nor your children/shall profit you upon the Day of Resurrection" (60:3), or, elsewhere: "And no burdened soul can bear another's burden, and if one heavy laden cried for (help with) his load, naught of it will be lifted even though he (unto whom he crieth) be of kin. . . . He who groweth (in goodness), groweth only for himself, (he cannot by his merit redeem others)" (35:18, Pickthall). The duties of faith create a unified ethical outlook, so that breaches can be remedied and achievements rewarded. Religion thus pre-scribes and proscribes for persons as individuals rather than becoming merely a function of ethnic or racial interest.

Education in its own sphere appeals to an identical principle of making the child's competence a matter of observing a personal code, the same code that guides the community in its relations with the school. In that respect Islam sows the seeds of personal ethical duty, so that a person's ultimate moral destiny rests not on lineage rank and tribal affinity but on individual merit (22:14; 36:54). Religious doctrine thus recognizes achieved results fixed in effort and enterprise, not acquired traits rooted in blood and soil.

Such ideas on ethical accountability could, with the right stimulus, inspire faith in personal freedom and ignite the impulse to explore and experiment, and that need not abandon the pattern of the "three C's" of moral education. However, with the rapid pace of change induced by Western contact well under way, chil-dren were destined to grow up in a world far less stable and self-assured than that of their elders. The sanctions of tradition derived their force from communal soli-darity based on kin and clan loyalty and established within fixed or sedentary territorial limits. Now, however, a new world order had arrived, requiring fresh symbols shaped by choice and personal freedom. With it, religion as authoritative transmission would not be exempt, for children would grow up having learned to question authority, absorbed in self-discovery and rejecting the old ways. This would create a form of commitment centered on self-knowledge rather than on received tradition.

Some children, though, were too loyal not to look for assurance from the old teachings and sanctions. They took encouragement from the fact that the word of God, which had the rod on it and from which they obtained divine *barakah*, would ensure their well-being against the enemy. Thus they washed their slates and consumed the holy water, and also sought for Teacher's approval and commendation. God's word contained *barakah* that was for their worldly benefit. *Barakah* as an ineffable resource comes into our midst mediated by numerous channels of principle and circumstance. Yet how could the children be sure that *barakah* would follow them into change and defiance? *Barakah* has as its opposite, *danka*, which is ill-omen, sometimes incurred by the curse but more often from the ill-will of those unjustly wronged, and it haunts and tracks down its subject. Between them *barakah* and *danka* conditioned the moral universe of children, carefully marking out those who might be their recognized agents. It was impossible to break completely free of the force of *barakah* and *danka*, and that was why even those of the children who enrolled in Western schools carried in their souls a double or bifurcated loyalty. There was the awful possibility that *danka* would fill the void which the Western school in its unfamiliarity with the world of *barakah* allowed to exist in their souls. If *barakah* was excluded from the new type of education and things went wrong, there was little remedy except self-blame, and that kind of reproachful individualism leaves victims, troubled, alienated souls torn up from their roots. Children cannot be thrown from the old system into the new without risking a grave identity crisis. And that was why generations of children in traditional society arrived in the new world of Western secularism with a sense of dissonance and alienation. In our particular case, change was in the offing, and we were destined for an extraordinary adventure far beyond the confines of our small, obscure school and its juvenile, motley convoy. What happened to us in Western schools of assimilation as well as rejection, of *barakah* and *danka*, left our families with painful ambivalence toward Western schools. Many traditional families continued to keep a wary distance from these schools, whatever the promises or incentives.

CHAPTER BIBLIOGRAPHY

Abuja, J. Bala. "Koranic and Modern Law Teaching in Nigeria," *Nigeria*, no. 37 (1951).

Brenner, Louis. "The Role of Language in West African Islam," *Africa*, vol. 55, no. 4 (1985).

_____. *West African Súfí: The Religious Heritage and Spiritual Search of Cerno Bokar Saalif Taal*. Berkeley and Los Angeles: University of California Press; London: Christopher Hurst Publishers, 1984.

Davidson, Basil. "West African Arabic Scripts," *West Africa*, no. 2433 (18 January 1964).

Goody, Jack. "The Impact of Islamic Writing on the Oral Cultures of West Africa," *Cahiers d'Études Africaines*, vol. 11, no. 3 (1971).

Harrison, Christopher. *France and Islam in West Africa: 1860-1960*. Cambridge: Cambridge University Press, 1988.

Kane, Cheikh Hamidou. *Ambiguous Adventure*. London: Heinemann, 1965.

Marty, Paul. *L'Islam en Guinée*. Paris: E. Leroux, 1921.

Monteil, Vincent. "Marabouts." In *Islam in Africa*. Edited by J. Kritzeck and W. H. Lewis. New York: Van Nostrand, 1969.

Osman El-Tom, Abdullahi. "Drinking the Koran: The Meaning of Koranic Verses in Berti Erasure," *Africa*, vol. 55, no. 4 (1985).

Şaul, Mahir. "The Quranic School Farm and Child Labour in Upper Volta," *Africa*, vol. 54, no. 2 (1984).

Sesay, S. I. "Koranic Schools in the Provinces, *Sierra Leone Journal of Education*, vol. 1, no. 1 (April 1966).

General Bibliography

Abdin, Tayyid Z. Al-. "The Implications of *Sharí'ah, Fiqh and Qánún* in an Islamic State." In *Religion, Law and Socety: A Christian-Muslim Discussion.* Edited by Tarek Mitri. Geneva: World Council of Churches, 1995.

_____. "The Role of Religious Institutions and *'ulamá'* in a Contemporary Muslim Society." In *Religion, Law and Socety: A Christian-Muslim Discussion.* Edited by Tarek Mitri. Geneva: World Council of Churches, 1995.

'Abduh, Muhammad. *The Theology of Unity.* Translated by K. Cragg and I. Musa'ad. London, 1965.

Abdul, Musa. *A Report on Arabic and Islamic Studies in Secondary Schools in Nigeria.* Unpublished M.S. thesis. Ibadan, 1965.

Abuja, J. Bala. "Koranic and Modern Law Teaching in Nigeria," *Nigeria*, no. 37 (1951).

Abul-Fadl, Mona. *Where East Meets West: The West on the Agenda of the Islamic Revival.* Herndon, VA: The International Institute of Islamic Thought, 1992.

Abu-l-Fazl, Mirza. *The Koran.* Bombay, 1955.

Abun-Nasr, J. *The Tijaniyya: A Sufi Order in the Modern World* Oxford: Oxford University Press, 1965.

Adams, C. C. *Islam and Modernism in Egypt.* London, 1933; repr. New York: Russell & Russell, 1968.

Adams, Charles J. *Reader's Guide to the Great Religions.* New York, 1965.

Adamu, Haroun al-Rashid. *The North and Nigerian Unity: Some Reflections on the Political, Social and Educational Problems of Northern Nigeria.* Lagos: Daily Times, 1973.

Adegbite, Lateef. "The Role of Muslim Leaders in the Government of Nigeria." Paper, Religious Studies Conference, University of Ibadan, 1978.

Adigwe, H.A. *Nigeria Joins the Orgnaization of Islamic Conference O.I.C.* Onitsha: Archdiocesan Secretariat, 1986.

AFD, Dossier no. 170: "Administrative Report of Kindia," 19 April 1911.

African Guardian, The, vol. 2, no. 48 (1987).

Ahmad, Khurshid. *Islam: Its Meaning and Message.* London, 1970.

Ahmad, Zahir. *Mohammad, Glimpses of the Prophet's Life and Times.* New Delhi, 1980.

Ahsan, 'Abdullah al-. *OIC: The Organization of the Islamic Conference.* Series no. 7. Herndon, VA: The International Institute of Islamic Thought, 1988.

Akinrinade, Olusola, and M. A. Ojo. "Religion and Politics in Contemporary Nigeria: A Study of the OIC Crisis," *Journal of Asian and African Affairs*, vol. 4, no. 1 (Fall 1992).

Alao, Nurudeen. "Education in Islam: The Challenge of Numbers, Breadth and Quality." In *Islam in Africa: Proceedings of the Islam in Africa Conference.* Edited by Nura Alkali, Adamu Adamu, Awwal Yadudu, Rashid Motem, and Haruna Salihi. Ibadan: Spectrum Books Limited, 1993.

Alharazim, M. Saif'ud Deen. "The Origin and Progress of Islam in Sierra Leone," *Sierra*

Leone Studies, old series, no. 21 (1939): 12-26.

'Ali, 'Abdallah Yúsúf. *Fundamentals of Islam*. Geneva, 1929.

_____ . *The Holy Qur'an*. 2 vols. Lahore, 1937/38.

_____ . *The Message of Islam*. London, 1940.

_____ . *The Personality of Muhammad*. Lahore, 1931.

'Ali, Hashim Amir. *The Student's Qur'an*. Hyderabad, 1959.

'Ali, Michael Nazir. *Frontiers in Muslim-Christian Encounter*. Oxford: Regnum Books, 1987; repr. 1991.

_____ . *Islam: A Christian Perspective*. Philadelphia: Westminster Press, 1984.

'Ali, Muhammad. *The Living Thoughts of the Prophet Muhammad*. London, 1947.

_____ . *Manual of Hadith*. Lahore, n.d.

Amin, Osman. *Muhammad 'Abduh*. Washington, 1953.

Aminu, Jibril. "Towards a Strategy for Education and Development in Africa." In *Islam in Africa: Proceedings of the Islam in Africa Conference*. Edited by Nura Alkali, Adamu Adamu, Awwal Yadudu, Rashid Motem, and Haruna Salihi. Ibadan: Spectrum Books Limited, 1993.

Ammah, R. "New light on Muslim Statistics for Africa," *Bulletin on Islam and Christian-Muslim Relations in Africa*, vol. 2, no. 1 (1984): 11-20.

Anasiudu, R., ed. *Christian-Muslim Relations in Nigeria: The Stand of the Catholic Bishops*. Lagos: Catholic Secretariat.

Anawati, G. C., and Louis Gardet. *Mystique Musulmane: Aspects et Tendances— Expériences et Techniques*. Paris: Librairie philosophique J. Vrin, 1961.

Anderson, E. "Early Muslim Education and British Policy in Sierra Leone," *West African Journal of Education*, vol. 14 (October 1970).

Anderson, J. N. D. *Islamic Law in Africa*. London, 1954; repr. Frank Cass Publishers, 1970.

Andrae, Tor. *Muhammad, the Man and His Faith*. Translated by T. Mentzel. New York, 1960.

Apter, David E. "Political Religion in the New Nations." In *Old Societies and New States: The Quest for Modernity in Asia and Africa*. Edited by Clifford Geertz. New York: Free Press, 1963.

Arberry, A. J. *The Holy Koran: An Introduction with Selections*. London, 1953.

_____ . *The Koran Interpreted*. 2 vols. London, 1955; New York, Macmillan, 1969.

_____ . *Revelation and Reason in Islam*. London: Allen & Unwin; New York, 1957.

Arinze, Francis A. *Sacrifice in Ibo Religion* Ibadan: Ibadan University Press, 1970.

Arnaud, Robert. "L'Islam et la politique musulmane française en Afrique occidentale française, suivi de la singulière légende des Soninkés." Paris, 1911.

Arnold, Thomas, and Guillaume, A. *The Legacy of Islam*. Oxford, 1931.

Asad, M. *Principles of State and Government in Islam*. Gibralter: Dár al-Andalus, 1980.

Asad, Muhammad. *The Message of the Qur'an*. Gibraltar, 1980.

Atabani, Ghazi Salahuddin. "Islamic Sharí'ah and the Status of Non-Muslims." In *Religion, Law and Socety: A Christian-Muslim Discussion*. Edited by Tarek Mitri. Geneva: World Council of Churches, 1995.

Atanda, J. A. "Paradoxes and Problems of Religion and Secularism in Nigeria: Suggestions for Solutions." In *Nigeria since Independence: The First Twenty-Five Years*, vol. ix, *Religion*. Edited by J. A. Atanda, Garba Ashiwaju, and Yaya Abubakar. Ibadan: Heinemann, 1989.

Augustine. *Confessions*. New York: Image Book/Doubleday and Anchor, 1960.

Ayubi, Nazih. *Political Islam: Religion and Politics in the Arab World*. London: Routledge & Kegan Paul, 1994.

Azad, Abu-l-Kalam. *Tarjuman al-Qur'an.* Translated by Syed Latif. 2 vols. Bombay, 1962.

Aziz, Mokhtar Ihsan. "Notes on *Sharí'ah, Fiqh* and *Ijtihád.*" In *Religion, Law and Socety: A Christian-Muslim Discussion.* Edited by Tarek Mitri. Geneva: World Council of Churches, 1995.

'Azzam, 'Abd al-Rahman. *The Eternal Message of Muhammad.* New York: Mentor Books, 1965.

Ba, Hampate, and J. Daget. *L'Empire Peul du Macina.* Paris, 1962.

Bah, Mohammad Alpha. "The Status of Muslims in Sierra Leone and Liberia," *Journal of the Institute of Muslim Minority Affairs,* vol. 12, no. 2 (July 1991).

Baillie, Neil B. E., ed. and tr. *Digest of Moohammadan Law: Containing the Doctrines of the Hanifeea Code of Jurisprudence.* 1869-75; reprinted Lahore: Premier Book House, 1974.

Bakalla, M. H. *Arabic Culture: Through Its Language and Literature.* London and Boston: Kegan Paul International, 1984.

Bakrí, al-. *Kitáb al-Masálik wa'l-Mamálik (Book of Routes and Realms).* Edited by M. G. de Slane. Algiers: A. Jourdan, 1913.

Balogun, Isma'íl A. B., tr. and ed. *The Life and Works of 'Uthmán dan Fodio.* Lagos: Islamic Publications Bureau, 1975.

Banton, Michael. "Adaptation and Integration in the Social System of Temne Immigrants in Freetown," *Africa* [Journal of the International African Institute] 26, 4 (October 1956): 354-68.

———. *West African City.* London: Oxford University Press for the International African Institute, 1957.

Barkatt, A. M. "Church -State Relation in an Ideological Islamic State," *The Ecumenical Review,* vol. 21 (1977).

Barker, Sir Ernest. *Principles of Social and Political Theory.* Oxford: Clarendon Press, 1951.

Barnes, Andrew E. "'Evangelization Where It is Not Wanted': Colonial Administrators and Missionaries in Northern Nigeria during the First Third of the Twentieth Century," *Journal of Religion in Africa,* vol. XXV, no. 4 (1995).

Bartels, F. L. *The Roots of Ghana Methodism.* Accra: Methodist Book Depot; London: Cambridge University Press, 1965.

Bascom, William. "Yoruba Religion and Morality." In *Presence Africaine.* Paris, 1972.

Batchelor, John. *The Ainu and Their Folk-lore.* London: The Religious Tract Society, 1901.

Battúta, Ibn. *Travels in Asia and Africa.* Translated and edited by H. A. R. Gibb. London, 1929; repr. London: Routledge & Kegan Paul, 1957.

Baydáwí, *Anwár al-Tanzíl.* Edited by H. O. Fleischer. Volume 2. Leipzig: F. C. G. Vogel, 1848.

Bell, Richard. *Introduction to the Qur'an.* Edinburgh, 1963; rev. and enl. W. M. Watt, Edinburgh, 1970.

———. *The Origin of Islam in Its Christian Environment.* London, 1926; repr. Frank Cass, 1968.

———. *The Qur'an,* 2 vols. Edinburgh, 1937/39.

Bello, Alhaji Sir Ahmadu, Sardauna of Sokoto. *My Life.* Cambridge: Cambridge University Press, 1962; repr. Zaria: Gaskiya Corporation, 1986.

Bello, Muhammad. *Infáq al-Maysúr.* Edited by C. E. J. Whitting. London: Luzac, 1957.

Benna, Umar G. "The Changing Patterns of Muslim Cities in Africa." In *Islam in Africa: Proceedings of the Islam in Africa Conference.* Edited by Nura Alkali, Adamu Adamu,

Awwal Yadudu, Rashid Motem, and Haruna Salihi. Ibadan: Spectrum Books Limited, 1993.

Bennabi, Malek. *Le Phénomène Coranique.* n.d.

Ben-Yunusa, Mohammed. "Secularism and Religion." In *Religion, Law and Socety: A Christian-Muslim Discussion.* Edited by Tarek Mitri. Geneva: World Council of Churches, 1995.

Betts, Robert Brenton. *Christians in the Arab East: A Political Study.* London: S.P.C.K., 1979.

Birks, J. S. *Across the Savannas to Mecca: The Overland Pilgrimage Routes from West Africa.* London: Christopher Hurst, 1978.

Bivar, A. D. H. "Arabic Calligraphy of West Africa," *African Language Review*, vol. 7 (1968).

Blachère, Regis. *Le Coran.* Paris, 1947.

_____. *Le Problème de Mahomet.* Paris, 1952.

Blasdell, R. A. "Use of Drum for Mosque Service," *Muslim World*, vol. 30 (1940).

Blasdoe, C. H., and K. M. Robey, "Arabic Literacy and Secrecy among the Mende of Sierra Leone," *Man*, vol. 21 (1986).

Blyden, Edward W. *Christianity, Islam and the Negro Race.* London 1887; repr. Edinburgh: Edinburgh University Press, 1967.

_____. "The Koran in Africa," *Journal of the African Society*, vol. 4 (January 1905).

Bonhoeffer, Dietrich. *Letters and Papers from Prison.* London: SCM, 1971. Reprinted.

Borrmans, Maurice. *Guidelines for Dialogue between Christians and Muslims.* Translated by R. Marston Speight. Rome: Pontifical Council for Interreligious Dialogue; New York: Paulist Press, 1990.

Bosworth, C. E., ed. *The Legacy of Islam.* New edition. Oxford, 1970.

Bovill, E. W. ed., *Missions to the Niger.* Volume IV: *The Bornu Mission 1822-25.* London (Hakluyt Society Series II vol. CXXX), 1966.

Bravmann, René A. "A Fragment of Paradise," *Muslim World*, vol. 78 (1988).

Breiner, Bert F. "Secularism and Religion: Alternative Bases for the Quest for a Genuine Pluralism." In *Religion, Law and Socety: A Christian-Muslim Discussion.* Edited by Tarek Mitri. Geneva: World Council of Churches, 1995.

_____. "*Sharí'ah* and Religious Pluralism." In *Religion, Law and Socety: A Christian-Muslim Discussion.* Edited by Tarek Mitri. Geneva: World Council of Churches, 1995.

Brenner, Louis. "Concepts of *Taríqa* in West Africa: The Case of the Qádiriyya." in *Charisma and Brotherhood in West African Islam.* Edited by D. B. Cruise O'Brien and C. Coulon. Oxford: Oxford University Press, 1988.

_____. "The Role of Language in West African Islam," *Africa*, vol. 55, no. 4 (1985).

_____. *West African Súfí: The Religious Heritage and Spiritual Search of Cerno Bokar Saalif Taal.* Berkeley and Los Angeles: University of California Press; London: Christopher Hurst Publishers, 1984.

Brown, Mervyn. *Madagascar Rediscovered: From Early Times to Independence.* Hamden, CT: Archon Books, 1979.

Brown, Stuart E. *Meeting in Faith: Twenty Years of Christian-Muslim Conversations Sponsored by the World Council of Churches.* Geneva: WCC, 1989.

Bruce, F. F. *Jesus and Christian Origins outside the New Testament.* Grand Rapids: Eerdmans, 1977. See especially chapters 9 and 10.

Buchanan, Pat. "The Global Ascent of Islam," *Colorado Springs Gazette* (August 20, 1989).

Bukhárí, al-, *Al-Sahíh.* Translated by Muhammad Muhsin Khan. 9 volumes. New Delhi: Kitab Bhavan, 1987.

Burckhardt, Jacob. *Force and Freedom: An Interpretation of History.* New York: Meridian Books, 1955.

Burrows, William R., ed. *Redemption and Dialogue: Reading* Redemptoris Missio *and* Dialogue and Proclamation. Maryknoll, NY: Orbis Books, 1993.

Burton, John. *The Collection of the Qur'án.* Cambridge, England, 1977.

Caillie, René. *Travels through Central Africa to Timbuctoo and across the Great Desert to Morocco, 1824-28.* 2 vols. Reprinted. London: Frank Cass, 1968.

Callaghy, Thomas. *The State-Society Struggle: Zaire in Comparative Perspective.* New York: Columbia University Press, 1984.

Calverley, E. E. *Islam: An Introduction.* Cairo, 1958.

Camps, Arnulf, "The Prayers for Peace at Assisi, October 27, 1986: What Was Shared?" In Jerald D. Gort, Hendrik M. Vroom, Rein Fernhout, and Anton Wessels, eds. *On Sharing Religious Experience: Possibilities of Interfaith Mutuality.* Amsterdam, 1992.

Carriere, Rene, and Paul Holle. *De la Senegambie Française.* Paris, 1955.

Carroll, K. *Yoruba Religious Carving.* London, 1967.

Chittick, William C. *Faith and Practice of Islam: Three Thirteenth Century Sufi Texts.* Albany: State University of New York Press, 1992.

Clapperton, Hugh. *Journal of a Second Expedition into the Interior of Africa.* London, 1829; repr. Frank Cass, 1966.

Cole, Ibrahim. "Muslim-Christian Relations in Sierra Leone," *Bulletin on Islam and Christian-Muslim Relations in Africa,* vol. 1, no. 4 (1983).

Collingwood, R. G. *The Idea of History.* London & New York: Oxford University Press, 1946.

Conrad, David C. "Islam in the Oral Traditions of Mali: Bilali and Surakata," *Journal of African History,* vol. 26 (1985): 33-49.

————, ed. *A State of Intrigue: The Epic of Bamana Segu According to Tayiru Banbera.* London: Oxford University Press for the British Academy, 1990.

Cragg, Kenneth. *The Call of the Minaret.* Revised edition. Maryknoll, NY: Orbis Books, 1985.

————. *Counsels in Contemporary Islam.* Edinburgh: Edinburgh University Press, 1965.

————. *The Event of the Qur'an.* London, 1970.

————. *The House of Islam.* 2d ed. Belmont, Cal., 1975.

————. *The Mind of the Qur'an.* London, 1973.

————, and R. Marston Speight. *Islam from Within.* Belmont, Cal. 1980.

Crollius, Ary A. R. *The Word in the Experience of Revelation in Qur'an and Hindu Scriptures.* Rome, 1974.

Curtin, Philip. *Economic Change in Precolonial Senegambia in the era of the Slave Trade.* Madison: University of Wisconsin Press, 1975.

Daiber, Hans. "Abú Hátim ar-Rází (10th century A.D.) on the Unity and Diversity of Religions." In Jerald D. Gort, et al., eds. *Dialogue and Syncretism: An Interdisciplinary Approach.* Amsterdam: Editions Rodopi; Grand Rapids: Eerdmans, 1989.

————. "Sharing Religious Experience as a Problem in Early Islamic Mysticism." In Jerald D. Gort, Hendrik M. Vroom, Rein Fernhout, and Anton Wessels, eds. *On Sharing Religious Experience: Possibilities of Interfaith Mutuality.* Amsterdam, 1992.

Daily Mail, 11 June 1975.

Davidson, Basil. *The Black Man's Burden: Africa and the Curse of the Nation State.* London: James Currey, 1992.

————. "West African Arabic Scripts," *West Africa,* no. 2433 (18 January 1964).

Dawisha, A., ed. *Islam in Foreign Policy.* Cambridge: Cambridge University Press, 1983.

Dawood, N. J. *The Koran.* London: Penguin Books, 1956.

Deeb, M-J. "Islam and Arab Nationalism in Al-Qaddhafi's Ideology," *Journal of South Asian and Middle Eastern Studies*, vol. 2, no. 2 (1978): 12-26.

_____. *Libya's Foreign Policy in North Africa*. Boulder: Westview, 1991.

Dehaini, A. R. *Report on Qur'an Schools in the Western State of Nigeria*. Unpublished manuscript. Ibadan, 1965.

Dennett, R. E. *Nigerian Studies*. London, 1910; repr. London: Frank Cass, 1968.

Derman, W. *Serfs, Peasants and Socialists: A Former Serf Village in the Republic of Guinea*. Berkeley and Los Angeles: University of California Press, 1973.

Dewey, John. *Democracy and Education: An Introduction to the Philosophy of Education*. New York: Macmillan Press, 1916; repr. Free Press, 1966.

_____. *Freedom and Culture*. Buffalo: Prometheus Books, 1989.

Diallo, Thierno. *Alfa Yaya: roi du Labé (Fouta Djallon)*. Paris, Dakar, and Abidjan, 1976.

Dieterlen, G. (with Solange De Ganay). *La Génie des Eaux chez les Dogons*. Paris, 1942.

Dieterlen, Germaine. "Mythe et organisation sociale en Afrique Occidentale," *J. Soc. Africanistes*, 29, I (1959).

Dilley, Roy M. "Spirits, Islam and ideology: A Study of a Tukulor Weavers' Song (Dillire)," *Journal of Religion in Africa*, vol. xvii, no. 3 (October 1987).

Dobbelaere, K. "Secularization: A Multi-dimensional Concept," *Current Sociology*, vol. 29, no. 1 (1981): 11-12.

Donald, Leland. "Arabic Literacy among the Yulanka of Sierra Leone," *Africa*, vol. 44 (January 1974).

Donaldson, Dwight M. *The Shi'ite Religion*. London, 1933.

Doornbos, M. "Linking the Future to the Past: Ethnicity and Pluralism," *Review of African Political Economy*, 52 (1991): 53-65.

Droogers, André. "Meaning, Power and the Sharing of Religious Experience: An Anthropology of Religion [sic] Point of View." In Jerald D. Gort, Hendrik M. Vroom, Rein Fernhout, and Anton Wessels, eds. *On Sharing Religious Experience: Possibilities of Interfaith Mutuality*. Amsterdam, 1992.

Duffy, James. *A Question of Slavery: Labour Policies in Portuguese Africa and the British Protest, 1850-1920*. Cambridge, Mass.: Harvard University Press, 1967.

Dumont, Fernand. *La Pensée réligieuse d'Amadou Bamba*. Dakar and Abidjan: Nouvelles editions Africaines, 1975.

Duniya, Francis. "The Politics of Sharia and the Constitution of Nigeria," *Encounter*, no. 169-170 (November-December 1990).

Earthy, E. D. "The Impact of Mohammedanism on Paganism in the Liberian Hinterland," *Numen* 2 (1955).

Economist, The. "Islam and the West." 6 August 1994.

Engineer, Asghar A. *Origin and Development of Islam: An Essay on Its Socio-Economic Growth*. Bombay, 1980.

_____. *"Tashrí'* (Process of Law-making) in Islam." In *Religion, Law and Socety: A Christian-Muslim Discussion*. Edited by Tarek Mitri. Geneva: World Council of Churches, 1995.

Enwerem, Iheanyi O. *The Politicization of Religion in Modern Nigeria: The Emergence and Politics of the Christian Association of Nigeria (CAN)*. Unpublished Ph.D. dissertation. York University, 1992.

Esin, Emil. *Mecca and Medina*. London, 1963.

Esposito, John. *The Islamic Threat to the West: Myth or Reality?* New York: Oxford University Press, 1990.

Fadera, al-Hájj Muhammad Fádilu. *Kitáb Tahdhíru Ummati 'I-Muhammadiyát min Ittibái 'l-firqati Ahmadiyát (A Warning to the Muslim Community on the Dangers of Following the Ahmadiyah Sect)*. Printed in Dakar, n.d.

Fafunwa, A. Babatunde. *A History of Education in Nigeria.* London: George Allen and Unwin, 1974.

Fahd, Toufic. *La Divination Arabe: Etudes Religieuses, Sociologiques et Folklorique sur la Milieu Natif de l'Islam.* Leiden: E. J. Brill, 1966.

Faksh, M. "Concepts of Rule and Legitimation in Islam," *Journal of South Asian and Middle Eastern Studies,* vol. 13, no. 3 (1990): 21-36.

Falconbridge, Alexander. *An Account of the Slave Trade on the Coast of Africa.* London, 1788.

Falconbridge, Anna Maria. *Narrative of Two Voyages to the River Sierra Leone During the Years 1791-1793.* London, 1794; repr. Frank Cass, 1967.

Fasholé-Luke, Edward W. "Christianity and Islam in Sierra Leone," *Sierra Leone Bulletin of Religion,* vol. 9, no. 1 (June 1967).

Fazlur, Rahman, *Islam.* London, 1961.

_____ . *Major Themes of the Qur'an.* Minneapolis, 1980.

Fernhout, Rein. "Can Faith in the 'Inspiration' of Holy Scripture Be Shared?" In Jerald D. Gort, Hendrik M. Vroom, Rein Fernhout, and Anton Wessels, eds. *On Sharing Religious Experience: Possibilities of Interfaith Mutuality.* Amsterdam, 1992.

Fisher, Humphrey J. *The Ahmadiyya.* London: Oxford University Press, 1963.

_____ . "Ahmadiyah in Sierra Leone," *S/L Bulletin of Religion,* vol. 2, no. 1 (June 1960).

_____ . "Conversion Reconsidered: Some Historical Aspects or Religious Conversion in Black Africa," *Africa* [Journal of the International African Institute] XLIII, no. 1 (January 1973).

_____ . "Dreams and Conversion in Black Africa." In *Conversion to Islam.* Edited by Nehemia Levtzion. New York: Holmes and Meier, 1979.

_____ . "Hassebu: Islamic Healing in Black Africa." In *Northern Africa: Islam and Modernization.* Edited by Michael Brett. London: Frank Cass, 1973.

_____ . "Islamic Education and Religious Reform in West Africa." In *Education in Africa.* Edited by Richard Jolly. Nairobi, Kenya, 1969.

_____ . "Liminality, Hijra and the City." In *Rural and Urban Islam in West Africa.* Edited by Nehemia Levtzion and Humphrey J. Fisher. Boulder: Lynne Rienner, 1987.

_____ . "A Muslim Wilberforce? The Sokoto *jihád* as Anti-slavery Crusade: An Enquiry into Historical Causes." In *De la traite à l'esclavage: Actes du colloque international sur la traite des Noirs, Nantes.* Edited by Serge Daget. 2 vols. Volume 2: Nantes and Paris, 1988, pp. 537-55.

_____ , and A. G. B. Fisher. *Slavery and Muslim Society in Africa.* London: Christopher Hurst Publishers, 1971.

Fitzgerald, Michael. "An African Brotherhood: Tijaniyya," *Encounter* [Rome], no. 167 (July-August 1990).

_____ , and Jacques Lanfry. "The Ahmadiyya Community and Its Expansion in Africa," *Encounter* [Rome], vol. 1, no. 2 (February 1974).

Flügel, Gustave *Corani Textus Arabicus.* Leipzig, 1883; repr. Farnborough, England: Gregg Press, 1965.

Fodio, Abdalláh dan. *Tazyín al-Waraqát.* Edited by M. Hiskett. Ibadan University Press, 1963.

Fodio, Uthmán dan. *Bayán Wujúb al-Hijrah 'Alá-l-Ibád.* Edited and translated by F. H. El-Masrí. Khartoum: Khartoum University Press and Oxford University Press, 1978.

Forde, Daryll. *African Worlds.* London: Oxford University Press, 1954.

Foy, Whitfield. *Man's Religious Quest.* Part 8. London: Open University, 1978.

Freetown Daily Mail, 24 March 1975.

Fyfe, Christopher. *A History of Sierra Leone.* London: Oxford University Press, 1962.

_____ , ed. *Sierra Leone Inheritance*. London: Oxford University Press, 1964.

Gabid, Hamid al-. "The Organization of Islamic Conference (OIC) and the Development of Africa." In *Islam in Africa: Proceedings of the Islam in Africa Conference*. Edited by Nura Alkali, Adamu Adamu, Awwal Yadudu, Rashid Motem, and Haruna Salihi. Ibadan: Spectrum Books Limited, 1993.

Gabrieli, Francesci. *Muhammad and the Conquests of Islam*. London: Widenfeld and Nicolson, 1968.

Galadanci, S. A. S. "Islamic Education in Africa: Past Influence and Contemporary Challenges." In *Islam in Africa: Proceedings of the Islam in Africa Conference*. Edited by Nura Alkali, Adamu Adamu, Awwal Yadudu, Rashid Motem, and Haruna Salihi. Ibadan: Spectrum Books Limited, 1993.

Gardet, Louis. *Connaître l'Islam*. Paris, 1958.

_____ , and Anawati, C. G. *Introduction à la Théologie Musulmane*. Paris, 1948.

Gay, Peter. *The Enlightenment: An Interpretation*. Vol. I: *The Rise of Modern Paganism*. New York: W. W. Norton, 1977.

Gbadamosi, T. G. O. *The Growth of Islam among the Yoruba: 1841-1908*. London: Longman, 1978.

Ghazálí, Abdul Karim, "A Muslim Propaganda Play: De Man Way De Play Gyambul Wit God," in *Sierra Leone Bulletin of Religion*, vol. 3, no. 2 (December 1961).

_____ , and L. Proudfoot. "A Muslim Propaganda Play and a Commentary," *Sierra Leone Bulletin of Religion*, vol. 3, no. 2 (December 1961).

Ghazálí, Abú Hamíd Al-. *Kitáb Ihyá 'Ulúm al-Dín*. Vol. 2. Translated by Al-Haj Maulana Fazul-ul-Karim. New Delhi: Kitáb Bharan, 1982.

_____ . *Taháfut al-Falásifah* [*The Incoherence of the Philosophers*]. Edited and translated by Sabih Ahmad Kamali. Lahore: Pakistan Philosophical Congress, 1963.

Gibb, H. A. R. *Muhammadanism: A Historical Survey*. New York, 1961.

_____ . *Studies on the Civilization of Islam*. Collected essays. Edited by Stanford J. Shaw and William R. Polk. London: Routledge & Kegan Paul, 1962. Chapter 10, "The Islamic Background of Ibn Khaldun's Political Theory," pp. 166-75.

_____ , et al. *The Encyclopedia of Islam*. New edition. The Hague, from 1954.

Gibbon, Edward. *The Decline and Fall of the Roman Empire*. 3 vols. New York: Modern Library, n.d.

Gitari, David. "The Church and Politics in Kenya," *Transformation: An International Evangelical Dialogue on Mission and Ethics* (July-September 1991).

_____ . "The Church's Witness to the Living God: Seeking Just Political, Social, and Economic Structures in Contemporary Africa," *Transformation: An International Dialogue on Evangelical Social Ethics* 5 (2) (April/June 1988).

Goldziher, Ignaz. *Etudes sur la Tradition Islamique*. Paris, 1952.

Goody, Jack. "The Impact of Islamic Writing on the Oral Cultures of West Africa," *Cahiers d'Études Africaines*, vol. 11, no. 3 (1971).

Goriawala, Mu'izz. "Maguzawa," *Orita: Ibadan Journal of Religious Studies*, IV/2 (December 1970).

Gort, Jerald D. "Liberative Ecumenism: Gateway to the Sharing of Religious Experience Today." In Jerald D. Gort, Hendrik M. Vroom, Rein Fernhout, and Anton Wessels, eds. *On Sharing Religious Experience: Possibilities of Interfaith Mutuality*. Amsterdam, 1992. Editions Rodopi, Grand Rapids, Michigan: Eerdmans, 1992.

Gray, Richard. *Black Christians and White Missionaries*. New Haven: Yale University Press, 1990.

Green, J. "Islam, Religio-politics and Social Change," *Comparative Studies in Society and History*, 27: 312-22.

Greenberg, Joseph. *The Influence of Islam upon a Sudanese Religion*. New York, 1946.

Grunebaum, G. E. von. *Modern Islam: The Search for Cultural Identity*. Berkeley, 1962.

Guardian, The, 27 January 1986.

Guillaume, Alfred. *The Life of Muhammad*. Translated from Ibn Isháq's *Sírat Rasúl Alláh*. Oxford, 1955.

———. *The Traditions of Islam*. Oxford 1924.

Gummi, Sheikh Abubakar Mahmud. Interview. *Quality Magazine*. Lagos (October 1987).

Gutiérrez, Gustavo. *Las Casas: In Search of the Poor of Jesus Christ*. Maryknoll, NY: Orbis Books, 1993.

Hailey, Lord. *An African Survey: Revised 1956*. Oxford: Clarendon Press, 1957.

Hallam, W. K. R. *The Life and Times of Rabih Fadl Allah*. Elms Court, Ilfracombe, England: Arthur H. Stockwell Ltd., 1977.

Hamidulláh, Muhammad. *The Battlefields of the Prophet Muhammad*. Woking, Surrey, 1957.

———. *Le Prophète de l'Islam*. 2 vols. Paris, 1955.

Hansen, Holger Bernt. *Mission, Church and State in a Colonial Setting: Uganda: 1890-1925*. London: Heinemann, 1984.

Hanson, John, and David Robinson. *After the Jihád: The Reign of Ahmad al-Kabír in the Western Sudan*. East Lansing: Michigan State University, 1991.

Harazim, S.D. al-. "The Origin and Progress of Islam in Sierra Leone," *Sierra Leone Studies*, Old Series, no. 21 (1939).

Harden, Blaine. *Africa: Dispatches from a Fragile Continent*. New York: W. W. Norton, 1990.

Harrison, Christopher. *France and Islam in West Africa: 1860-1960*. Cambridge: Cambridge University Press, 1988.

Hastings, Adrian. *The Church in Africa: 1450-1950*. Oxford: Clarendon Press, 1994.

———. *A History of African Christianity: 1950-1975*. Cambridge: Cambridge University Press, 1979.

Haykal, Muhammad Husain. *Life of Muhammad*. Translated by A. Wessels. New York, 1976. *International Congress for the Study of the Qur'an*. Series 1. Canberra, 1982.

Haynes, Jeff. *Religion in Third World Politics*. Boulder: Lynne Rienner Publishers, 1994.

Hiskett, Mervyn. *The Development of Islam in West Africa*. London: Longman, 1984. Chapters 13, 16, and 17.

———. "The Islamic Tradition of Reform in the Western Sudan from the 16th to the 18th Century." *Bulletin of the School of Oriental African Studies* XXV, 3 (1962).

———. "The Maitatsine Riots in Kano, 1980: An Assessment," *Journal of Religion in Africa*, vol. xvii, no. 3 (October 1987).

———. "Problems of Religious Education in Muslim Communities in Africa," *Oversea Education*, vol. xxxii, 3 (October 1960).

———. *The Sword of Truth: The Life and Times of Shehu Usuman dan Fodio*. New York: Oxford University Press, 1973.

Historical Society of Ghana. Volume 7, part 7 (1964).

Hocking, William Ernest. *The Coming World Civilization*. New York: Harper, 1956.

Hodgkin, Thomas. "The Fact of Islamic History (II): Islam in West Africa," *Africa South*, vol. 2, no. 3 (1958): 88-99.

———. "Islam and National Movements in West Africa," *Journal of African History*, vol. 3, no. 2 (1962).

———. "Islam, History and Politics," *Journal of Modern African Studies*, vol. 1, no. 1 (1963).

———, ed. *Nigerian Perspectives: An Historical Anthology*. London: Oxford University Press, 1960.

Honko, Lauri, ed. *Science of Religion: Studies in Methodology*. The Hague: Mouton, 1979.

Hopewell, James F. *Muslim Penetration into French Guinea, Sierra Leone and Liberia before 1850*. Unpublished Ph.D. dissertation. Columbia University, New York, 1958.

Hopkins, J. F. P., and Nehemia Levtzion, eds. *Corpus of Early Arabic Sources for West African History*, Cambridge: Cambridge University Press, 1981.

Horton, Robin. "African Conversion." *Africa* [Journal of the International African Institute] XLI, no. 2 (April 1970).

_____ . *Patterns of Thought in Africa and the West: Essays on Religion and Science*. Cambridge: Cambridge University Press, 1993.

Huntingdon, Samuel P. "The Clash of Civilizations?," *Foreign Affairs* (Summer 1993).

Hunwick, John O. "The Influence of Arabic in West Africa," *Transactions of the Historical Society of Ghana*. Vol. 7, pt. 7. 1964.

_____ . "Religion and State in the Songhay Empire: 1464-1591." In *Islam in Tropical Africa*. Edited by I. M. Lewis. London: Oxford University Press for the International African Institute, 1966.

_____ . *Report on the Seminar on the Teaching of Arabic in Nigeria*. Unpublished manuscript. Ibadan, 11-15 July 1965.

_____ . *Sharí'a in Songhay: The Replies of al-Maghílí to the Questions of Askiya al-Hájj Muhammad*. London: Oxford University Press for the British Academy, 1985.

Ibn 'Ata'lláh, *The Book of Wisdom*. Edited and translated by Victor Danner. Classics of Western Spirituality series. New York: Paulist Press, 1978.

Idowu, E. Bolaji. *African Traditional Religion: A Definition*. London: SCM Press, 1973.

_____ . *Olodumaré, God in Yoruba Belief*. London: Longman, 1962.

Ikenga-Metuh, Emefie. "Muslim Resistance to Missionary Penetration in Northern Nigeria, 1857-1960," *Mission Focus*, vol. 3, no. 2 (1986).

Ingham, K. *Politics in Modern Africa: The Uneven Tribal Dimension* London: Routledge, 1990.

Iqbal, Muhammad. *The Reconstruction of Religious Thought in Islam*. Lahore, 1944.

Isichei, Elizabeth. "The Maitatsine Risings in Nigeria, 1980-1985: A Revolt of the Disinherited," *Journal of Religion in Africa*, vol. xvii, no. 3 (October 1987).

Issawi, Charles. *An Arab Philosophy of History*. London: George Allen & Unwin, 1963.

Izutsu, T. *Ethico-Religious Concepts in the Qur'an*. Montreal, 1966.

_____ . *God and Man in the Qur'an*. Tokyo, 1964.

Jah, al-Hájj U. N. S. "Christian-Muslim Relations: An Islamic Point of View," *Bulletin on Islam and Christian-Muslim Relations in Africa*, vol. 5, no. 4 (1987).

James, C. L. R. *American Civilization*. Cambridge, Mass., and Oxford: Blackwell, 1993.

James, William. *Varieties of Religious Experience*. New York: Mentor Books, 1958.

Jansen, G. H. *Militant Islam*. London: Pan Books, 1979.

Jeffery, Arthur. *Islam: Muhammad and his Religion*. New York, 1958.

_____ . *Reader in Islam*. The Hague, 1962.

Jimeh, S. A. "A Critical Appraisal of Islamic Education with Particular Reference to Critical Happenings on the Nigerian Scene," *Nigerian Journal of Islam*, vol. 2, no. 1 (July 1971-January 1972).

John Paul II. *The Speech of the Holy Father John Paul II to Young Muslims during His Meeting with them at Casablance (Morocco)*. 19 August 1985. Rome: Islamochristiana.

Johnson, S. *The History of the Yorubas*. London: Routledge & Kepan Paul, 1921, 1969.

Jomier, Jacques. *Bible et Coran*. Paris, 1959.

_____ . *Le Commentaire Coranique du Manar.* Paris, 1955.

_____ . *La Place du Coran dans la Vie Quotidienne en Egypte.* Tunis, 1952.

Jones, Trevor. *Ghana's First Republic: The Pursuit of the Political Kingdom.* London: Methuen, 1976.

Jusu, B.M. "The Haidara rebellion of 1931," *Sierra Leone Studies, New Series,* vol. 3, no. 4 (December 1954).

Kamara, Sheikh Moussa. *L'Islam et le Christianisme.* Translated from the Arabic by Amar Samb, Dakar: *Bulletin de l'Institut Fondamental de l'Afrique Noire,* vol. 35, sér. B, no. 2 (1973).

Kane, Cheikh Hamidou. *Ambiguous Adventure.* London: Heinemann, 1965.

Kasim, Alhaji M.S., ed. *Songs and Prayers for Muslim Schools, Nigeria.* Reprinted Ijebu-Ode, July 1969.

Kastfelt, Niels. "African Resistance to Colonialism in Adamawa," *Journal of Religion in Africa,* vol. viii, no. 1 (1976).

_____ . *Religion and Politics in Nigeria: A Study in Middle Belt Christianity.* London: British Academic Press, 1994.

_____ . "Rumours of Maitatsine: A Note on Political Culture in Northern Nigeria," *African Affairs,* LXXXVIII (1989): 83-90.

Ka'ti, Mahmúd al-. *Ta'ríkh al-Fattásh.* Translated and edited by O. Houdas and M. Delafosse. Paris: Librairie d'Amérique et d'Orient Adrien-Maisonneuve, 1964.

Kenny, Joseph. "Shari'a in Nigeria: A Historical Survey," *Bulletin on Islam and Christian-Muslim Relations in Africa,* vol. 4 (January 1986).

Kerr, Malcolm. *The Arab Cold War: Gamal 'Abd al-Nasir and His Rivals: 1958-1970.* 3d edition. London: Oxford University Press for the Royal Institute of International Affairs, 1971.

Khaldún, Ibn. *Al-Muqaddimah: An Introduction to History.* 3 vols. Translated by Franz Rosenthal. Princeton: Princeton University Press, 1968.

Khalidi, Tarif. "Islamic Views of the West in the Middle Ages," *Studies in Interreligious Dialogue,* vol. 5, no. 1 (1995).

Khan, Muhammad Zafrullah. *Muhammad, Seal of the Prophets.* London, 1980.

Khwaja, Jamal. *Quest for Islam.* Bombay, 1977.

Kimball, Charles. *Striving Together: A Way Forward in Christian-Muslim Relations.* Maryknoll, NY: Orbis Books, 1991.

Kindí, Abd al-Masíh ibn Isháq al-. *The Apology.* Edited and translated by Sir William Muir. London: S.P.C.K, 1887.

Kitagawa, Joseph. "Ainu Bear Festival (Iyomante)." *History of Religion* 1, no. 1 (Summer, 1961).

Klaaren, Eugene M. *The Religious Origins of Modern Science.* Lanham, Md.: University Press of America, 1985.

Klautzke, Heinz. "Religion and Secularization: Introductory Remarks from a Western-Christian Perspective." In *Religion, Law and Socety: A Christian-Muslim Discussion.* Edited by Tarek Mitri. Geneva: World Council of Churches, 1995.

Koch, Adrienne, and William Peden, eds. *The Life and Selected Writings of Thomas Jefferson.* New York: The Modern Library, Random House, 1993.

Kokole, Omari H. "Religion in Afro-Arab Relations: Islam and Cultural Changes in Modern Africa." In *Islam in Africa: Proceedings of the Islam in Africa Conference.* Edited by Nura Alkali, Adamu Adamu, Awwal Yadudu, Rashid Motem, and Haruna Salihi. Ibadan: Spectrum Books Limited, 1993.

Kreutzinger, Helga. *The Eri Devils in Freetown, Sierra Leone.* Vienna: Österreichische Ethnologische Gesellschaft, 1966.

Kumo, Suleimanu, "Shar'ia [sic] under Colonialism-Northern Nigeria." In *Islam in Africa: Proceedings of the Islam in Africa Conference*. Edited by Nura Alkali, Adamu Adamu, Awwal Yadudu, Rashid Motem, and Haruna Salihi. Ibadan: Spectrum Books Limited, 1993.

Kup, P. *A History of Sierra Leone, 1400-1787*. Cambridge: Cambridge University Press, 1961.

Laitin, David D. *Hegemony and Culture: Politics and Religious Change among the Yoruba*. Chicago: University of Chicago Press, 1986.

Lammens, Henri. *Islam, Beliefs and Institutions*. Translated by E. D. Ross. London, 1926; repr. Frank Cass, 1968.

Lane Poole, S. *Studies in a Mosque*. London, 1893.

Langewiesche, William. "Turabi's Law," *Atlantic* (August 1994): 26-33.

Langley, J. Ayodele, ed. *Ideologies of Liberation in Black Africa: 1856-1970*. London: Rex Collings, 1979.

Last, Murray. "Aspects of Administration and Dissent in Hausaland: 1800-1968," *Africa*, XL, 4 (October 1970).

——— . *The Sokoto Caliphate*. London: Longman, 1967.

Lawuyi, Tunde. "Nigeria in the 1980s: Religion and National Integration." In *Religion and Society in Nigeria: Historical and Sociological Perspectives*. Edited by Jacob K. Olupona and Toyin Falola. Ibadan: Spectrum Books Limited, 1991.

Lemu, B. A. "Islamisation of Education: A Primary Level Experiment in Nigeria," *Muslim Educational Quarterly*, vol. 2 (1988): 70-80.

Levine, D. "Religion and Politics in Comparative Perspective," *Comparative Politics* (October 1986): 95-122.

Levtzion, Nehemia. "'Abd Allah ibn Yasin and the Almoravids." In *Studies in West African Islamic History*. Volume 1. Edited by John Ralph Willis. London: Frank Cass, 1979.

——— . *Muslims and Chiefs in West Africa: A Study of Islam in the Middle Volta Basin in the Pre-colonial Period*. Oxford: Clarendon Press, 1968.

Lewis, Bernard. *Islam from Muhammad to the Capture of Constantinople*. 2 vols. New York: Oxford University Press, 1974.

Lewis, C. S. *English Literature in the Sixteenth Century*. In *Oxford History of English Literature*. London and New York: Oxford University Press, 1954.

——— . *Surprised by Joy*. London: Collins, 1975.

Lewis, Ewart. *Medieval Political Ideas*. 2 vols. New York: Cooper Square Publishers, 1974. Volume 1.

Lings, Martin. *Muhammad, His Life Based on Earliest Sources*. New Delhi, 1983.

Little, Kenneth L. "A Muslim Missionary in Mendeland," *Man. Journal of Royal Anthr. Inst.* (September-October 1946).

Locke, John. *A Letter concerning Toleration*. Buffalo, NY: Prometheus Books, 1990.

——— . *Two Treatises of Government*. Edited by Peter Laslett. Cambridge: Cambridge University Press, 1963; New York: Mentor Books of the New American Library, 1965.

Lugard, Lady (*nee* Flora Shaw). *A Tropical Dependency*. London, 1906; repr. London, 1964.

Lynch, H. R. *Edward Wilmot Blyden: Pan-Negro Patriot*. New York: Oxford University Press, 1967.

Macdonald, Duncan Black. *The Development of Muslim Theology and Jurisprudence*. Beirut: Khayat Books, 1965.

Mala, Sam Babs, and Z. I. Oseni, eds. *Religion, Peace and Unity in Nigeria*. Ibadan: Nigerian Association for the Study of Religions, 1984.

Malcolm X (with Alex Haley). *Autobiography.* London: Penguin Books, 1968.

Malik, Charles. *God and Man in Contemporary Islamic Thought.* Beirut, 1972.

Málik, Imám, *Al-Muwatta.* London: Diwan Press, 1982.

Mallia, J. "Fundamentalists Rejoice but Sudan's Millions Starve," *The Guardian*, 15 July 1991.

Manga, Al-Amin Abu. "Resistance to the Western System of Education by the Early Migrant Community of Maiurno (Sudan)." In *Islam in Africa: Proceedings of the Islam in Africa Conference.* Edited by Nura Alkali, Adamu Adamu, Awwal Yadudu, Rashid Motem, and Haruna Salihi. Ibadan: Spectrum Books Limited, 1993.

Maranz, David E. *Peace Is Everything: The World View of Muslims and Tradionalists in the Senegambia.* Dallas: International Museum of Cultures, 1993.

Maritain, Jacques. *Man and the State.* Chicago: University of Chicago Press, 1951.

Martin, B. G. *Muslim Brotherhoods in 19th century Africa.* Cambridge: Cambridge University Press, 1976.

_____. "A Muslim Political Tract from Northern Nigeria: Muhammad Bello's *Usúl al-Siyása.*" In Daniel F. McCall and Norman R. Bennett, eds. *Aspects of West African Islam*, vol. 5. Boston: Boston University Press, 1971.

Martin, David. *The Religious and the Secular.* London: Routledge, 1969.

Marty, Paul. *Les Mourides d'Amadou Bamba.* Paris, 1913.

_____. *L'Islam en Guinée.* Paris: E. Leroux, 1921.

Masrí, F. H. El-. "The Life of Shehu Usuman dan Fodio before the Jihad," *Journal of the Historical Society of Nigeria* (1963).

Masson, D. *Le Coran et la Révélation Judéo-Chrétienne Comparée.* 2 vols. Paris, 1958.

Maudúdí, Abú-l-'Alá. *Islamic Law and Constitution.* Karachi, 1955.

_____. *Towards Understanding Islam.* Lahore, 1940.

Mauny, R. *Tableau géographique de l'ouest africain.* Dakar, 1961.

Mazrui, Ali A. "African Islam and Comprehensive Religion: Between Revivalism and Expansion." In *Islam in Africa: Proceedings of the Islam in Africa Conference.* Edited by Nura Alkali, Adamu Adamu, Awwal Yadudu, Rashid Motem, and Haruna Salihi. Ibadan: Spectrum Books Limited, 1993.

Mbiti, John S. *African Religions and Philosophy.* London: Heinemann Publishers, 1969, 1985.

_____. *New Testament Eschatology in an African Background.* London: Cambridge University Press, 1971.

_____. *Prayers of African Religion.* Maryknoll, NY: Orbis Books, 1975.

McCarthy, Richard. *The Theology of Al-Ash'arí.* Beirut. 1953.

McKenzie, Peter Rutherford. *Inter-religious Encounters in West Africa: Samuel Ajayi Crowther's Attitude to African Traditional Religions and Islam.* Leicester: Leicester University Bookshop, 1976.

_____. "Thomas Freeman's Attitude to Other Faiths," *Ghana Bulletin of Theology*, vol. 3, no. 8 (1970).

McIlwain, Charles H. "Medieval Institutions in the Modern World." In *The Renaissance: Medieval or Modern?* Edited by Karl H. Dannenfeldt. Problems in European Civilization Series. Boston: D. C. Heath, 1959.

Medhurst, K. "Religion and Politics: A Typology," *Scottish Journal of Religious Studies*, I, vol. 2, no. 2 (1981): 115-34.

Meek, C. K. *The Northern Tribes of Nigeria.* 2 vols. London: 1929; repr. Frank Cass, 1971.

Merkl, Peter H., and Ninian Smart, eds. *Religion and Politics in the Modern World.* New York: New York University Press, 1985.

Mews, S., ed. *Religion in Politics*. Harlow: Longman Publishers, 1989.

Michel, Thomas. "Differing Perceptions of Human Rights: Asian-African Interpretations at the Human Rights Conference." In *Religion, Law and Socety: A Christian-Muslim Discussion*. Edited by Tarek Mitri. Geneva: World Council of Churches, 1995.

Miller, Walter. *Have We Failed in Nigeria?* London: Lutterworth Press, 1947.

―――― . *Reflections of a Pioneer*. London: CMS, 1936.

Miskin, Tijani, El-. "Da'wa and the Challenge of Secularism: A Conceptial Agenda for Islamic Ideologues." In *Islam in Africa: Proceedings of the Islam in Africa Conference*. Edited by Nura Alkali, Adamu Adamu, Awwal Yadudu, Rashid Motem, and Haruna Salihi. Ibadan: Spectrum Books Limited, 1993.

Mitchell, Peter K. "A Note on the Distribution in Sierra Leone of Literacy in Arabic, Mende and Temne," *African Language Review*, vol. 7 (1968).

Mitri, Tarek, ed. *Religion, Law and Socety: A Christian-Muslim Discussion*. Geneva: World Council of Churches, 1995.

Molla, Claude F. "Some Aspects of Islam in Africa South of the Sahara," *International Review of Mission*, vol. 56, no. 224 (October 1967).

Mollien, Gaspard. *Travels in Africa to the Sources of the Senegal and Gambia in 1818*. London, 1820.

Momoh, C. S., et al., eds. *Nigerian Studies in Religious Tolerance*. 4 vols. Ibadan, 1989.

Monteil, Vincent. *L'Islam noir*. Paris: Seuil, 1964.

―――― . "Marabouts." In *Islam in Africa*. Edited by J. Kritzeck and W. H. Lewis. New York: Van Nostrand, 1969.

Moore, Kathleen M. *Al-Mughtaribun: American Law and the Transformation of Muslim Life in the United States*. Albany: State University of New York Press, 1994.

Motte, Mary. "Diversity and Truth: A Missiological Perspective," *Missiology*, vol. xxiii, no. 1 (January 1995).

Mourey, Charles, and August Terrier. *L'Expansion Francaise et la Formation Territoriale*. Paris: E Larose, 1910.

Moyser, G., ed. *Politics and Religion in the Modern World*. London: Routledge, 1991.

Muir, William. *Life of Mahomet*. 4 vols. London, 1858-61; new abridged ed., Edinburgh, 1923; rev. ed., New York, 1975.

Mulk, Nizám al-. *The Book of Government for Kings (Siyását Náma)*. London: Routledge & Kegan Paul, 1960.

Nadel, Siegfried F. *A Black Byzantium: The Kingdom of Nupe in Nigeria*. London: Oxford University Press, 1942; repr. 1969.

―――― . *Nupe Religion*. London: Oxford University Press for the International African Institute, 1954.

Nadví, Abul Hasan. *Life of Muhammad*. Lucknow, n.d.

Nation, The, 11 June 1975.

New York Times, 14 April 1990.

New York Times, "A Fundamentalist Finds a Fulcrum in Sudan," 29 January 1992.

Nida, Eugene. *Message and Mission*. New York: Harper & Brothers, 1960.

―――― , and Reyburn, William D. *Meaning across Cultures*. New York: Orbis Books, 1981.

Niebuhr, H. Richard. *Radical Monotheism and Western Culture*. New York: Harper and Brothers, 1960.

Nielsen, Jørgen S. "*Sharí'ah*, Change and Plural Societies." In *Religion, Law and Socety: A Christian-Muslim Discussion*. Edited by Tarek Mitri. Geneva: World Council of Churches, 1995.

Noibi, D.O.S. "Muslim Youth and Christian-Sponsored Education," *Bulletin of Islam and Christian-Muslim Relations in Africa*, vol. VI, no. 3: 3-25.

Norris, H. T. *The Arab Conquest of the Western Sudan*. Oxford: Oxford University Press, 1986.

_____. *The Tuaregs: Their Islamic Legacy and Its Diffusion in the Sahel*. Warminster, 1975.

Numání, Shibh. *Muhammad*. Karachi, 1975.

Oberhammer, Gerhard. "Hermeneutics of Religious Experience." In Jerald D. Gort, Hendrik M. Vroom, Rein Fernhout, and Anton Wessels, eds. *On Sharing Religious Experience: Possibilities of Interfaith Mutuality*. Amsterdam, 1992.

O'Brien, Conor Cruise. *God Land: Reflections on Religion and Politics*. Cambridge: Harvard University Press, 1987.

_____. "The Wrath of Ages: Nationalism's Primordial Roots," *Foreign Affairs* (November-December 1993), pp. 142-49.

O'Brien, Donal Cruise. *The Mourides of Senegal*. Oxford: Clarendon Press, 1971.

_____. "A Versatile Charisma: The Mouride Brotherhood 1967-1975," *Archives européenes de sociologie* 18 (1977).

Ofonagoro, W. I. *The Great Debate: Nigerian Viewpoints on the Draft Constitution 1976/77*. Lagos: Times Publication, 1978.

Okunola, Muri. "The Relevance of Shar'ia [sic] to Nigeria." In *Islam in Africa: Proceedings of the Islam in Africa Conference*, Edited by Nura Alkali, Adamu Adamu, Awwal Yadudu, Rashid Motem, and Haruna Salihi. Ibadan: Spectrum Books Limited, 1993.

Olayiwola, R. O. "Religious Pluralism and Functionalism among the Ijesha-Yoruba of Nigeria," *Asia Journal of Theology*, vol. VI, no. 1: 141-53.

Olupona, Jacob K., ed., *Religion and Peace in Multi-Faith Nigeria*, Ile-Ife: Obafemi Awolowo University, 1992.

_____ , and Toyin Falola, eds. *Religion and Society in Nigeria: Historical and Sociological Perspectives*. Ibadan: Spectrum Books Limited, 1991.

Onaiyekan, J. "Christians and Muslims: Human Rights and Responsibilities: the Nigerian Situation," *Islamochristiana*, vol. IX (1983): 181-99.

_____ , ed. *Religion, Peace and Justice in Nigeria: Breaking New Grounds*. Communique of the Catholic Bishops' Conference of Nigeria. Ilorin, February 1989.

Oseni, Z. I. "Islamic Scholars as Spiritual Healers in a Nigerian Community," *Islamic Culture*, vol. 62, no. 4 (1988).

Osman El-Tom, Abdullahi. "Drinking the Koran: The Meaning of Koranic Verses in Berti Erasure," *Africa*, vol. 55, no. 4 (1985).

Osuntokun, J. "The Response of the British Colonial Government in Nigeria to the Islamic Insurgency in the French Sudan and Sahara during the First World War," *Bulletin de l'Institut Fondamental d'Afrique Noire*, sér B, vol. XXVI (Janvier 1974): 14-24.

Owen, Nicholas. *Journal of a Slavedealer, 1746-57*. Edited by E. Martin. London, 1930.

Oyelade, Emmanuel O. "Islamic Theocracy and Religious Pluralism in Africa," *Asia Journal of Theology*, vol. VII, no. 1 (1993): 149-60.

_____ . "Sir Ahmadu Bello, the Sardauna of Sokoto: The Twentieth Century Mijaddid (Reformer) of West Africa," *Islamic Quarterly*, vol. XXVII, no. 4 (1983): 223-31.

_____ . "Trends in Hausa/Fulani Islam since Independence: Aspects of Islamic Modernism in Nigeria," *Orita*, vol. XIV, no. 1 (1982): 3-15.

Ozigi A., and L. Ojo. *Education in Northern Nigeria*. London, 1981.

Paden, John N. *Ahmadu Bello, Sardauna of Sokoto: Values and Leadership in Nigeria*.

London: Hodder & Stoughton, 1986.

_____ . *Religion and Political Culture in Kano.* Berkeley and Los Angeles: University of California Press, 1973.

Parrinder, G. *African Traditional Religion.* London: Hutchinson's University Library, 1954.

_____ . *Africa's Three Religions.* London: Sheldon Press, 1969.

_____ . *Jesus in the Qur'an.* London: Faber & Faber, 1965.

_____ . *Religion in Africa.* Harmondsworth, Middlesex: Penguin Books, 1969.

_____ . *West African Religion.* London: Epworth Press, 1969.

Parsons, Robert T. "Death and Burial in Kono Religion," *Sierra Leone Bulletin of Religion,* vol. 3, no. 2 (December 1961).

Peel, John D. Y. *Aladura: A Religious Movement among the Yoruba.* London: Oxford University Press for the International African Institute, 1968.

_____ . *Ijeshas and Nigerians: The Incorporation of a Yoruba Kingdom, 1890s-1970s.* Cambridge: Cambridge University Press, 1983.

Peterson, John. *Province of Freedom.* London, 1969.

Piscatori, J. F. *Islam in a World of Nation States.* Cambridge: Cambridge University Press, 1986.

Poston, Larry. *Islamic Da'wah in the West: Muslim Missionary Activity and the Dynamics of Conversion to Islam.* New York: Oxford University Press, 1992.

Pro Mundi Vita Bulletin. "The Muslim-Christian Dialogue of the Last Ten Years," no. 74 (September-October 1978). Brussels.

Pro Mundi Vita Dossiers. "The Church and Christians in Madagascar Today," Africa Dossier 6 (July-August 1978).

Proctor, J. E. *Islam and International Relations.* London, 1965.

Proudfoot, Leslie. "Ahmed Alhadi and the Ahmadiyah in Sierra Leone," *Sierra Leone Bulletin of Religion,* vol. 2, no. 2 (December 1960).

_____ . "An Aku Factional Fight in East Freetown," *Sierra Leone Bulletin of Religion,* vol. 4, no. 2 (1962).

_____ . "Mosque-building and Tribal Separatism in Freetown," *Africa,* XXIX, no. 4 (1959).

_____ . "Towards Muslim Solidarity in Freetown," *Africa,* XXXI (1961).

_____ , and H. S. Wilson. "Muslim Attitudes to Education in Sierra Leone," *Muslim World,* vol. 50, no. 1 (1960).

Qayrawání, Ibn Abí Zayd al-. *La Risálah: ou épitre sue les éléments du dogme et de la loi de l'Islam selon le rite malikte.* Edited and translated by Léon Bercher. Algiers: 1952. Éditions Jules Carbonel, 1952. English edition: Joseph Kenny, ed. and tr. *The Risálah.* Minna, Nigeria: The Islamic Educational Trust, 1992.

Quadri, Y. A. "The Qadiriyyah and Tijaniyyah Relations in Nigeria in the Twentieth Century," *Orita,* vol. XVI, no. 1 (1984): 15-30.

_____ . "A Study of the Izalah: A Contemporary Anti-Sufi Organisation in Nigeria," *Orita,* vol. XVII, no. 2 (1985): 95-108.

Qur'án, The Meanings and Commentary in English translation. Medina: Ministry of Hajj and Endowments, 1411 H (1990/91), Kingdom of Saudi Arabia.

Rahbar, Daud. *God of Justice, Ethical Doctrine of the Qur'an.* Leiden: E. J. Brill, 1960.

Rahnama, Zayn al-'Ábidín. *Payambar: The Messenger.* Translated by L. P. Elwell Sutton. Lahore, 1964.

Rahner, Hugo. *Church and State in Early Christianity.* San Francisco: Ignatius Press, 1992. Translated from the German by Leo Donald Davis, *Kirche und Staat im Frühen Christentum: Dokumente aus acht Jahrhunderten und ihre Deutung.* Munich: Kösel Verlag, 1961.

Raji, R. A. "The Nigerian Association of Teachers of Arabic and Islamic Studies (NATAIS): An Appraisal of Its Effects on Muslim Minority Education," *Muslim Education Quarterly*, vol. VII (Winter 1990): 57-71.

Ramadan Vision, The. Freetown, July 1947.

Rasmussen, Lissi. *Religion and Property in Northern Nigeria.* Copenhagen: University of Copenhagen, 1990.

Reeck, Darrell L. "Islam in a West African Chiefdom: An interpretation," *Muslim World*, vol. 62, no. 3 (1972).

Rippin, A., and J. Knappert, eds. *Textual Sources on Islam.* Manchester: Manchester University Press; Chicago: Chicago University Press, 1986.

Roberts, H. "Radical Islamism and the Dilemma of Algerian Nationalism: The Embattled Arians of Algiers," *Third World Quarterly*, vol. 10, no. 2 (1988): 567-75.

Roberts, S. H. *The History of French Colonial Policy: 1870-1925.* London, 1929.

Robinson, David. "Beyond Resistance and Collaboration: Ahmadu Bamba and the Murids of Senegal," *Journal of Religion in Africa*, vol. xxi, no. 2 (May 1991).

_____ . *The Holy War of 'Umar Tal: The Western Sudan in the Mid-Nineteenth Century.* Oxford: Clarendon Press, 1985.

Robinson, Francis. *Atlas of the Islamic World since 1500.* London, 1982.

Rodinson, Maxine. *Mohammed.* Translated by A. Carter. New edition. London: Penguin, 1971.

Rosenthal, E. I. J. *Islam and the Modern National State.* Cambridge: Cambridge University Press, 1965.

_____ . *Political Thought in Medieval Islam.* Cambridge: Cambridge University Press, 1958.

Rubin, B. "Religion and International Affairs," *The Washington Quarterly*, vol. 13, no. 2 (1990): 51-63.

Ruete, Emily. *Memoirs of an Arabian Princess from Zanzibar.* New York: Markus Wiener Publishing, 1989.

Ruxton, F. H.. *Maliki Law.* London, 1916.

Ryan, Patrick J., S.J. *Imale: Yoruba Participation in the Muslim Tradition.* Montana: Scholars Press, 1979.

Sa'dí, 'Abd al-Rahmán al-. *Ta'ríkh al-Súdán.* Translated and edited by O. Houdas. Paris: Librairie d'Amérique et d'Orient, Adrien-Maisonneuve, 1964.

Sahliyeh, E., ed. *Religious Resurgence and Politics in the Contemporary World.* Albany: State University of New York Press, 1990.

Saif, Walid. "Human Rights and Islamic Revivalism." In *Religion, Law and Socety: A Christian-Muslim Discussion.* Edited by Tarek Mitri. Geneva: World Council of Churches, 1995.

_____ . "*Sharí'ah* and Modernity." In *Religion, Law and Socety: A Christian-Muslim Discussion.* Edited by Tarek Mitri. Geneva: World Council of Churches, 1995.

Sale, George. *The Koran.* Introductory essay and translation. Many editions since the eighteenth century.

Sambe, Amar. *Diplôme d'études supérieures.* Faculté des Lettres, Université de Paris, 1964.

Sanneh, Lamin. "The Domestication of Christianity and Islam in African Societies," *Journal of Religion in Africa* 11/1 (1980).

_____ . "Futa Jallon and the Jakhanke Clerical Tradition. Part I: The Historical Setting," *Journal of Religion in Africa* 12/1 (1981): 53.

_____ . *The Jakhanké Muslim Clerics: A Religious and Historical Study of Islam in Senegambia.* Lanham, Md.: University Press of America, 1989.

———— . "The Origins of Clericalism in West African Islam." *Journal of African History* XVII, 1 (1976).

Santerre, R. *Pédagogie Musulmane de l'Afrique Noire*. Presse Universitaire de Montreal (1975).

Sarwar, H. G. *The Holy Qur'an*. Singapore, 1929.

———— . *Life of the Holy Prophet*. Lahore, 1937.

———— . *Philosophy of the Qur'án*. Lahore, 1938.

Saul, Mahir. "The Quranic School Farm and Child Labour in Upper Volta," *Africa*, vol. 54, no. 2 (1984).

Sawyerr, Harry. "Do Africans Believe in God?" *Sierra Leone Studies*, New Series, no. 15 (December 1961).

———— . "Sacrificial Rituals in Sierra Leone," *Sierra Leone Bulletin of Religion*, 1 (June 1959).

———— . "The Supreme God and Spirits," *Sierra Leone Bulletin of Religion*, vol. 3, no. 2 (December 1961).

Sayeed, Khalid Bin. *Western Dominance and Political Islam*. Albany: State University of New York Press, 1994.

Schimmel, Annemarie. *Mystical Dimensions of Islam*. Chapel Hill: University of North Carolina Press, 1975.

Schlenker, C. F. *Collection of Temne Traditions, Fables and Proverbs*. London, 1861.

Schultze, Arnold. *The Sultanate of Bornu*. Translated from the German. London, 1913; repr. Frank Cass, 1968.

Schuon, F. *Understanding Islam*. Translated by D. M. Matheson. London, 1963.

Sekyi, Kobina. *The Parting of the Ways*. In J. Ayodele Langley, *Ideologies of Liberation in Black Africa: 1856-1970*. London: Rex Collins, 1979.

Sell, Edward. *The Faith of Islam*. 4th ed. London, 1920.

Sesay, S. I. "Koranic Schools in the Provinces, *Sierra Leone Journal of Education*, vol. 1, no. 1 (April 1966).

Sharpe, Eric. "Dialogue and Faith," *Religion*, vol. 3 (1973).

Sheard, Robert B. *Interreligious Dialogue in the Catholic Church Since Vatican II: An Historical and Theological Study*. Lewiston, NY: Edwin Mellen Press, 1987.

Shipton, Parker. *Bitter Money: Cultural Economy and Some African Meanings of Forbidden Commodities*. Washington, D.C.: American Anthropological Association, 1989.

Sierra Leone Bulletin of Religion, vol. 4, no. 2 (1962).

Sierra Leone Weekly News [Freetown], vol. 9 (January 1889).

Sivan, E. *Radical Islam*. New Haven: Yale University Press, 1985.

Skinner, David E. "Islamic Education and Missionary Work in the Gambia, Ghana and Sierra Leone During the Twentieth Century," *Bulletin on Islam and Christian-Muslim Relations in Africa*, vol. 1, no. 4 (October 1983).

———— . "Islam in Sierra Leone During the 19th Century," Ph.D. thesis. Berkeley, 1971.

———— . "Mende Settlement and the Development of Islamic Institutions in Sierra Leone," *International Journal of African Historical Studies*, vol. 11, no. 1 (1978).

Slater, B., and R. Shultz, eds. *Revolution and Political Change in the Third World*. London: Adamantine, 1990.

Smart, Joko H. M. "Place of Islamic Law within the Framework of the Sierra Leone Legal System," *African Law Studies*, vol. 18 (1980).

Smith, D. E. *Religion and Political Development*. Boston: Little, Brown & Co., 1970.

Smith, Jane. *An Historical and Semantic Study of the Term 'Islam' as Seen in a Sequence of Qur'an Commentaries.* Cambridge, Mass., 1975.

_____ , and Y. Y. Haddad. *Islamic Understanding of Death and Resurrection.* Albany, 1981.

Smith, Jane Idleman, and Yvonne Yazbeck Haddad, eds. *Muslim Communities in North America.* Albany: State University of New York Press, 1994.

Smith, Mary, ed. *Baba of Karo.* New Haven: Yale University Press; London: Faber, 1954.

Smith, R. Bosworth. *Mohammed and Mohammedanism.* 2d edition. London: Smith and Elder Co., 1876.

Smith, Wilfred C. *The Faith of Other Men.* New York: Harper Torchbooks, 1963.

_____ . *The Meaning and End of Religion: A New Approach to the Religious Traditions of Mankind.* New York: Mentor Books, 1963.

_____ . *Questions of Religious Truth.* London: Victor Gollancz Ltd., 1967.

_____ . "Can Believers Share the Qur'an and the Bible as Word of God?" In Jerald D. Gort, Hendrik M. Vroom, Rein Fernhout, and Anton Wessels, eds. *On Sharing Religious Experience: Possibilities of Interfaith Mutuality.* Amsterdam, 1992.

Speelman, Gé. "Muslim Minorities and *Sharī'ah* in Europe." In *Religion, Law and Socety: A Christian-Muslim Discussion.* Edited by Tarek Mitri. Geneva: World Council of Churches, 1995.

_____ , Jan van Lin, and Dick Mulder, eds. *Muslims and Christians in Europe: Breaking New Ground: Essays in Honour of Jan Slomp.* Kampen: Uitgeverij, 1993.

Stackhouse, Max. "Politics and Religion," *Encyclopedia of Religion,* vol. 11, Mircea Eliade, ed. New York: Macmillan, 1987.

_____ . *Public Theology and Political Economy: Christian Stewardship in Modern Society.* Grand Rapids: Eerdmans, 1987.

Stanton, H. U. W. *The Teaching of the Qur'án.* London, 1919.

St. Croix, F. W. de. *The Fulani of Nigeria.* Lagos, 1945.

Stewart, Desmond. *Mecca.* New York, 1980.

Stock, Eugene. *A History of the Church Missionary Society.* Vols. ii and iii. London, 1916.

Strolz, Walter. "The Incomparability of God as Biblical Experience of Faith." In Jerald D. Gort, Hendrik M. Vroom, Rein Fernhout, and Anton Wessels, eds. *On Sharing Religious Experience: Possibilities of Interfaith Mutuality.* Amsterdam, 1992.

Swartz, Merlin. *Studies in Islam.* New York, 1980.

Sweetman, David. *Women Leaders in African History.* London: Heinemann Publishers, 1984.

Sweetman, J. W. *Islam and Christian Theology.* London, part I, vol. 1, 1945; part I, vol. 2, 1947; part II, vol. 1, 1955.

Swift, R. "Fundamentalism," *New Internationalist* (August 1990).

Tangban, O. E. "The Hajj and the Nigerian Economy: 1960-1981," *Journal of Religion in Africa,* vol. xxi, no. 3 (August 1991).

Taylor, A. J. P. *The Habsburg Monarchy: 1808-1918.* 1948; reprinted London: Penguin Books, 1990.

Taylor, John V. *The Primal Vision.* London: SCM, 1963.

Thieman, Ronald R. *Constructing a Public Theology: The Church in a Pluralistic Culture.* Louisville: Westminster/John Knox Press, 1991.

Thomas, Owen C., ed. *Attitudes towards Other Religions: Some Christians Interpretations.* London: SCM, 1969.

Tibi, Basam. *Islam and the Cultural Accommodation of Social Change.* Boulder: Westview, 1990.

Tocqueville, Alexis de. *Democracy in America.* Translated by George Lawrence. Edited by J. P. Mayer. New York: Harper Perennial, 1988. Published by Harper & Row, 1966.

Torrey, C. C. *Jewish Foundation of Islam.* New Haven, 1933.

Tremearne, A. J. N. *Ban of the Bori.* London, 1914; repr. Frank Cass, 1968.

Trimingham, John Spencer. *A History of Islam in West Africa.* London: Oxford University Press, 1962.

————. *The Influence of Islam upon Africa.* Beirut: Librairie du Liban; London: Longman Publishers, 1968.

————. *Islam in West Africa.* Oxford: Clarendon Press, 1959.

————. *The Sufi Orders in Islam.* Oxford: Clarendon Press, 1971.

————, and Christopher Fyfe. "The Early Expansion of Islam in Sierra Leone," *Sierra Leone Bulletin of Religion,* vol. 2, no. 1 (June 1960).

Turner, Harold W. *History of an African Independent Church: Church of the Lord (Aladura).* 2 vols. Oxford: Clarendon Press.

Turner, Victor. *Dramas, Fields and Metaphors: Symbolic Action in Human Society.* Ithaca, 1983. See especially the chapter "Metaphors of Anti-Structure in Religious Culture."

————. *The Ritual Process: Structure and Anti-Structure.* Ithaca, NY: Cornell University Press, 1972.

"Universal Islamic Declaration," *The Times,* London, 14 April 1980.

Usman, Yúsúf Bala. *The Manipulation of Religion in Nigeria, 1975-1987.* Kaduna: Vanguard Publisher, 1987.

Vatikiotis, P. *Islam and the State.* London: Routledge, 1991.

Voll, J., and F. von der Mehden. "Religious Resurgence and Revolution: Islam." In *Revolution and Political Change in the Third World.* Edited by B. Slater and R. Shultz. London: Adamantine, 1990.

Vroom, Hendrik M. "Sharing Religious Experience: Recapitulation, Comments and Questions." In Jerald D. Gort, Hendrik M. Vroom, Rein Fernhout, and Anton Wessels, eds. *On Sharing Religious Experience: Possibilities of Interfaith Mutuality.* Amsterdam, 1992.

Waardenburg, J. J. *L'Islam dans le Miroir de l'Occident.* The Hague, 1963.

Waddy, Charis. *The Muslim Mind.* New York, 1976.

————. *Women in Muslim History.* New York, 1980.

Waldman, M. W. "The Church of Scotland Mission at Blantyre, Nyasaland: Its Political Implications," *Bulletin of the Society of African Church History,* 2/4 (1968).

Waqidi, Muhammad ibn 'Umar al- (752-829). *Muhammad in Medina.* Translated and abbreviated. Wellhausen, Berlin, 1882.

Warburg, Gabriel R. "Ideological and Practical Considerations regarding Slavery in the Mahdist State and the Anglo-Egyptian Sudan: 1881-1918." In *The Ideology of Slavery in Africa.* Edited by Paul Lovejoy. Beverly Hills, Cal.: Sage Publications, 1981.

————. *Islam, Nationalism and Communism in a Traditional Society: The Case of the Sudan.* London: Frank Cass, 1978.

Watt, W. Montgomery. *Christian-Muslim Encounters: Perceptions and Misperceptions.* London: Routledge, 1991.

————. *Companion to the Qur'an.* Edinburgh, 1968.

————. *The Formative Period of Islamic Thought.* London, 1973.

————. *Islam and Christianity Today.* London: Routledge, 1983.

————. *Islamic Fundamentalism and Modernity.* London: Routledge, 1990.

————. *Islamic Philosophy and Theology.* Edinburgh: Edinburgh University Press, 1962.

————. *Muhammad at Mecca.* Oxford: Clarendon Press, 1953.

_____ . *Muhammad at Medina*. Oxford: Clarendon Press, 1956.

_____ . *Muhammad, Prophet and Statesman*. London, 1961.

We Yone [newspaper], 11 June 1975.

Weaver, Richard. *Ideas Have Consequences*. Chicago: University of Chicago Press, 1948.

Wensinck, A. J. *Handbook of Early Muhammadan Tradition*. Leiden, 1960.

_____ . *The Muslim Creed*. Cambridge, England, 1932; repr. Frank Cass, 1965.

Wessels, Anton. "The Experience of the Prophet Mohammed." In Jerald D. Gort, Hendrik M. Vroom, Rein Fernhout, and Anton Wessels, eds. *On Sharing Religious Experience: Possibilities of Interfaith Mutuality*. Amsterdam, 1992.

West Africa [weekly magazine], 17 September 1979.

Westerlund, David, ed. *Questioning the Secular State: The Worldwide Resurgence of Religion in Politics*. London: Christopher Hurst and Co, 1995.

Westermarck, E. A. *Pagan Survivals in Mohammadan Civilization*. London, 1933.

Williams, J. A. *Islam*. London, 1961.

Willis, John Ralph. "*Jihád fí sabíl li-lláh*: Its Doctrinal Basis in Islam and Some Aspects of Its Evolution in Nineteenth Century West Africa," *Journal of African History*, vol. 8 (1967).

_____ . *The Passion of al-Hájj 'Umar: An Essay into the Nature of Charisma in Islam*. London: Frank Cass, 1989.

Woodhouse, A. S. P., ed. *Puritanism and Liberty: The Army Debates (1647-9) from the Clarke Manuscripts*. London: J. M. Dent & Sons Ltd., 1974.

Wurie, A. "The Bundukas of Sierra Leone," *Sierra Leone Studies*, n.s., vol. 1, no. 4 (December 1953).

Wyndham, H. A. *The Atlantic and Slavery*. Oxford: Oxford University Press, 1935.

Yadudu, Auwalu Hamisu. "The Prospects for Shar'ia [sic] in Nigeria." In *Islam in Africa: Proceedings of the Islam in Africa Conference*. Edited by Nura Alkali, Adamu Adamu, Awwal Yadudu, Rashid Motem, and Haruna Salihi, Ibadan: Spectrum Books Limited, 1993.

Yahya, Dahiru. "Colonialism in Africa and the Impact of European Concepts and Values: Nationalism and Muslims in Nigeria." In *Islam in Africa: Proceedings of the Islam in Africa Conference*. Edited by Nura Alkali, Adamu Adamu, Awwal Yadudu, Rashid Motem, and Haruna Salihi. Ibadan: Spectrum Books Limited, 1993.

Yamusa, S. *The Political Ideas of the Jihad Leaders: Being a Translation, Edition and Analysis of* Usúl al-Siyása *by Muhammad Bello and* Diya al-Hukkum *by Abdullahi b. Fodio*. M.A. thesis. Abdullahi Bayero Collehe, Kano, 1975.

Yúsúf, Bilikisu. "Da'wa and Contemporary Challenges Facing Muslim Women in Secular States-A Nigerian Case Study." In *Islam in Africa: Proceedings of the Islam in Africa Conference*. Edited by Nura Alkali, Adamu Adamu, Awwal Yadudu, Rashid Motem, and Haruna Salihi. Ibadan: Spectrum Books Limited, 1993.

Zaehner, R. C. *Hindu and Muslim Mysticism*. New York: Schocken Books, 1972.

_____ . *Mysticism, Sacred and Profane: An Inquiry into Some Varieties of Praeternatural Experience*. London: Oxford University Press, 1973.

_____ . *At Sundry Times: An Essay in the Comparison of Religions*. London, 1958.

_____ . *The Teaching of the Magi*. London: Oxford University Press, 1956.

Ziadeh, Khalid. "On the Urgency of *Ijtihád*." In *Religion, Law and Socety: A Christian-Muslim Discussion*. Edited by Tarek Mitri. Geneva: World Council of Churches, 1995.

Zwemer, Samuel. *Arabia: The Cradle of Islam*. New York, 1900.

_____ , ed. *The Mohammedan World of Today*. New York, 1906.

Index

Abayomi-Cole, 77, 78
Abdallah, 39
Abraham: in passages on revelations at
  Medina, 43
Acheampong, Gen., 90, 94
Afghání, Jalál al-Dín, 121
Afonso I (king), 93
Africa: capture of religion by state in,
  91-97; Christian communities of, 1;
  cross-cultural and comparative nature
  of religious practice in, 82-83;
  dialogue with Islam in, 23-24; early
  church fathers from, 75; historical
  encounter of Islam or Christianity
  with, 11-12; history of Islamic
  da'wah in, 26; impact of Islam on
  personal and social life of, 70, 73-77;
  impact of secular state in, 89-90;
  interfaith issues in Muslim *da'wah* in,
  5-27; mediation between Islam and
  Western secularism, 3; mobilizing
  Qádiriyah *tariqah* in Muslim, 58;
  Muslim interactions with Christians
  in, 1; Portuguese immmigration into,
  92; response to Christianity and Islam
  by, 76; role of religion in mass
  movements of, 81; Western political
  influence in, 85; Western secular
  influence in, 85-86
African Christian Independency:
  apocalyptic theme in, 21-22;
  comparative dimension with *jihád*,
  22-23; and modernist reaction, 22;
  structural factors in, 22
African Islam: missionary movements in,
  17
Africans: esteem for religion held by, 16;
  as missionary pioneers and spokes-
  man, 9
Agbebi, Mojola, 106n42

Ahmadiyah Muslim missionary move-
  ment, 18
Ainu, ancient: religion of, 62
'A'ísha, 45
Akan, the: proverbs of, 107, 108
Akus. *See* Muslim Creoles
Alexandria: Christian community in, 49
Algeria: Muslim radicalism in, 81
Alhadi, Ahmed, 78
Ali (fourth caliph), 39
Almohad dynasty: collapse in North
  Africa, 100
Alphabet: teaching of, in Qur'án school,
  152
Amara, Almami, 78
America: Tocqueville's observance on
  religious practice in, 115, 118
Amin, Gen. Idi, 94
Aminah, 39
Andrae, Tor, 34
Angola: declares independence from
  Portugal, 92; enacts freedom of
  religion, 94
Anthropology: of religious experience,
  60, 64
Antioch: Christian community in, 49
Apocalyptic theme: in African Indepen-
  dency and *jihád*, 21-22
Apologetics: and Islam and Christianity,
  8
Aqsá mosque: and arson, 131
Arab League: OIC distinctive from, 131
Aristotelianism: Islamic extension of, 98
Aristotle, 98
Arnold, Sir Thomas, 12
Artisan, The: text of Freetown debate in,
  67, 68
'Asabiyáh (solidarity): importance
  Khaldún attaches to, 102, 103
Athens: Christian community in, 49

Joseph: in passages on revelations at
  Medina, 43
Jurisprudence, Islamic: founder of, 47
Ka'ba: as *qiblah*, 45; trade center at, 43
Kalimah (or *shahádah*), 29
Kánemí, Muhammad al-, 122
Ka'ti, Mahmúd al-, 14
Kenya: church and state tensions in,
  94
Khadíjah, 40, 43
Khaldún, Ibn (Abú Zayd al-Rahmán),
  13, 17, 58-59, 125; life and work of,
  100-102; *Muqaddimah*, 146; on
  nature of Christian mission, 10;
  Prolegomena to Universal History,
  101; views on religion and politics of,
  100, 102-105, 137
Khalwah, 58, 59
Khattáb, 'Umar ibn, 121
Khumayní, Ayátullah, 120, 121
Kings: and clerics, 14-17
Kinship: Khaldún's defense of, 102
Knowledge: modern West and view of,
  147; Muslim view of, 146
Language: and mission, 8-9; symbolic
  use of, 61
Lara, Lúcio, 92
Learning: joined with religion in Muslim
  tradition, 146, 166, 171; stages
  teachers in Qur'án schools undergo,
  158-59. *See also* Education; Knowl-
  edge
Lebanon: Muslim populations in, 131
Letter concerning Toleration (Locke),
  115-17
Liberals: and state power, 111
Liberia: coup d'état topples President
  Doe in, 94
Liberty: Lockean view of, 125
Lienhardt, Godfrey, 76
Lives of the Saints (Butler), 48
Locke, John, 137; *A Letter concerning
  Toleration*, 115-17; on religious
  triumphalism, 122-23; *Second
  Treatise on Civil Government*, 119
Lockean views: of liberty, 125; of
  religion and politics, 140
"Love, Peace, and Unity: A Christian
  View of Politics in Kenya," 94
Luwum, Archbishop Lanani, 94
Machiavelli, Niccolò, 85, 89

Madrasas, 78
Mahdí, Sádiq al-, 97, 120
Majlis: names for, 18
Malams, 18
Malcolm X: conversion to Islam of, 63-
  64
Mali: Islamic conversion in, 13; Islam in
  ancient, 18; Islamic influence on
  rulers in ancient, 14-15; roots of the
  Gambia in medieval, 148
Ma'mún, Caliph al-, 122
Mandinka clerics, 159
Marsiglio of Padua, 89, 90
Marty, Paul, 124
Marxist-Leninism: in Angola, 92, 93
Maslahah: Muslim reformers appeal to,
  60
Mauny, Raymond, 148
Mauritania: incarceration of Muslim
  scholars in, 19
Mbiti, John, 75
Mecca: antagonism toward Muhammad
  in, 43; Malcolm X's pilgrimage to,
  64; Muhammad's taking of, 45
Meccans: material cynicism of, 42
Medina: impact on Islam and Muham-
  mad, 43; Muhammad reaches, 44;
  Muhammad's revelations at, 43;
  passages on revelations occurring at,
  43
Memory and reminiscence, religious:
  and poetic hyperbole, 34
Merkl, Peter, 96
Methodism, 73
Militancy: and Islam, 17-21; and
  religion, 122, 123, 124
Miller, Walter, 20
Milton, John, 118; on goal of learning,
  147
Miltonian view: of religion and politics,
  140
Missionaries: and conflicts with slave
  traders and liquor and arms mer-
  chants, 73
Missionary movements: in African
  Islam, 17; and rise of modern
  Christianity, 112; and Western
  religious influence in Africa, 85, 87-
  88
Missions: educational reforms of
  Western Christian, 2; and indigenous

Other Titles in the Faith Meets Faith Series

Toward a Universal Theology of Religion, Leonard Swidler, Editor
The Myth of Christian Uniqueness, John Hick and Paul F. Knitter, Editors
An Asian Theology of Liberation, Aloysius Pieris, S.J.
The Dialogical Imperative, David Lochhead
Love Meets Wisdom, Aloysius Pieris, S.J.
Many Paths, Eugene Hillman, C.S.Sp.
The Silence of God, Raimundo Panikkar
The Challenge of the Scriptures, Groupe de Recherches Islamo-Chrétien
The Meaning of Christ, John P. Keenan
Hindu-Christian Dialogue, Harold Coward, Editor
The Emptying God, John B. Cobb, Jr., and Christopher Ives, Editors
Christianity Through Non-Christian Eyes, Paul J. Griffiths, Editor
Christian Uniqueness Reconsidered, Gavin D'Costa, Editor
Women Speaking, Women Listening, Maura O'Neill
Bursting the Bonds?, Leonard Swidler, Lewis John Eron, Gerard Sloyan, and
  Lester Dean, Editors
One Christ—Many Religions, Stanley J. Samartha
The New Universalism, David J. Krieger
Jesus Christ at the Encounter of World Religions, Jacques Dupuis, S.J.
After Patriarchy, Paula M. Cooey, William R. Eakin, and Jay B. McDaniel, Edi-
  tors
An Apology for Apologetics, Paul J. Griffiths
World Religions and Human Liberation, Dan Cohn-Sherbok, Editor
Uniqueness, Gabriel Moran
Leave the Temple, Felix Wilfred, Editor
The Buddha and the Christ, Leo D. Lefebure
The Divine Matrix, Joseph A. Bracken, S.J.
The Gospel of Mark: A Mahāyāna Reading, John P. Keenan
Revelation, History and the Dialogue of Religions, David A. Carpenter
Salvations, S. Mark Heim
The Intercultural Challenge of Raimon Panikkar, Joseph Prabhu, Editor
Fire and Water: Women, Society, and Sprituality in Buddhism and Christianity,
  Aloysius Pieris, S.J.